Qi Stagnation - Signs of Stress: Readers' Reviews

*These quotes are either from Amazon sites or from direct communications. Some reviews of the original **Kindle** edition were critical because of the layout and accessibility, now (August 2017) remedied, I hope.*

*****5.0 out of 5 stars* This is a revelatory book, I highly recommend it! By Foo Chi on December 2, 2014
Format: Kindle Edition | Verified Purchase
Very informative for those who are under constant stress, or suffer grief, depression, and who have come to know an allopathic approach doesn't get to the psycho-organic dynamics of what's going on, and how to work on and with it.

———
*****5.0 out of 5 stars* The clearest and most accessible book on the subject that I've ever read By Liz on 13 May 2014
Format: Paperback
This book is a must for those who are embarking on a course of study of Traditional Chinese Medicine and Medical Qigong. At last I have been able to visualise and understand concepts which are quite challenging for a Western mind. Great book!

———
*****5.0 out of 5 stars* Excellent book By kim mcdaniel on May 8, 2017
Format: Paperback | Verified Purchase
I am new to acupuncture but this helped me understand

where my qi is not working. Even showed it to my acupuncturist and he was pleased as well.

___

A must read for good health of mind and body By GJLeale on 21 October 2015
Format: Kindle Edition | Verified Purchase
This book explains the Chinese acupuncture model of the body clearly and simply. It is thorough, helpful and provides much food for thought, and many ways to improve health sensibly. Clearly the western world has much to learn from this system and it is a great shame so many western scientists, medics and governments actively seek to discredit it. .... I will recommend to anyone who wants to understand the body as an intricate energetic system which it truly is rather than a mechanical vehicle for big pharma.

___

*****5.0 out of 5 stars Excellent Meridian Overview By CaroinDorset on 9 July 2015
Format: Paperback | Verified Purchase
An excellent book giving detailed insight into the workings of the meridians, explanations and suggestions for dealing with problems. Comprehensive and well written, easy to follow. Very pleased I ordered this book. Next day delivery too. Brilliant service.

___

*****5.0 out of 5 stars Five Stars By Teri Powell on May 30, 2015
Format: Paperback | Verified Purchase
Nice book. I am studying herbalism & Chinese medicine so this is a nice addition to my other books.

___

*****5.0 out of 5 stars Five Stars By anns on May 4, 2015
Format: Kindle Edition | Verified Purchase

Excellent book. A must-read.

*****5.0 out of 5 stars highly
recommended By J.A.Golden on March 1, 2015
Format: Kindle Edition | Verified Purchase
Great book. Very detailed and clear on the subject.

*****5.0 out of 5 stars Qi stagnation
book By Blueflame on 10 January 2015
Format: Kindle Edition | Verified Purchase
Very interesting to anyone interested in Qi Stagnation

*****5.0 out of 5 stars Glad to have it in my
library By Olga Rodina on 12 December 2014
Format: Paperback | Verified Purchase
Thank you, the book is very informative. Glad to have it in
my library.

****4.0 out of 5 stars Worth reading if you don't want to
rely on drugs By Nik Jones on 10 December 2014
Format: Kindle Edition | Verified Purchase
I'm a huge advocate of helping myself with any ails I have
and have found that getting to the root problem rather
than just suppressing the symptoms far more sustainable
than just reaching for the paracetamol – read this book if
you are of a similar mind or want to change the way you
feel/are.

*****5.0 out of 5 stars Brilliant book for people who would
like to know more about TCM. By Yavor Lazarov on May
17, 2014
Format: Kindle Edition | Verified Purchase
I was able to use the principles mentioned in this book to
reverse and completely eradicate a lifelong chronic illness.

The book is very empowering in the way that it helps you take responsibility of your own health and helps you diagnose yourself whenever you feel sick or simply under par and would like to get better. The author does a wonderful job of explaining traditional Chinese medicine in simple terms so that it is available for people with no prior medical background.

———

From Sherry Mcleod on May 7, 2014
I just started seeing an acupuncturist last week and was baffled why a few needles made such a difference in how I felt. I looked online to see if there was a book that could help explain how acupuncture worked and came across this one. It is well-written and easy to understand. I recommend it to anyone wanting to know how energy stagnation starts and how it affects your health.

———

*****5.0 out of 5 stars*best book about qi stagnation **By choongchang on 26 April 2014
Format: Paperback | Verified Purchase
It was so insightful to understand about my body/energy field, why I have those symptoms and ways to improve them. I could rate more stars than 5 if I may.

———

*****5.0 out of 5 stars* Illuminating reading! **By Elektra Perkins on 15 March 2014
Format: Paperback | Verified Purchase
The best answers to all of your digestive problems. Really worthy to buy it! Great explanation of many hidden symptoms, that regular doctors have no clues.

———

*****5.0 out of 5 stars* Real information to understand and deal with stress **By J. Buis on 2 March 2014
Format: Paperback | Verified Purchase

... This book very clearly explained my problem ..: "Lung Qi stagnation". ... The author explained exactly what I was dealing with and came with many ways to 'cure' the problem. I have taken a few serious, particularly more physical exercise and breathing exercises, and for the first time in 6 years I sleep well most nights. What I love about the book is that it clearly explains the causes of the problems and simple ways to deal with it. ... For me this book is absolutely priceless. And a nice side effect: I am now making regular physical exercise a priority in my life no matter how busy I am with work. Nice to know: the book has many other suggestions too for those that are not that much into sports. Highly recommended for anyone suffering from stress-related problems!

by Barbara (Ontario, Canada)

I did buy Qi Stagnation from Amazon, but I regret, I'm too taken up with exploring further to take the extra time to go and add my comment from Amazon's site. However, I am a self-certified Amazon purchaser.

I have one real comment I want to make. I love the idea you have put in my head that Qi stagnation has a very positive attribute in that it represents a tremendous, banked up, potential power resource.

We are generally so hung up on the downside of everything, especially when our bodies don't feel good.

You have transferred the idea that our dis-eases are a power bank, just waiting for us to release the dams, in order to fuel our dreams. AND – that figuring out how to let the Qi go could actually be FUN, That is a pretty exhilarating idea! Therein lies the way towards health.

Perhaps your book will be one of the transformative agents which will set the world alight (Water fuelling Wood, fuelling Fire!)and get us all moving again. (I also appreciated the crash course in Chinese medicine. It seems to be based on considerable practical experience and it is experience which teaches, not books.)

.

by Thevra Assiotis (Cyprus)
I wanted to read this book through before i wrote a review...Well what can I say...It's been the best book I have read in this field by far, money well spent. Easy reading,although I wanted to take my time in reading it because I wanted to clearly understand every sentence I didn't really have to.

It has helped me understand the way my body functions and has made me see Chinese medicine in a completely different way. My husband has strabismus and double vision and reading this book has helped us understand where the underlying problem is, quite amazing really.

I would highly recommend this book, it really is worth buying. Five stars for me on this one. Thevra Assiotis

By Jonathan Clogstoun-Willmott
Qi Stagnation – Signs of Stress is **Book 1** in the Series
Chinese Medicine in English

Contents

Introduction

The main purpose of this book is to help readers understand stress as the ancient Chinese viewed it. They thought of it in terms of what happens to Qi (pronounced *'TCHEE!'*) when it stagnates. (More on Qi in Appendix 1.)

There are many kinds of stress, not just the 'heart pounding, breathing faster, forehead sweating' kind.

If stress is seen as Qi stagnation, a whole range of physical sensations and emotions and the illnesses they lead to makes sense.

Making sense of these sensations and emotions means you can often work out how to help yourself.

Take an example. An article (The Digital Obsession that's driving us Crazy: p2 News Review, Sunday Times 15 July 2012) describes how many teenagers get ill because of their obsession with the Internet.

It talks about the Internet's harmful effects on the mind, and how internalised and obsessive thoughts about computer games or what others think can take over a person's thinking.

Worse, that many become addicted to the Internet or to their cell-phone and its latest message.

Maintaining a digital reputation through Facebook or Linked-In is an effort. The speed with which news and views break across the Internet can be both exciting and terrifying – particularly when you are the target of abuse.

The article describes the emotional and depressive states into which users can sink, how even a few hours on the Net appears to rewire their brains. The article said teenagers were particularly prone to these ills.

But adults are susceptible too. As an extreme example, a young couple let their infant baby die while they reared a virtual baby online ('Girl starved to death while parents raised virtual child' Guardian 5 March 2010).

Many people report phantom cell-phone vibration. Others are diagnosed with Internet-related psychosis.

Some countries have noticed how many people spend more time online than they do on any other activity, including sleeping; how they think it normal to text during social meetings with friends or while dining with parents.

To Chinese medicine, these states into which people get themselves were described over 3,000 years ago. We have just invented new ways to reach them.

A large part of how we get into these states, how they evolve and how they can be changed and treated comes down to a syndrome that Chinese Medicine calls Qi Stagnation.

'Syndrome' is the word used to describe a particular condition in Chinese Medicine. 'Qi Stagnation' is a syndrome.

More money has probably been made from Qi Stagnation than any other syndrome in Chinese medicine!

Everyone knows what it is like but few stop to think about its consequences. Perhaps only Chinese medicine understands it in terms of *energy*.

It cannot be prevented. It is part of life and often good. Dealing with its early stages is easy. Individual susceptibility to disease governs our ability to stop it deteriorating into other syndromes.

Those other syndromes are where the trouble starts. They are often where chronic illness begins.

For governments, the cost of stress can be huge, making it a political and social, as well as a biological and physiological problem.

Depending on your view, you regard stress as being, on one hand, the responsibility of the state or some other organisation, such as your employer; on the other an individual matter.

What happens when Qi stagnates?

There is a phenomenon called a 'Standing' or a 'Stationery' Wave. You can look it up on the Internet, where it tends to be explained in terms of physics and mathematical equations.

A particular example of this is a so-called 'shock-wave traffic jam'. Suppose you are driving along a motorway. You are behaving yourself, driving at a steady pace and within the speed limit, like everyone else.

Suddenly you see rear brake-warning lights in traffic ahead. You slow down, along with all the other drivers around you.

Then, for a time, you crawl along, stop-starting. This can continue for miles – and hours. Eventually, everyone speeds up and you get under way again, unable to account for the delay.

Well, there is a reason for the delay!

Some time, possibly hours, before you reached the slowdown, someone braked, perhaps to prevent an accident. The following cars also braked.

In their turn the cars still further back, all of whom until then had been driving along steadily like you within the speed limit, had to brake and slow down too.

So, for a mile or more, sometimes tens of miles, everyone slowed.

Because people react in different ways, some of the cars actually stopped. That created further ripples back down the motorway.

And then you came across one of those ripples. This was not a moving ripple, it was still, like the ripple effect in sand when the tide goes out.

You too had to slow down and endure the ripple. In fact, you were part of the ripple. Not just you, but hundreds of other motorists, bus, van and lorry drivers. All were affected.

You cannot speed round it or through it.

You just have to endure it.

Eventually you emerge at the far end of it. So nothing happened; there was no accident. Just the whole energy of all the cars and lorries 'stagnated' for a while before it got going again.

Tim Rees of TRL, a UK traffic research firm, is quoted (New Scientist 4 March 2008) as commenting on a Japanese experiment:

"I suspect that the trigger would either be a particular driver who was more nervous than the rest, or a particular location... where the capacity was slightly lower."

Likewise, energy can stagnate in your body. You cannot see it stagnating, but you can see its effect as in all the people and their cars who became part of the shock-wave traffic jam.

On the motorway, what do you see going on around you when you are in the stationery wave?

Some drivers just sit there looking glum. Others shout at their mobiles, or pick their noses. Children get restless.

Some cars overheat, some drivers get cross and hot and open windows to let cool air circulate. If you live in a hot climate, you turn on the air-conditioning.

So the volume of noise goes up, more energy is used, some of the cars overheat, and people get restless: all for no progress.

As Tim Rees commented, had the road been wider it might have accommodated more vehicles, so have been no cause for a queue.

But it was not wider at that point so pressure just built up.

Actually, what builds up is emotional pressure. After all, the cars do not mind – their owners do the minding!

In your body, stagnant Qi causes a sensation of *fullness*, of being *blocked-up, swelling or distension*.

Some people describe it as *stuffiness*.

However, these adjectives do not really do justice to the range of sensations people get when they feel stressed.

Some people say they do not get any of the above. However, if you ask people to explain carefully what they do feel, they may admit to something like one (or more) of the following symptoms *as the stress pressure builds up:*

- Adam's apple seems to want to push up into mouth
- Alone: desire to be alone/get away; claustrophobia
- Bladder 'full' feeling; sudden urge to pee
- Women's breasts feel too big as before the monthly period
- Breathing feels tight
- Ears: oppressive feeling, as in a lift descending fast
- Eyes feel too big, need to blink
- Forehead feels squeezed, as if trying to push out
- Guts tighten or cramp
- Heart pounds as if too big
- Jaw feels stiff
- Limbs feel rigid, hands get hot or cold

- Nose feels narrower on one or both sides
- Rectum feels urge to pass a stool, or tightens
- Shoulders get taut
- Swallowing, urge to
- Throat tightens
- Voice feels strangled

Think about yourself and how you react to stress. Do any of the above fit with how you feel? If not, watch yourself next time you are in a difficult situation, such as where

- someone barges into a queue just in front of you
- you receive unexpected criticism or abuse
- your job suddenly requires much more effort or time when you had already made other plans
- you find yourself having to make an unexpected speech

However, that is only the first phase.
   What HAPPENS NEXT?
   Chinese medicine has here two main kinds of second phase: the names they gave them were WIND and HEAT.

PRESSURE BECOMES *WIND*

Qi in the form of WIND shows up as movement.
   Think of the wind as you experience it, as it blows on trees, over grass, through your hair, rattles doors and windows.
   How do you know it is the wind? Because it moves things. It presses on you. You cannot see it but you know it is there.
   In the body, the pressure build-up tries to escape as some kind of motion or escape, such as:

- Getting busy, always doing something (mental or physical or diversionary), obsessive movements
- Blinking rapidly, winking
- Picking the nose; biting fingernails
- Bowel movements: passing stools, diarrhoea
- Breathing deeply or faster
- Burping, eructations
- Company: talking (hot air!): conversation: gossiping
- Cool air: desire to open windows or turn on air-conditioning
- Crossing/uncrossing of legs/arms, combing hair
- Crying
- Dancing around (obvious in children, for example)
- Trying to hawk what feels like phlegm in the throat
- Nervous, hurried motions (when trying to seem calm)
- Restlessness, change of position; babies want to be carried
- Rhythmic movement, continued motion, flexing limbs
- Rubbing, pressing or scratching eyes/skin/nose/ears
- Orgasm – sexual release (alone or with another)
- Smoking tobacco, take medication or social drugs
- Sneezing/coughing/yawning/sighing
- Stretching out or bending backwards (body/arms/head)
- Swallowing/eating/drinking
- Tapping fingers or foot
- Teeth: grinding or chattering
- Stuttering speech
- Tremor/twitches (eyelid/cheek/mouth/nostril/upperlip)

- Walking (often, walking away from the problem)
- Washing hands repeatedly
- Wind: often want a cool breeze but dislike strong wind

PRESSURE BECOMES *HEAT*

The other main way Qi stagnation pressure is experienced is through HEAT. Symptoms you might notice include:

- Bleeding (eg nosebleed) or between menses
- Blushing
- Desire for cool air/water/bathing/weather
- Desire to be fanned
- Discharges e.g. need to urinate or stool – cools you down
- Avoiding hot food, conditions or states
- Eructations, burping, farting – foul-smelling gas
- Diarrhoea – offensive smell
- Fasting (i.e. going off food) or eating less
- Redness of skin
- Sweating
- Increased thirst
- Uncovering, or need to loosen clothing or belt

Of course, the above WIND and HEAT symptoms are mainly physical. Emotions, too, play out in many ways either to release or to try to contain pressure:

- Clam up ie refuse to talk or reason or say what you feel
- Cry

- Laughter, usually hysterical or inappropriate

- Shout

- Talk, talk, talk, usually fast

- Whimper

If the situation causing this cannot be resolved, or if you have to live or work with a situation like this all the time, the symptom(s) can become entrenched.

They may become painful. In Chinese medicine, Heat and Wind (just two of the many forms of Qi) can turn into more serious syndromes of illness. These can become chronic and debilitating.

You will read about them later in this book, but when they occur they usually show up in ways for which Western Medicine has names – disease conditions.

For example: irritable bowel syndrome, hypertension, ulcers.

Of course, these conditions often have other explanations in Chinese medicine, but even then, Qi Stagnation often makes them worse or prolongs them, making them chronic.

What is Qi?

Modern science says there is no such thing as Qi.

So what? If it behaves as if it exists, and you can find ways of using it as if it exists, calling it Qi is a convenient way of describing it.

Once you have an idea that you can use repeatedly to explain things, which can be used to predict behaviour, including the progress between disease and health, you are well on the way to having a theory.

Mathematics is full of theories, using invisible and imaginary factors, like the square root of minus one: ($\sqrt{-1}$).

Nobody insists that they see physical evidence of the

square root of '-1' before they use it. However, for mathematicians it is a vital device, intrinsic to many theories and calculations.

The same goes for Qi. Whether it exists or not is a moot point (for more on this see appendix 1), but the theory of Qi can explain many kinds of illness.

What is more, Qi does not have to be purely physical in form.

In fact, the ancient Chinese were perfectly clear that Qi itself takes many forms including thoughts and emotions. (See appendix 3 for more on this.)

It is a good theory. There has been plenty of time to develop it. Acupuncturists and practitioners of Chinese and other kinds of medicine have been using it for thousands of years.

Perhaps someone will one day explain it in ways acceptable to modern science. Then we may call it something else.

Stress

Doctors think of stress in terms of its longer-term, more serious consequences, like chronic illness and insanity.

Though doctors recognise stress, they lack a clear definition for it and, surprisingly, there is no agreed understanding of the mechanism that builds stress. (For a discussion of the history of stress over the last two hundred years from the Western Medical perspective, see appendix 8.)

Chronic illness – illness that the body cannot itself cure without external treatment – burdens our health systems.

All the more important to teach people how to recognise and deal with Qi stagnation early on, to realise when it transforms into something more serious, and to devise ways to prevent, ameliorate or reverse further deterioration.

Equally important is to find ways to lessen our susceptibility to Qi stagnation in the first place.

Comparison of the different approaches of Chinese and Western medicine

Whereas Western medicine recognises the long-term results of stress, Chinese medicine's model also recognises the early stages. The model predicts how symptoms may progress at first mildly, then become more serious, to the point where Western medicine recognises them.

Two apologies

1/ I repeat myself a number of times throughout the book. This is because I doubt if many people will read it cover-to-cover, unless they are practitioners – but this book was intended for patients and others interested in a different way of looking at their health: not practitioners, who have much weightier tomes to inform them. Some matters occur frequently under different headings. Always to refer readers to the original page is tedious.

Equally, in some chapters, points are reiterated several times both to make them more readable and to emphasise them.

2/ I over-simplify some matters!
For example, the Liver Energy Organ does not merely ascend Qi, and there seems to be no real agreement over which way Gall-Bladder sends it, though I think it is upwards.

This book explains from the perspective of Chinese medicine our susceptibility to Qi Stagnation, how it starts, its symptoms, the different types, the more serious syndromes it can turn into, and the consequences for modern health systems.

It explores how it affects us and what we can do about it.

If you are reading this because you wonder how to help yourself, I hope you will find that help here. I hope from reading this that you will realise what you can do for yourself, whether you need outside help, where you may be able to get treatment, how to decide what treatments are conducive to better health and which may be less appropriate for you.

Request!

First, when you have read this book, may I ask you to review it?

This will help others decide if they might benefit from it. Please post your opinion on Amazon or anywhere else you think would reach prospective readers. Of course I hope you will write a positive or at least constructive opinion!

However, if you have major reservations or criticisms, do let me know! Then I can improve the book for the next readers. Reach me through http://www.acupuncture-points.org/book-review-contact-page.html .

How to read this book

If you hesitate to wade through the whole book to find which chapters apply to yourself, you might find the tables on the next pages helpful.

Concerning Table A

Tip: sometimes you will not be the best person to assess yourself: especially to recognise the emotional state(s) to which you frequently or habitually succumb.

If you are not sure, and even if you are sure, ask a close friend or partner to tell you to which uncomfortable emotions you are most susceptible in their judgement.

Several of the following are not emotions but states of

being, like 'Desk: always working over a desk' and 'Shock'. The latter might apply if you have had a sudden shock or bad news (or even, for some people, good news).

This is because our emotions often lead to Qi stagnation, and knowing which emotions can help explain our symptoms.

Table A is much more important than Table B. Use Table B only as a back-up, because the chapters you should read depend far more on your symptoms and emotions than on your position or stage in life.

However, your position or life-stage often makes you susceptible to certain syndromes and Table B suggests what those might be.

You may of course not be typical in which case Table B will not work for you! In any case, I suggest you read all of the first 8 chapters because they lay the groundwork for what follows.

See which emotion, in the left-hand column of Table A, most easily matches you. Then read the suggested chapters listed in the columns to the right.

TABLE A

Most frequent emotion	First … read chapter numbers:	Then … read chapter number:	Later read chapter number(s):
Anger	1 2 3 4 5 6 7	8	12, 11, 10
Angry while eating	1 2 3 4 5 6 7	8	11, 12, 10
Anxious	1 2 3 4 5 6 7	15	8, 13, 10
Brooding	1 2 3 4 5 6 7	13	9, 10

Desk work ie always working over a desk	1 2 3 4 5 6 7	13	9
Envious	1 2 3 4 5 6 7	13	8, 10
Fearful	1 2 3 4 5 6 7	15	10
Frustrated	1 2 3 4 5 6 7	8	13, 12, 11, 10
Grieving	1 2 3 4 5 6 7	9	10
Jealous	1 2 3 4 5 6 7	13	8, 10
Moody	1 2 3 4 5 6 7	8	13, 11, 10
Moral crisis	1 2 3 4 5 6 7	12	8
Obsessive	1 2 3 4 5 6 7	13	9, 10
Over-intellectualising	1 2 3 4 5 6 7	13	9, 10
Pre-menstrual syndrome	1 2 3 4 5 6 7	8	13, 11
Resentful	1 2 3 4 5 6 7	8	10, 13, 15
Sad	1 2 3 4 5 6 7	9	8, 10
Shock	1 2 3 4 5 6 7	10	15
Worrying	1 2 3 4 5 6 7	13	9, 8, 10

Table B: *please note that Table B (below) is much less important than Table A. However, if you cannot decide from Table A which predominant emotions cause your Qi stagnation, this may help.*

However, do realize that the chapters in Table B listed in the right-hand two columns are only suggestions.

Everyone is different and your susceptibilities may make you prone to syndromes other than those indicated.

Too bad: you may just have to read the whole book to find which chapters are relevant for you!

.

TABLE B

Position	First ... read chapter numbers:	Then ... read chapter number:	Later ... read chapter number(s):
Wealthy, no need to work	1 2 3 4 5 6 7	8	10, 15
Entrepreneur	1 2 3 4 5 6 7	8	13, 10, 15
Business, big property or investment owner	1 2 3 4 5 6 7	13	8, 10, 15
Professional	1 2 3 4 5 6 7	13	12, 11, 15, 8
Manager	1 2 3 4 5 6 7	13	8, 9, 10, 11, 15
Technician	1 2 3 4 5 6 7	12	13, 9, 8
Office worker	1 2 3 4 5 6 7	9	8, 13, 11
Writer, artist, composer	1 2 3 4 5 6 7	9	10, 13, 15
Manual worker	1 2 3 4 5 6 7	11	12, 13, 10
Unemployed jobseeker	1 2 3 4 5 6 7	8	16, 11, 13, 15
Unemployed, not job-seeking	1 2 3 4 5 6 7	9	11, 8, 10, 12, 15
Retired with adequate income	1 2 3 4 5 6 7	13	10, 15
Retired without adequate income	1 2 3 4 5 6 7	11	9, 14, 16, 15

Doctor, therapist (orthodox)	1 2 3 4 5 6 7	9	13, 11, 12, 10, 8
Therapist (unorthodox)	1 2 3 4 5 6 7	13	15, 12, 10, 8
Male	1 2 3 4 5 6 7	8	15, 10
Female	1 2 3 4 5 6 7	8	13, 10, 15, 14, 11
Baby	1 2 3 4 5 6 7	11	12, 13, 9, 8
Child	1 2 3 4 5 6 7	11	8, 9
Teenager	1 2 3 4 5 6 7	8	9, 13, 11

The Natural Movement of Qi

Alice became a patient when medicines from her doctor made her ill. She was in her late thirties and looked robust: not prone to panics, you would have thought.

"Something from my belly grabbing my throat so I can't breathe", she said.

She thought she had something alive living in her.

The year before, her husband had been waking in the night suddenly unable to breathe, greatly alarming his family. One acupuncture treatment cured it, though he later returned for more acupuncture to deal with other problems.

Anyway, here was Alice, with her husband, both very anxious.

How do you diagnose something from your belly grabbing your throat and stopping you breathing?

You can understand why her doctor, after lots of tests on Alice, suggested she see a psychiatrist. Before she saw the psychiatrist, her husband suggested she visit me in case I could help.

Chinese medicine has an explanation for Alice's strange sensation. It is called *running piglet disorder!*

You can look it up on the Internet, but basically it is a sensation which starts in the abdomen and rushes up to your chest, where it feels as if you cannot breathe, then tightens your throat so you feel throttled.

IF this happened to me, I would feel alarmed.

The explanation in Chinese medicine is that it is your own energy, running amok. Your energy, your Qi, they say, should run smoothly, so you do not notice it.

That is, when you are healthy.

When you are ill, or in pain, your Qi does not flow smoothly. That is either because it is blocked, or because there is not enough of it, or because there is too much of it, creating a feeling of fullness, excess or throbbing.

Or, as with Alice, it flows in the wrong direction.

So, for health, it should flow 'naturally'.

·

You could say that the definition of health in Chinese medicine is when you have enough Qi and it runs smoothly, without symptoms. However, the more you know about it, the more you realise that you need a balance between Qi and Blood, and also between Yin and Yang.

·

So what is the natural flow of energy in the body and why does orthodox (ie Western) medicine not recognise this idea?

Ever since they started thinking about it, perhaps 3000 years ago, the Chinese have said that everything that exists, and all life, is an expression of energy. (Modern science agrees: Einstein and others sorted that out.)

But Chinese medicine developed an entire understanding of health and disease around this idea.

Over 3000 years, they have developed many ingenious ways to treat ill people by using it.

Western medicine finds the basic idea, in the form presented by the Chinese, very hard to accept. There is no obvious sign of this 'Qi-energy', nor a way to measure it, and it is hard to monitor because it is so subjective. Western medicine is inclined to dismiss it as nonsense, as at best a pseudo-science.

Anyway, in Chinese medicine, we are made of energy, and that energy should flow naturally, back and forth.

Actually, they are much more precise about it than that.

In Traditional Chinese Medicine, the energy in your body is said to move in 4 ways: up and down, in and out.

When energy moves the wrong way – for example, energy that should be going down starts instead to ascend, you get pathology: illness, pain or discomfort of some kind.

In a healthy person, energy flows in ordered directions, up, down, in or out. When Qi stagnates it can flow in the wrong direction.

That pathology can affect your Zang-fu[1] organs, which I call your 'Energy Organs'. It may affect part or the whole of your body.

The power that makes energy move in the first place is generated by the Energy Organs. It flows, or is said to flow, along the channels of acupuncture.

What does this mean? Let us take an analogy.

In a car with an internal combustion engine (i.e. the normal non-electric kind of engine) one cylinder fires, followed immediately afterwards by another then another and so on, each turning the engine's crankshaft.

Once the engine fires up, the car comes 'alive'.

We might say that the purpose the car was made for only then becomes possible. It can go forwards and backwards, drive fast or slow, it can warm up and cool down, and light up the countryside at night.

It can become an expression of its driver. Once the engine turns, all this becomes possible.

1. Zangfu organs. I have translated Zangfu as Energy Organs to keep as much as possible in this book in English. For more on zangfu see http://www.acupuncture-points.org/zang-fu.html Enter your footnote content here.

Your body is much the same, though much more sophisticated.

Your Energy Organs

In Traditional Chinese Medicine, you have the equivalent of an engine with 12 cylinders.

These are the twelve Energy Organs -Heart, Spleen, Lungs, Kidneys, Liver, Small Intestine, Stomach, Large Intestine, Bladder, Gall-bladder – plus a couple which you probably do not recognise as physical organs, the Pericardium and Three Heater.

I give the names of all these Energy Organs Capital first letters. So it's Heart, not heart, Spleen not spleen etc. If you see heart or spleen etc written with a lower type, it means the heart organ, or the spleen organ. This will make sense as you read on.

As these Energy Organs create and pass the energy around between them, like turning the crankshaft in an engine, the body 'fires' up.

Energy is said to pass around all of them every 24 hours, so in effect they each take the strain for 2 hours at a time.

However, here the analogy with the car breaks down because your car is made of metal and stuff, whereas your body is integrated and living.

In your body, each Energy Organ is said to be in charge of one of the many functions that make your body work.

But let us stay with the car analogy a little longer.

For example, we could say that cylinder no 11 (we shall call it the 'Stomach' energy) is also in charge of the carburetor, which measures the fuel and sends it down to the spark plug chamber.

However, because we are humans and everything clings together, in you and me our Stomach energy is also in charge of choosing the fuel we take in, as well as digesting it.

Another Analogy – to flesh out how the Energy Organs are understood to work:

Take a ship such as used in the 16th Century in Europe. For long distances, these were powered by the wind, with sails.

Every two hours, let us say, there was a new officer-of-the-watch. (In fact, this was usually a 4-hour slot, not two hours, but let us say it was 2 hours.)

During that 2-hour slot, a member of the crew was required to keep the ship on course, with the sails trimmed as necessary. There were, let us say, twelve crew-members and they all took one two-hour slot in turn.

Of course, each crew-member had other duties. Together with the duties of all the other crew-members, the business of the ship carried on.

For example, if the chef did not do the cooking, the crew would starve, or at least the food would be less palatable, when someone less skilled had to cook it instead.

If the Captain could not decide where they were going, the crew might fall out, they would not make meaningful progress and the whole enterprise might founder.

If the engineer and chief repair-man was unable to do his job, the rudder would not steer because of lack of maintenance, the ship would start leaking seriously and they might have to stop for major repairs.

The Channels or Meridians of Acupuncture

Each Energy Organ was also responsible for its associated channel, sometimes called a 'meridian'.

The channels (or meridians) of acupuncture are like rivers carrying our energy out to and back from our extremities and giving them life. Energy ("Qi") is said (in Chinese medicine) to flow along them.

Many books talk about acupuncture 'meridians', but the word

'channel' is better. So 'acupuncture channel' and 'acupuncture meridian' mean the same thing.

The acupuncture channels connect one with the next, creating a circuit.

The Energy Organs are like the crew-members in the ship analogy above. Each Energy Organ has a two-hour slot, after which the next Energy Organ takes over.

And as in the car analogy, you come alive when all your Energy Organs – your cylinders – are firing.

In this acupuncture circuit, the flow is ceaseless and run by a different energy system every two hours. For instance, the Stomach energy takes over between 7am and 9am, the Bladder energy between 3pm and 5pm.

For more on this ancient idea see Appendix 5.

What matters is that if you know which Energy Organ is below par, you might expect its associated Channel to have problems along its path, such as pain, stiffness, swelling, skin problems, discolouration, heat or cold.

Conversely, where you have pain along a Channel, it often suggests its associated Energy Organ may be in trouble.

In general then, when Qi stagnates in an Energy Organ, you often find pain in the regions traversed by its Channel.

Stomach

When the Stomach energy is taking the strain between 7am and 9am, what happens to the other 11 cylinders, or Energy Organs? Are they asleep?

Not at all! They still do their job. It is just that each has a particular time of day or night when it takes on this additional job: it is on duty then, just as an officer of the watch in the navy might be on duty.

However, it can mean that 12 hours after its 'watch' time that Energy Organ is less active.

For instance, sometimes problems at 3am are due to problems with the Organ that starts 'duty' at 3pm. That is what happened to Alice's husband. He was waking up, unable to breathe, at 3am, but it was treatment on his 3pm Energy Organ that cured his problem.

HOWEVER, PLEASE! IF YOU WAKE AT 3AM OR HAVE ANY OTHER SYMPTOM DESCRIBED IN THIS BOOK, IT IS NOT SENSIBLE TO DIAGNOSE YOURSELF ON THE BASIS OF WHAT YOU READ HERE.

FOR ONE THING, IT IS VERY HARD TO BE OBJECTIVE ABOUT YOUR SYMPTOMS AND FOR ANOTHER, DOCTORS AND ACUPUNCTURISTS TAKE MANY YEARS TO LEARN HOW TO DIFFERENTIATE DISEASE PATTERNS TO TREAT PROBLEMS.

IF YOU HAVE ANY HEALTH PROBLEM, GO AND SEE SOMEONE PROFESSIONAL WHO KNOWS ABOUT IT.

It is the same in your body. There is a flow of energy that just goes quietly on and on, day and night. It is handled by different Energy Organs at different times.

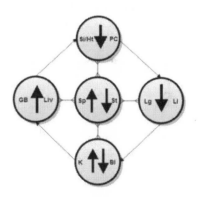

As a result, those Energies just calmly doing their work enable your body to function physically and mentally and in relation to others.

Each Energy Organ also has a specific direction in which it normally moves energy within the body: up, down, in or out. This is sometimes quite different to the direction of flow along the channels.

The diagram "Direction of Energy Flow in Healthy Energy

Organs" and table show what this direction should be in terms of Up and Down.

Figure 1: Direction of Energy Flow in Healthy Energy Organs

Qi Flow Direction	Energy Organ	Energy Organ	Qi Flow direction
.?.	Three heater – TH	Gall-bladder – GB	Up
Down	Pericardium – PC	Liver – Liv	Up
Both Up and Down	Kidney – K	Lungs – Lg	Down
Down	Bladder – Bl	Large Intestine – Ll	Down
Down	Small Intestine – Si	Stomach – St	Down
Down	Heart – Ht	Spleen – Sp	Up

Table 1: Direction of Energy Flow in Healthy Energy Organs

When it comes to stagnation of Qi, it is the direction the Energy Organ sends Qi when healthy that matters. Problems arise when, because of Qi stagnation, energy goes in the wrong direction, or exceeds specifications!

In the above diagram, the arrows show the directions the Energy organs push Qi when healthy. Those sending it up are the Kidney, Gallbladder, Liver and Spleen.

(Just to remind you, the direction of flow along an acupuncture 'channel' or 'meridian' is a different matter altogether. For instance, if you imagine someone standing with hands above his head, the Heart channel flows upwards (from the chest area to the small finger), but the normal direction in which the Heart Energy Organ sends Qi is downwards. To take the Ship analogy you could say that the Chef takes his turn at the helm from 7-9am but his job is to order and cook the food, then make sure food goes down and doesn't come up!)

The Kidney sends energy both up and down – but for different kinds of Qi.

As for the Three Heater Energy organ? You will notice a query against it! The Chinese are not sure about this, even though they have had nearly 3000 years to consider the matter. So it is not shown on the arrow diagram.

(In fact, this is about this book's only mention of the Three Heater energy organ because to explain it would have added too much to the book which is long enough already. Besides, almost nobody understands it.)

And if you look carefully, you will notice that the PC -Pericardium – doesn't appear in the diagram. For the moment, just take it as being like the Ht – Heart. Read more about it in chapter 16.

Bit of Technical Stuff: you may wonder why I have arranged the table above on Qi Flow Direction as it is. One reason is that it conforms to the Chinese Clock (see appendix 5) but it also pairs up Mother-Child connections from the 5 Phase or Element diagram which you will read more about in chapter 5 and in appendix 4.

Clear and Turbid Qi

Qi manifests in many ways. Two important forms are 'Clear' Qi and 'Turbid' Qi.

According to Chinese medicine, clear Qi is sent upwards to allow our sense organs to work properly, including our Mind.

For the eyes to see, the nose to smell, the ears to hear, the tongue to taste, and the Mind to think, Clear Qi (actually it should be described as Clear Yang) must ascend smoothly. See Table 2.

Ascending Clear Qi (or Yang)

If clear Qi fails to ascend to our eyes, our vision is blurred.

When clear Qi fails to ascend to our ears, we cannot hear well.

If clear Qi fails to reach our nose, we lose our sense of smell.

When clear Qi does not ascend to the mouth, we lose our sense of taste.

When clear Qi fails to reach our Mind, we cannot think straight, we become forgetful, we cannot concentrate and we get confused.

Descending Turbid Qi

Turbid Qi, in the form of phlegm, mucus, wax, urine and stools, must descend.

When turbid Qi fails to descend from our eyes, they get sticky or painful.

If turbid Qi fails to descend from our ears, excess wax blocks them up.

When turbid Qi fails to descend from the nose, the nose runs or is blocked.

When turbid Qi fails to descend from the mouth, we get a sticky taste.

When turbid Qi fails to descend from the Mind, we feel confused, heavy, blocked up, possibly dizzy.

	Symptoms when Clear Qi Fails to Ascend	Symptoms when Clear Qi Fails to Descend
Eye	Vision Blurred	Sticky and painful
Ear	Cannot hear well	Excess wax
Nose	No sense of smell	Runs or blocked
Mouth	No sense of taste	Sticky taste
Mind	Confused, cannot think straight	Heavy, blocked, or dizzy

Table 2: Symptoms when Clear Qi fails either to ascend or descend

You have almost certainly experienced some of these symptoms on waking up after a poor night's sleep, when it takes you a little time to come round, your mind takes its time to register reality, and you have sticky eyes or lack your sense of smell. Chronic smokers frequently recognise these symptoms.

Qi enters and exits

Qi permeates every part of the body and for health, Qi must be able to change or move. This book is about Qi stagnation, when Qi stops moving or cannot change, slows down or goes in the wrong direction. Consequently, for health, every bone, tissue and organ must have a constant flow of Qi, in and out, up and down.

Most important message in this book?

**For health,
Qi must be able to change or move!**

When Qi stops moving through every bone, organ or tissue, both inwards and outwards, firstly that part of the body stops performing as it should, but secondly, Qi builds up often in the form of fluids, described as Dampness[2] or Phlegm[3].

More about movement in and out?

Not only does this movement takes Qi in and out of the various body structures, like the bones, tendons, joints, membranes, fat tissues and so on, keeping them alive and refreshing them, it also occurs between different channels as they traverse the body.

2. http://www.acupuncturepoints.
   org/damp.html
3. http://www.acupuncturepoints.
   org/phlegm.html

Qi Stagnation -Signs of Stress

At the hip, for instance, the leg-Yang[4] channels (the Bladder, Gall Bladder and Stomach channels) traverse the anterior-lateral, the lateral and posterior of the hip.

If one of these is malfunctioning, the other two will take the strain to some extent.

Summary so far

You have twelve Energy Organs, each of which takes its turn to run the show. Each has its own job to do besides taking that '2 hour watch' once in every 24 hours.

Each is associated with an acupuncture Channel and each if working properly sends energy either up, down, in or out.

If Qi stagnates in a given Energy Organ, we may expect problems not just specifically related to that Energy Organ, but also in the direction that Energy Organ moves Qi.

A quick example? When your Stomach energy is stagnating, instead of allowing food to descend, its healthy direction, it may cause it to ascend instead, causing nausea or vomiting.

Another example: your Heart Qi normally sends energy down, keeping you calm and steady. When your Heart Energy organ malfunctions because of Qi stagnation, energy ascends instead of descending: your heart races and you become anxious and unable to think clearly.

What happens if Qi stagnates for too long?

If Qi stagnates for too long, the *first thing* that happens is that it pushes out and cooks.

4. You will gradually become used to the words Yin and Yang, but there is more about how they work in chapter 4.

Cooking produces Heat and Heat expands and rises. If that process is prevented, it will seek outlet somewhere, just as increasing the air pressure in a rubber tyre will eventually burst it.

Usually that means that something more serious happens, although at the time it may not seem so. Also, modern Western medicine is very good at removing – or 'suppressing' – symptoms caused by Qi stagnation. Usually this does not cure them.

The unpleasant sensation may 'disappear' but it will reappear, perhaps in some other form, more serious, later. That is unless the underlying Qi stagnation and its causes are resolved.

Here are real-life examples, but please do not assume that Qi stagnation always turns out like this, or that Qi stagnation is always the cause of the consequences described.

.

Example 1. Long-standing anxiety and pressure at work, lead first to abdominal pains and constipation.

Medical treatment to 'move' the stools was highly effective and this improved the abdominal pain.

Time went by and the work pressure continued. Next came sleep disturbances, also treated successfully with medication, but she was now on two forms of medication.

Then began depression, and this was followed – despite the medication for sleep – by waking in panics, hot and sweaty. On four medications now.

Eventually, when she reached me, she was on five regular medications and one for occasional panics. And she'd been diagnosed with a variety of problems, including Irritable Bowel Syndrome, Raynaud's syndrome and Depression.

The point is this. Those conditions became progressively more difficult to treat. They went, if you like, deeper, eventually affecting her mind (depression and the panics).

It started with abdominal pain and constipation. Qi stagnation was the cause and if treated could probably have prevented what followed. Instead, her body put up conditions that were more and more serious, each successively suppressed by medication.

By the time she reached me, her condition had progressed, in terms of Chinese medicine, to include not just Qi stagnation but also other syndromes like Internal Heat and the beginning of Kidney deficiency, with Heart Qi and Heart Blood deficiencies.

At this stage, just treating Qi stagnation was not enough. A whole lot more had to be done and it took time.

Eventually she found the courage to apply for and take another job, which greatly helped what I was doing.

However, by this stage, even a pleasant job with little or no Qi stagnation could not ameliorate the other syndromes[5], 'Kidney deficiency[6]' and 'Heart Blood deficiency[7]' are technical terms used in diagnosing and treating patients in Chinese medicine. Although they are technical terms with fairly precise meanings, I think they are often easier to understand than many of the Latin-based terms used in Western medicine, once you know a little about them.[/footnote] that had developed; Kidney, Heart and Heart Blood deficiencies. These needed a number of treatments.

So, while Qi stagnation and its symptoms are definitely unpleasant, they are not in themselves causes of major ill-health.

But if Qi stagnation is ignored or suppressed, the pent-up energy will go somewhere else, almost certainly deeper.

Then it can become more serious.

.

5. Syndromes like 'Internal Heat'[footnote]http://www.acupuncture-points.org/Heat.html
6. http://www.acupuncture-points.org/kidney-syndromes.html
7. http://www.acupuncture-points.org/heart-blood.html

Example 2. A family situation (the need to move home to care for an ill parent and take a part-time job paying much less than before, so stymieing a woman's career) led to considerable tension, mainly from disappointment but also suppressed anger that she'd been put in this situation.

She started getting short of breath, with tightness in her lungs and a need to swallow because of what she thought was phlegm in her throat.

Here the stagnating Qi pushed up into the chest and throat. The lump feeling in her throat made her even more anxious and she became worse at interviews when she was applying for better jobs.

This started producing panics whenever she was apprehensive, which was often. She found she could not swallow properly, so cut down on the foods that she ate.

Then she got stomach cramps. So now the stagnating Qi was not just pushing upwards into her chest, causing the chest, throat and now heart palpitations that accompanied the panics, but sideways into the stomach.

By the time she saw me she was on a number of medications. Because of loyalty to her parents it took us, working together, some time to unravel the causes of her problem.

Meantime, I had worked out that her cause was Qi stagnation, not least because she always felt so much better after vigorous exercise, even if only temporarily.

Treatment to move the Qi greatly reduced her symptoms but until her parent was taken into a care home (which itself caused huge and unpleasant repercussions) she needed regular treatments.

I still see her occasionally, when parental pressure, (it now concerns the other parent) builds up.

Example 3. A company director found himself taking the flak from annoyed creditors when the finance director was too 'relaxed' to honour the company's debts, even though the company had the money to pay them.

Over several years this and the general unreliability of the finance director, who was also the major shareholder of the company, led my patient into sudden bouts of extreme fury.

He started waking at night to torture himself over the ramifications of his situation.

Physically, he overstrained a muscle in his calf (positioned on the Liver channel).

Then he got frequent hot and urgent diarrhoea (the Qi stagnation turned to Heat that attacked his bowels causing offensive and frequent diarrhoea).

He started grinding his teeth in his sleep. (Qi stagnation was now attacking through the Gall Bladder channel, which goes through the muscle in the mandibular joint).

He began getting headaches, which he'd never suffered from before (Qi stagnation forced Yang energy upwards along the Liver and Gall Bladder channels).

He had been seeing a counsellor for some months by the time she recommended he see me.

Remarkably, at least for me, was that a few sessions of acupuncture made a huge difference. He got so much better that he stopped coming for about 6 months.

Subsequently he returned for two more treatments, by which time he had resigned his directorship and was already feeling so much better that he probably did not really need the treatments I gave.

I could give many more examples of how a relatively mild condition caused by Qi stagnation can progress inwards.

Stagnant Qi fails to transform via Four/ Five Phase system

The *second* thing that happens when Qi stagnates is that it stops or impedes the natural process of transformation and change.

The *normal* or natural process of transformation and change is like this:

- The seasons change in a continuous cycle (e.g. winter – spring – summer – autumn – winter)

- The farmer's earth goes through different processes and transformations (rests; nurtures growth as seed draws from it; transforms via the seed into green shoots; those shoots mature as vegetable or fruit; is eaten; is digested and becomes flesh and blood; is discharged as urine, sweat, air, faeces, skin; decomposes back to earth)

- Our lives alter as we grow older (conception-waiting-baby- child-teenager-young adult-adult-retire-die)

- Our actions vary through the day (e.g. sleep-rise-wash-eat-work-eat-work-eat-rest-play-sleep)

- Our mood or behaviour adjusts as we deal with children, (support them, direct them, humour them, help them, teach them, rest them)

These are the natural way of things as life proceeds.

But when Qi stagnates, the Chinese noticed that this process either slows down, goes wrong or stops.

For example, psychologists realise that people get stuck in certain phases:

- Adults commonly dislike ageing and strive to remain young-looking

- Some young people seem to miss out on play in childhood and proceed straight to serious adulthood

- Some people seem only able to play, to enjoy themselves, unable to take responsibility when appropriate
- Other people seem unable to act other than in a nurturing or mothering role
- Some people are always angry.

The (ancient) Chinese said that these people were stuck in one of the phases of what they called a **Five Phase** cycle, also known as the **Five Element** system. For more on this see appendix 4 and chapter 5. (Please note that, depending on context, I sometimes call this the **Four Phase** system.)

Treatment for Qi Stagnation via the Five Phase System

If Qi stagnates for too long, disease ensues. In its early stages it is usually relatively easy to 'un-stagnate' it.

The longer Qi stagnation persists, the more likely it becomes that, as explained above, there will be pain and discomfort, illness and physiological changes to the structure of the body.

By then it will have become much harder for prolonged cure. All the more important, then, to assist Qi to proceed normally!

This can be done in many ways, as you will read throughout the book. Broadly speaking they fall into three categories:

1. The 'Mother' phase: change the environment that caused your condition of Qi stagnation to emerge. This was the original, or what they called the 'Mother', phase.
2. The 'Stagnant' phase: help you adjust to your situation better via relaxation or stimulation, mental conditioning or physical modification. This is the phase in which you are 'stuck'.

3. The 'Child' phase: help your Qi to move gracefully into the next phase – the 'Child' phase.

If the Qi can be encouraged to move on round the Five Phase cycle, then change and transformation recommence and health returns, together with happiness.

Chinese medicine and in particular acupuncture, one of the methods of treatment developed in Chinese medicine, has a particularly clear understanding of this.

Acupuncture uses acupuncture points that can often move stagnant Qi on round the Five Phase cycle, when employed correctly. There are also many other acupuncture points that help stagnant Qi symptoms to resolve naturally.

Summary

If ignored or if its symptoms are suppressed[8] for too long (for example by disregarding them or by ill-considered use of orthodox or other medicine), Qi stagnation can transform into disease.

It becomes more serious because like pressure in a balloon, stagnant Qi needs to expand and to be released.

Failing that it pushes out against other Energy Organs in the body, or turns to – what are called in Chinese medicine – 'Wind' (movement of some kind) or 'Heat' (inflammation, for example).

Often, Qi stagnation in an Energy Organ means it sends Qi in the wrong direction with neither Clear Qi ascending nor Turbid Qi descending properly.

8. Suppression is a word that you may see several times in this book and refers to a condition when symptoms are seemingly made to disappear, but unfortunately, the underlying causative condition continues. Eventually it may happen that, even if the original causative condition has disappeared, symptoms continue, like a car alarm that goes on ringing even after the storm that caused it has long since passed. However, do not condemn your doctor! His training makes him highly skillful in many ways and able to help you. It is just a problem that his medicines are sometimes unintentionally suppressive. For more on this, read http://www.acupuncture-points.org/suppression.html

*Remember the analogy of the shock-wave traffic jam on
a motorway, from the Introduction? Now suppose that after hours,
even days of being unable to escape, some of the motorists drive
off the motorway, pushing sideways as it were. Worse, some turn
round and try to drive back up the motorway, against the flow of
traffic.*

.

Stagnant Qi also prevents what should be natural transformation round what is called the Five Element cycle.

Recognise this progression, do something about it early, and you prevent the occurrence of more severe conditions, conditions that in time might even become fatal.

Lastly, if you have symptoms of Qi Stagnation, try to view them positively. It is your own energy that is stagnating; nobody else's! Those symptoms represent your energy awaiting release. If you can find an effective resolution, you will feel much more positive and energised.

There may be downsides to your solution, but there will be upsides too, possibly immense. What that means is that you may have to give up something you value but the compensating benefits may far exceed the costs.

Often Qi stagnation symptoms are like the feelings you might get in a plane awaiting take-off when the pilot puts the throttle to full speed but keeps the brakes on until the engines are at full power. As a passenger you feel the plane shuddering, almost ripping itself apart as it tries to hold still.

When the brakes are released, suddenly it realises its potential as it takes to the air.

.

Why do we get sick? Read the next chapter.

CHAPTER 2

Susceptibility

This chapter is about why we get ill in ways that are individual to us. Put another way, why do we not all get ill the same way?

We may think, believe or wish that we enter life untarnished in mind and body but we do not. Our genes hand us a cocktail of abilities and susceptibilities. Starting there, we make do!

Some of us need more help than others, some are taught to expect help when they do not really need it, and others learn not to expect it when they do.

The personalities, wealth and knowledge of our parents and our environment affect what we become.

For health, Qi must flow. When it flows slowly, there can be temporary pleasure or pain.

When unable to flow, it stagnates. The consequences are initially discomfort, later pain, ultimately disease.

Organic Change

Finally, there follows organic change to accommodate the stagnation of Qi.

By organic change I mean that there are

recognisable permanent alterations in the shape of the body or its structures and in how the mind works.

Organic change could include

- the appearance of polyps in the bowels
- loss of elasticity in the lungs (eg emphysema, in which the air sacs where oxygen is exchanged stop doing their job, so less oxygen is absorbed)
- the pathological effects of hypertension and ulcers

None of these is a direct consequence of Stagnant Qi, but may follow when Qi takes on some other form. Once there has been organic structural change, cure becomes harder and may be impossible.

And after surgery to reduce the appearance of organic change, a complete return to health is more difficult.

Your Constitution

Your 'constitution' is your body and how well its genes and its health protect you from disease. To some extent it is also how tough you are.

Remember the Princess and the Pea?

The Princess came from Royal stock and had been – we presume -properly fed and watered.

However, as the story goes, she was a spoilt brat!

As a spoilt brat she wanted everything her way, and could not tolerate pain, even a minute amount of discomfort.

Was it 17 mattresses that lay between her and the pea? Accounts differ!

Unfortunately, at least in my opinion, the Prince's mother, the Queen, made the wrong recommendation.

She judged that only a really Royal girl would be able to feel the pea even through 17 mattresses.

I think the Prince might have done better to wed a Princess who could sleep perfectly well without any mattresses, even if right on the pea.

She would have been a far tougher, more resilient girl, almost certainly with a better constitution, more able to bear his Royal children and much less inclined to complain about little inconveniences.

I am sure every Palace has its share of little inconveniences.

So mental toughness has to be there.

Increasing research shows the importance of the mind in helping the body resist disease[1].

Formative Experience

Chris Beardshaw (a garden designer and TV presenter) asked his students to play different kinds of music to see how it affected plant growth. In one greenhouse they played Cliff Richard music. In another Black Sabbath: a third greenhouse was silent, as a control. He told BBC Radio 4 Question Time "The ones with Black Sabbath – great, big, thumping noise, rowdy music – they were the shortest but they had the best flowers and the best resistance to pest and disease.
Those in the Cliff Richard house all died.
Sabotage was suspected but we couldn't prove it."

.

Even a weak body, through supportive nurture, nutrition, exercise and regulation, can be greatly strengthened.

Indeed, 25 years of research[2] have shown that the genes you are born with, good or bad, do not have to behave as you would expect. Each gene, or at least a good many of them, have switches on them, like the light switches in your house.

1. See Who Gets Sick by Blair Justice (Jeremy P. Tarcher) and works by Hans Selye
2. Epigenetic transgenerational inheritance of altered stress responses (Crews, Giullette, Scarpino, Mankkam, Savenkova and Skinner: PNAS June 5, 2012 Vol 109 no 23)

Under certain circumstances, environmental factors can switch some of them on or off. The changes can be carried forward in the genes your children inherit from you.

Unfortunately, some unfavourable environmental factors such as, it would appear, certain chemicals habitually used in developed countries, can affect the mother if she is exposed to them while carrying the foetus at 10 – 12 days.

Her baby then becomes sensitised to them. At certain crucial stages of its life as the child matures, if again exposed to the substance in question, the gene's adverse effect may be switched on in the baby.

Then, at least in the genes of the animals in the experiments, that undesirable effect may carry down the generations indefinitely – and we do not yet know how to turn off the gene's adverse effect.

For example? The tendency to obesity.

This research challenges most thinking in this field over the last 100 years.

Repeated Adverse Circumstance

The body's resistance can be reduced through circumstances – but it can also be increased by them. With small to moderate levels of adversity, the body and mind grow stronger. Beyond a certain level, however, if the adversity continues for too long, resistance weakens. BBC Horizon TV programme reported an experiment in America. A group of males, all over 75, were tested for physical and mental abilities.

Then they were taken to premises specially prepared so that their living conditions would mimic those of 20 years ago, and they had to behave as if they were 20 years younger.

For example, when the bus arrived at the new premises, which were up steps from the bus stop, without a lift, they were told to carry their luggage up themselves, individually.

If this was difficult they could unpack and take their possessions up one by one instead – but there was no help available. They had to do it themselves.

Similarly, they had to walk as they had walked 20 years earlier – no sticks allowed. There was no help with cooking, opening tins, making beds; anything.

After a week, they were re-tested. There was a 61% increase in mental ability, and a marked reduction in dependence on help. One man decided to throw away his stick for good.

All were measurably healthier and fitter. Now, of course, these were volunteers and the act of volunteering for something like this at that age may itself be a sign of fitness.

The point is that it is easy to become dependent on free help, to be passive rather than active, to watch rather than to do.

And not using our body and mind – indeed not regularly stretching them to close to their maximum capacity to stimulate our defensive Qi (our immune system) – leads to greater susceptibility to disease: less resistance in life.

Stretching you to your limit?

Tai Qi (pronounced 'Tie Tchee') is a system of movements developed in China. It stretches you gently up to your limit every time you do it. Those who practise it regularly over the years are adamant about its benefits for their health.

.

The path of dependence runs downwards. It takes effort to avoid it, but effort is rewarded by fitness, as your Qi then flows more strongly round its obstacles.

Continuing and strong adversity is different. It harms and can kill. The fitter you are beforehand, the longer you can take it, and people's capacity to absorb adversity varies.

Mental fitness is the most important form. Physical harm beyond the body's ability to resist it leads to disease and, if continued powerfully, death. To some diseases we have no resistance. Perhaps our forbears adapted to them, but we have lost that resistance.

Immunization is modern science's answer to this, but its long-term effects on the health of future generations is unknown.

Also, whereas some diseases if caught and suffered in childhood conferred almost 100% immunity for life, immunization has to be repeated, sometimes expensively[3].

It is hard to know whether the cost of repeated immunizations and dealing with adverse reactions to them matches the cost of caring for people who suffered badly from the original illness.

I also look forward to evidence disproving that all those generations that survived a childhood dose of measles or mumps handed to succeeding generations a better chance of surviving them or other ills without dangerous consequences.

If we immunize future generations, how fast shall we lose that inherited genetic advantage – if it exists? Does any inherited resistance confer other advantages we might lose?

Antibiotics may no longer be able to defend us. Bacteria adapt to them faster than we can produce new ones.

There are many diseases for which modern medicine has few treatments or the treatments it does have are becoming less effective as the parasite or bacteria adapts to overcome them. These include plague and bilharzias. Even for the common cold there is as yet no effective treatment in modern medicine, as with most virus-caused illnesses.

We owe it to ourselves to keep as healthy as possible against the day when it is only our inbuilt and self-

---

3. Recent research shows the pertussis vaccine provides only limited protection after say, ten years. Scientific American, Oct 2013: 23-24

improved resistance to disease that stands between us and disaster.

Contribution by Chinese medicine to the Stress debate

Western medicine recognises diseases only when they reach a certain stage. This is when there are observable and measurable changes in the body such as

- tissue change or destruction
- abnormal behavioural alterations
- reduced efficiency from invasion by external pathogens
- intense or chronic pain or distress
- measurable alterations in physiology such as hypertension
- measurable alterations in cortical hormone release

Stress generates, from the perspective of Western medicine, temporary or mild abnormalities not amounting to 'disease'.

Examples of what may happen when stress culminates in recognisable diseases include arthritis, asthma, fibromyalgia, irritable bowel syndrome, lowered immune response, myocardial infarction and skin disease.

Western psychologists have speculated on the earlier stages of stress before it amounts to a recognised Western disease. Their theories cover what circumstances lead to stress and who is susceptible to it: and if so, with what symptoms.

Following on from that is the link from individual susceptibility to medically recognisable conditions. For example, what are called 'Type A' people are known to have combative personalities that predispose them to hypertension. Hypertension is a condition that may lead to other disease conditions like myocardial infarction and stroke.

Type B people are the opposite: laid-back, relaxed, sociable, but prone to procrastination and the pursuit of pleasurable activities. Their health problems come, for example, from over-eating. They are not stressed to the same extent as Type A people. But they do get ill eventually though their diseases are still not recognised until later on.

How Chinese Medicine approaches Stress

Chinese medicine recognises the potential for disease at a far earlier stage. It does not relate it to particular kinds of people but to disturbances in the function of their Energy Organs. You will remember the car analogy from the last chapter: twelve cylinders, each equally important in its own way and with a range of functions. These are the Energy Organs. Depending on circumstances, they work in different ways. For instance, they work in a circuit, taking energy round in a loop as in an electrical circuit. This is how they work through 24 hours, each taking two-hour turns as in the Navy analogy.

However, they also work in pairs as in the Five Element system – see appendix 4. (In another arrangement of pairs called the Six Stages[4], they work to defend the body by putting up resistance at different levels as disease tries to penetrate within.)

·

Chinese medicine has many ways to diagnose the early stages of ill-health and many ways to treat it.

·

By recognising which Energy Organ is out of balance you can make predictions. For example –

- what kind of behaviour is brought on by stress

4. http://www.acupuncture-points.org/six-stages.html

- what additional symptoms may appear if the underlying cause cannot be resolved
- how the condition may develop into other syndromes
- what Western medically recognised diseases may then arise
- what therapy or action on your part may ameliorate your condition

Which syndrome matters to you depends on your individual susceptibility. However, certain stages of life, certain emotions and certain work or living patterns may provoke or unbalance your energy system in a recognisable pattern.

Amongst these energetic imbalances is one very similar to the Type A personality, for which the Chinese medical model explains why the behaviour ends up with potential heart problems.

Summary

A small stimulus produces growth, strength and resistance whereas a large stimulus overwhelms or kills[5]. That being so, we should not allow ourselves to become dependent on our doctors and our national health service too soon. We can almost certainly improve our health and well-being by pushing ourselves beyond the point of comfort.

*In the next chapter, you will read what is meant by
Qi stagnation, and how to recognise it.*

5. Hans Selye: read Appendix 8 for other views.

CHAPTER 3

The Meaning of Qi Stagnation

This chapter is an introduction to the basic idea behind this book. If you can grasp it, the rest follows. Fortunately, it is not that difficult to understand because we all suffer from it.

However, how Chinese medicine describes it seems strange to many of us educated in the West.

The idea of stagnation of Qi is foreign to Western Medicine. However, Western medicine actually treats it all the time, often diagnosing it as stress.

Because Western Medicine lacks an understanding of how Qi behaves, its treatment often tends to suppress the symptoms rather than cure the condition[1].

Perhaps also, Western Medicine does not appreciate how one form of Qi can turn into another, more dangerous form. (Chapter 6 explains how what starts as a little nuisance can turn into something more serious.)

Early recognition of the form Qi stagnation takes may prevent further deterioration, or enable a doctor to suggest precautionary action.

---

1. This may be unfair on our doctors who I'm sure often recognise what's happening but who are called on by patients to prescribe medication which tends to suppress symptoms rather than cure the problem.

In Chinese medicine, Qi stagnation can be a major cause of disease, or at least of the susceptibility that leads to disease.

Just as often, however, it is a secondary cause that aggravates an underlying susceptibility such as *Kidney deficiency* or *Liver Blood deficiency*[2], and brings those symptoms out more clearly. By 'secondary cause' I mean that the Kidney deficiency may have been there before but only very mildly until the Qi stagnation exacerbated it.

Once the Qi stagnation becomes apparent, it is often assumed to be the prime cause. If so, treating it will help, but it will not cure the patient until the underlying syndrome is also dealt with.

An Example of Kidney deficiency

For instance, someone may have Kidney deficiency[3], with hot sweats at night, tinnitus, joint and back pain. This syndrome often starts as we grow older, but can occur after a number of fevers, a severe illness or some major over-strain.

Typically, people with Kidney deficiency get more tired, and their symptoms often grow stronger, later in the day, the Kidney 'time ' of day[4] being 5pm to 7pm.

Suppose a woman with weak Kidney Qi has children who get hungry and fractious late in the afternoon just as her Kidney Energy Organ deficiency symptoms peak.

Very often, confronted by her tired and irritable children, she will develop temporary signs of Liver qi stagnation, from even a small stimulus.

2. Kidney Deficiency and Liver Blood deficiency are syndromes in Chinese medicine. Each is a form of weakness or susceptibility to illness, and their symptoms, aetiologies and treatments have been well studied in Chinese medicine.
3. There are actually two kinds of Kidney deficiency, being Kidney Yang deficiency http://www.acupuncture-points.org/kidney-yang-deficiency.html and Kidney Yin deficiency http://www.acupuncture-points.org/kidney-yin-deficiency.html. For simplicity here I have made them into a composite syndrome.
4. See the Chinese Clock, appendix 5.

(Why Liver Qi stagnation? Weak Kidney Qi often predisposes you to Liver Qi stagnation. For reasons why, read chapter 15 and appendix 4.

The stronger your Kidney Qi is, the less susceptible you may be to Liver Qi stagnation.)

For instance, she might find her appetite for junk food increases, she bites her lips, she feels tense and a little breathless, she is more irritable and so on.

These signs are at first temporary. They may go away when her spouse returns from work. (Of course, it is quite possible that the woman is the wage-earner and the husband looks after the children and that it is he who gets these symptoms, not her!) But whichever of them it is, this late afternoon spot is very trying.

If her returning husband is not interested in helping with the children, just wants peace and quiet, then she will eventually start feeling hard done by, a classic pre-condition for developing a more full-blown Liver Qi stagnation.

So now she has two syndromes, slight Kidney deficiency and Liver Qi stagnation. Her Kidney deficiency has been slow to develop and may take some time to worsen whereas Liver Qi stagnation can quickly become predominant.

At that stage she needs a good rest away from the children, lots of attention from her husband, and time to recover.

Unfortunately, that is not always what she gets.

Alcohol relieves!

In many homes the woman starts taking a little alcohol, which works just fine.

Alcohol, in small quantities, helps Qi flow and that is great, except that eventually she needs a little more – and more.

What started as an occasional sip or two becomes a habit that leads to other syndromes in Chinese medicine and some recognised conditions in Western medicine.

How can a doctor or therapist deal with this?

Anyone treating her would now need several arrows to his bow. He needs to be able to listen, counsel and inspire. He should be able to recommend foods and supplements that help her body overcome any nutritional deficiencies she has developed.

He could suggest exercise. He could broach the subject of getting better support from her husband. And then he can treat her, for example with acupuncture, which is often brilliant for both parts of the syndrome picture.

What is Qi, and how does it stagnate?

Because Qi has neither shape nor form, it is hard for Western medicine to recognise or accept the idea of Qi. Indeed, only when it stagnates can one see its effect.

An analogy may help us to understand it.

Imagine a happy, healthy child, running and playing safely out in the park or garden.

You know he's there, but you cannot hear him. He's pursuing his interests vigorously, perhaps with friends.

They play cops and robbers, or cowboys and Indians, or dig tunnels or whatever.

Occasionally they get thirsty or hungry, may need to sit or rest awhile, then off they go again.

They are good watchmen too. If they see something going on, they tell you so you can check it. Perhaps someone breaks into the garden, or water starts to leak from a pipe. You can be sure that they will tell you, usually loudly.

But what happens when they are not allowed out? Perhaps it is raining or they have been 'grounded'.

Now there is noise and commotion in the house, and more likelihood of tempers and frustrations. Things get broken. Children, who were supposed to stay in their rooms, expand their area of activity to include any cupboards on the landing, the bathroom and other bedrooms.

Or they're in the lounge, hugely and restlessly, wanting far more food and drink than if they'd been out of doors. They watch TV, play computer or interactive TV games; There is noise, they take up space, they eat and drink more, the foods they eat make them fidgety and eventually fractious.

They start spilling over into your space.

You, of course, just want to work quietly at your desk, but you keep getting bothered by them. You start feeling put upon. You cannot get your work done. You have targets to meet and cut-off dates for your work. You cannot spend all your time soothing disputes.

Now you get tension in your shoulders, and you start grinding your teeth. You start nibbling food that you normally would not. If it is a wet summer, you will have indigestion by the time the children return to school. You will also be taking painkillers for headaches, and possibly a laxative.

Failing that, perhaps you will have taken to drink!

So, here was Qi, at first running smoothly so there were no symptoms – children outside and you quietly working.

Then the Qi got constrained (children stuck indoors) and began to stagnate (commotion, things broken, tempers frayed).

That meant noise, swelling (more space needed by the children), more appetite for junk food, restlessness, tension, indigestion, headache and so on...

In health, we have enough Qi. Each of our Energy Organs has its own Qi and together they make Blood from what we eat. That Blood is led around your body by your Qi, which keeps it in place, moving along nicely.

When Qi stagnates, things stop moving. There is a build-up of emotion. That means tension.

Take another analogy.

You are in your car, travelling across town for an appointment.

You have had breakfast and you have left home in plenty of time, well-prepared for your interview.

You are happy and in a state of pleasant anticipation.

It is a sunny day and you enjoy the drive. All the other cars and buses are moving along steadily, with just temporary stops for traffic lights.

But then the traffic pattern changes. There is a queue of traffic and you stop.

You cannot see what the cause is, and you remain stopped. The minutes tick by. You check your watch. You tune into your local radio. It tells you about emergency road works.

Worse, there has been an accident.

Surrounding you now there are increasing numbers of irritable drivers. They all have appointments to reach.

Pedestrians have to wait longer for buses, and start walking if they can. Everyone complains. No cars or buses can move for miles around and there are tail-backs into and out of the city. People miss their train and plane connections. Blame is apportioned freely.

You abandon the car and walk, at least as far as the other side of the disturbance. But once you arrive, all the taxis have gone. Now you worry about the safety of your car. Indecision: wait for another taxi or return to your car and abandon the appointment? Furrowed brow, anxiety, tension. Eventually indigestion, headache and shallow breathing. Stuffy chest. Restlessness.

Right there! That is the Qi stagnating in you. It blocks digestion, pushes up to your head and prevents free movement of air. That restlessness – 'wind' – is a sign of your Qi wanting to move.

But so far, no real damage done.

Damage happens only if the condition continues indefinitely. Then there may be organic changes to your body as it adapts. Unfortunately, such adaptation is not beneficial in the long term, but may work in the short term.

For example? Your blood pressure goes up because of the

stress. When traffic starts flowing again and you reach your appointment in time, your blood pressure slowly reduces.

But what if your life is made up of constant frustrations with no real chance to calm down? Then your blood pressure may remain raised, in time possibly harming your heart.

Summary

Life is full of inconvenience. Long[5] exposure to it leads to Qi stagnation, often experienced as tension and tightness, eventually pain and disease. Chinese medicine has mapped out the ways this stagnating Qi causes further symptoms and explains them in what are called 'syndromes[6]'.

If one or more syndromes are diagnosed, they suggest possible aetiologies, treatment strategies, and tactics for the patient to help himself. These need not include the powerful prescribed medications or self-prescribed social drugs that cost societies so much.

However, left to 'cook' for too long, the consequences of that Qi stagnation may require treatment over an extended period. Even Chinese medicine is not a panacea.

In the next chapter we look at a vital idea in Chinese thought and medicine that may help you appreciate where our problems come from.
It introduces the Chinese approach to what has been a long-standing debate in the West on the best approach to stress: whether it is better and if so how to reduce the incidence of stressors (the things or actions that cause stress) or to concentrate on reducing the symptoms when you get stressed.

5. 'Long' is a relative term. One person exposed for five minutes might reach an explosive point; another might tolerate it with equanimity.
6. Syndromes are what practitioners of Chinese medicine treat. They have many different names, partly depending on which school of Chinese medicine you attend. Well-known syndromes include Liver Qi stagnation, Kidney Yin deficiency, Invasion of Wind-Heat.

The Chinese evolved a theory that is, I believe, a useful way of categorising external factors in relation to the individual. This theory can be used, and has been used for at least 2000 years, to make predictions about possible outcomes.

CHAPTER 4

Yin, Yang and Life

How did we all get ourselves into this mess? ... Well, that bothered the ancient Chinese too. They took it seriously. Here is what they came up with, and it is just as relevant today as it was back then.

This chapter is a meagre introduction to both the ideas and the application of Yin, Yang and Qi stagnation in both life and politics. It represents my own ideas rather than seeking to reinterpret somebody else's.

Without Yin and Yang, there would be no philosophical foundation for Qi, nor for life's vicissitudes. Yin and Yang help to explain how external factors lead to Qi stagnation in us.

So not just in you and me – in individual persons, but in whole countries too we get Qi stagnation. If your country's Qi stagnates, it is more likely there will be circumstances that make your individual Qi stagnate.

What is the essential idea behind this chapter?

Change: in time, everything changes. If you are open to it and can adapt to it, your Qi will not stagnate.

However, that means you may lose what you have. Few of us want to lose what we have – we prefer our comfort zones! – so we resist change. That means Qi stagnation: stress! Change comes almost entirely from Yang factors – these are mainly ideas and beliefs. Yin factors, if they accede to it, provide the means for change to take place steadily.

If we refuse to change, we stultify and ultimately we die.

If we can change, we learn, grow and mature beyond what we thought of ourselves capable.

Root or classical texts for this approach

The root texts for this include the I Ching or Book of Change[1] which explores symbolically the different ways a given situation can emerge from the one before it. Another main classical text is the Dao de Jing[2].

The I Ching has traditionally been used for 'divinatory' purposes but can be read purely for its observations on how life turns out.

'Divinatory'?

"Fortune-telling" to our baser modern minds!? But the ancient sages saw the I Ching more as a way to understand and adjust themselves to the inevitability of life, with suggestions for possible actions and their consequences. Many modern philosophers, psychologists and others have found the comments and reflections in these ancient books of immediate relevance to their lives.

1. (yi jing)There are many translations of this text into English. A famous one by Wilhelm, Richard and Baynes, Cary F, Princeton Univ. Press 1967 is not that easy to read but has a forward by Carl Jung. More recent is by Karcher, Stephen and Ritsema, Rudolf, Element Books 1994. For its introduction and suggestions about how to use the book read the Book of Change by Blofeld, John, Dutton, 1965. An excellent recent book - Yin-Yang Code - by Dr Ning Lu gives it a mathematical introduction. However, the English in the first few chapters is sometimes almost incomprehensible. There are many other editions, and in many languages. Everyone has his own favourite. Every I Ching scholar thinks all translations except his own are inaccurate and then humbly admits that his own one is not right either.
2. The Tao Te Ching, Daodejing, or Dao De Jing (.. :. dào "way";. dé "virtue ";. jing "classic" or "text"). Many translations: hundreds. Compare some of them at http://www.duhtao.com/sidebyside.html. It can, however, be argued that Qi was the basic idea and that Yin and Yang were a way of understanding how Qi changed.

First, a reminder of the origin of this idea of Qi and Qi stagnation. The basic idea that the Chinese developed to explain life, the universe and everything, was that of Yin and Yang. This idea goes back at least to the second millennium BC.

What are Yin and Yang?

Yin and Yang are concepts. They are representations of two aspects of a single idea; two sides of an idea.

Like 'left' and 'right', each depends on the other. You cannot meaningfully say something is on the 'right' unless there is something else to its left.

Equally, 'up' and 'down', or 'heavier' and 'lighter', or 'male' and 'female'. With the latter, if everyone was of the same sex you could not have someone of the 'opposite' sex because the opposite would not exist.

But this Yin and Yang idea goes further. It defines how the two sides relate: indeed it defines how all pairs interrelate.

Yin and Yang:

- Appear to oppose one another: they are opposites
- Are mutually interdependent
- Support one another
- Supply the means for the other to exist

Like two sides of a coin, neither would exist without the other. So far, so good, because these qualities apply to all the pairs listed above (let/right; up/down; heavier/lighter etc.)

However, there is one other quality with Yin and Yang:

Yin and Yang **change** into one another. This is a bit harder to understand because it seems to imbue Yin and Yang with an energy, as if they are not just a state of being or a relationship, like left or right, but dynamic.

Consider:

At birth, our bodies are energetically growing and learning (a Yang state) whereas at death they are the opposite (Yin).

After death, the cells that formed our bodies eventually break apart (a Yang process) and

- go back into the food chain (a Yin process)
- to find their way up the food chain eventually to be
- absorbed by two parents (Yin process)
- who after sex (Yang process)
- and incubation (Yin process)
- produce (Yang process, at least for the mother)

... their next progeny.

Another example:

A political party at its birth is fizzing with ideas and energy (Yang state) but years, possibly centuries later, those ideas are found stale, old and wanting (Yin state), to be discarded.

However, aspects of them will continue, either as part of something new, or by sparking ideas that oppose them or prompt new thinking (Yang process).

Another example:

Physicists say that at the beginning of time, there was what we now call a Big Bang. Before that event, there was nothing meaningful, or at least, it is impossible to know.

The Big Bang started from what is thought to have been an infinitesimally small point, with an act of creation (Yang).

Because there was no Yin acting in balance this Yang act created Yin, the first forms of which were Time and Space.

Actually, you can probably forget about Time, which by some is considered merely an adaptation or aspect of Space[3].

Politicians seeking election can afford to be flexible and experimental (Yang) in their thinking; they promise great changes and improvements. At the birth of a political party, its parents imagine all the potential (Yin) inherent in the life they have created (Yang).

Once elected, they become part of the status quo, responsible for the whole country so inevitably they become more conservative and Yin. (As you mature, you grow a bigger body, not so quick to learn as when a baby, but stronger and more resilient.)

If they continue to be too creative (Yang), they will find that their civil service (Yin) will either resist or must be replaced (Yang process).

Countries where the civil service[4] is replaced usually enter hugely disruptive phases (Yang) before settling down to some new kind of status quo (Yin).

Your body can take a huge amount of stress, as athletes in training know, to achieve superb results.

However, everybody has a point beyond which damage occurs, when his body either resists further change – often through trauma – or fails.

The same goes for a country and its government.

Yin, Yang, Blood and Qi in the body

The process by which this idea of Yin and Yang manifests in the body is through the interplay of Qi and Blood.

Although, in this chapter, I am looking at how this might apply to the political economy and how this is reflected in the body, we start with the body.

Qi and Blood are also concepts. You may think you

3. Read 'The End of Time' by Julian Barbour Weidenfeld and Nicolson 1999.
4. Civil services are usually replaced following violent revolutions. For example the French Revolution; over throw of Tsarist Russia; Pol Pot.

know what Blood (capital B) is, but unless you study quite a lot of Chinese Medicine, you probably do not.

·

Qi comes first. Everything is a manifestation of Qi, but for convenience, in the body we say you have Qi and Blood, even though Blood is just a thicker form of Qi. And indeed, there are many other forms of Qi...

·

Blood (capital B) is not just the red stuff in your arteries and veins – blood. It represents a good deal more.

Blood itself is a form of Qi.

Indeed, everything is Qi in one form or another. In the study of the body, we use Blood and Qi as separate concepts, because in Chinese Medicine Blood represents a special and important kind of Qi, understood by practitioners.

Though still a kind of Qi, Blood is relatively Yin in relation to many other forms of Qi in the body.

In a country, one might say that Qi is the thoughts and actions of the people and the equivalent of Blood might be the people[5] themselves.

If that is all a bit abstruse, do not worry! Let us just stick with Qi and say that Qi represents the different forms of Yin and Yang as they inter-relate, support one another, oppose one another and change into one another.

Qi in health

For health, Qi should move freely. This means that Yin and Yang factors interplay smoothly. Neither takes precedence.

Energy flows between them, back and forth in its

5. 'Time is Blood' is a remark attributed to General Chuikhov, Commander of the 62nd (Soviet) Army when confirming he understood that his job was to defend Stalingrad or die in the attempt. His main weapons were cunning and the people. See The Second World War by Antony Beevor, Orion Publishing Group – 2012.

different forms, without too much opposition and without stagnation.

In a country what prevents this? The following is my attempt to equate what happens in the body with what happens in a political Identity.

Qi in the Body

Qi in the body takes many forms, including blood, sinews, brain and bone. It also carries ideas, warmth, inspiration and action, and how we hold our memories, how our minds work. Qi takes on the structure available to it.

Other vital forms of Qi in Chinese medicine are *defensive* qi (rather like your immune system), *inherited* qi (rather like your genetic makeup) and so on. That is in your body.

Qi in the political economy

For health, Qi must move.

It must be free to take on its different forms, being ideas one day, form or movement and change the next.

If it is moving and able to change its form as it moves, then you have a healthy economy.

If healthy, everyone in a country is happy and well, the country is stable, its people are adaptable, it can defend itself, and its needs are met.

That country can face opposition or competition creatively by

- adapting to it
- responding to it
- advancing
- retreating
- sometimes standing firm and sometimes changing.

As such it will, as a country, sometimes favour one part of its people over another.

Sometimes it will honour one part, sometimes another, and its people will comply because the government perfectly reflects the needs and opinions of its people. Wonderful!

Except, as everyone knows, that is not how it works. For one thing, sometimes a government has to send its people off to war to protect itself from loss or to gain something.

War can mean, first, diplomatic discussion and pressure. When that fails, it means people dying: hence General Chuikhov's perceptive but terrible comment, "Time is Blood", mentioned above.

And it is all very well to talk about being perfectly adaptable to the needs of the situation, but some of us do not like change much. Mostly these are the older or richer among us, the more Yin-like.

Most 'comfortable' people fear war. However, many of those who survived the Second World War without too much damage or misery actually had the times of their lives.

War (a Yang state of change, death and destruction, victory and profit) certainly gets your adrenalin going: an exciting feeling. This release of Qi can be enormously satisfying at the time[6].

Young people like excitement more than old people, making Young people more Yang. Yang people adapt better to change, and often want it.

More Yang	Less Yang	Less Yin	More Yin
Babies and Children	Teenagers and young adults	'Mature' people	Older, slower people

They see imperfections and strive to do something about them.

6. For more on this read the work done by Lawrence E. Hinckle 'The effect of exposure to culture change, social changes and changes in interpersonal relationships on health' in Stressful Life Events: Their Nature and Effects by DS & BP Dohrenwend, Wiley 1974.

That means Yang change for everyone else.

The young are willing to undergo these changes in aid of their ideals (the word 'ideal' is a Yang word).

Sometimes inspirational people, some of whom are fanatics, put forward ideas that threaten the status quo.

If the country is sufficiently mature and stable, it can absorb (Yin word) and manage these firebrands.

It does this either by letting them vent or by controlling them, limiting their movement, imprisoning them or expelling them.

More Yang	Less Yang	Less Yin	More Yin
Ideas of fanatics, zealots, and revolutionaries	New Ideas	Accepted Ideas	State-controlled ideas and religions: priests, police and army

Too much change, as governments know to their cost, can be destructive. New governments usually want change but if they are sensible they begin it gradually so nobody complains too much.

In terms of Yin and Yang, they control the speed at which Yang turns into Yin and vice versa. They let Qi flow but not so fast that people get hurt.

More Yang	Less Yang	Less Yin	More Yin
Philosophy, Abstruse thinking	Education	Teaching Colleges	Institutions, Associations, Trade Unions

Change can be Yin-like. In fact, Yin change is as important as Yang-like change, but it occurs less obviously.

For example, I decide my garden should enjoy daffodils next Spring. That is the originating Yang idea. Then I plan where to put them, which kinds to buy, how to prepare the soil.

That is also Yang-like: it is still all in the mind. Next, we get to the Yin phase.

In late Autumn, I prepare the soil, and buy and plant the bulbs.

Look! That is me labouring in the garden, carrying out the changes I planned.

Now I am a more Yin-like process, just working away steadily, digging and preparing, planting and watering. Then comes the Yin-like change. We wait. We wait.

My young children inspect where I planted the bulbs every day. Eventually they get bored. Nothing! For months, nothing!

More Yang	Less Yang	Less Yin	More Yin
Let us plant Daffodils!	Yes, yes, let's! Where shall we put them and what kinds shall we buy and please, what are daffodils? And are they nice with ice-cream? Can I have a chocolate one?	Sight of my back, bent over the soil as I plant the damned things.	We wait and we wait. We replant those the squirrels unearthed (allegedly). Then we go on waiting until everyone is bored and has forgotten the whole thing. Meanwhile...

Then, a miracle. Sometime in February or so, a green shoot. Then more. Then one day, we wake to Spring and the glory the plants bestow.

The Yin-like change took place under our noses. We hardly noticed until reality reflected my original Yang-like idea.

Sources of discord, of Qi stagnation

Any government has to balance its ideas with its means. As we are discovering, discord builds when there are huge differences between one segment of society and another, and when one group notices and resents these differences.

More Yang	Less Yang	Less Yin	More Yin
The Poor			The Rich

For example, if some (a few) people are too rich and many are too poor by comparison, what happens?

Eventually, the poor will change the situation. They will do this through electing politicians who change the status quo.

Failing that, they will take matters into their own hands in protest, failing which, ultimately, they start a revolution.

A strong government leader or dictator can prevent change for a considerable period of time, during which the people suffer, but he cannot hold it back forever.

Either a dictator goes, or he dies, or the people die.

More Yang	Less Yang	Less Yin	More Yin
Community Politics	Regional Councils	National Government	Dictators

Many rich people are aware of this kind of dynamic and live in gated communities.

I have a friend who moved to Bulgaria.

Unlike many other ex-patriots he refused to put a wall round his property. He did his best to interact and relate to the surrounding community by buying from and selling to them, employing them and learning their language.

While not always successful, he became respected and sought out for his qualities. When he fell on hard times (accident

– kicked by a horse; a bad harvest, together with an unfortunately dyslexic mistake with his bank) he was able to seek the community's support.

This contrasted with many expats living near him in gated communities who mingled only with their own and bought their food at supermarkets in distant cities. These 'rich' people were seen as fair game by the local 'entrepreneurs'.

My friend, when he fell on hard times, found that the community rallied round, looked after his animals and protected his farm and stock from theft.

Although when he originally arrived in Bulgaria he was, in local perceptions, much wealthier than they, he traded with them, lived among them and shared what he had with them.

His living standards were slightly above theirs but not hugely so: certainly not enough to rouse their envy and resentment.

The exchange of friendship, goods and work kept him at one with this community.

.

So here Qi moved evenly, neither Yang nor Yin becoming excessive or reaching a tipping point.

Contrast that with the gated communities (Yin) seen as targets by Yang entrepreneurs leading to crime.

Crime is one way of resolving Qi stagnation, where criminals see 'them' and 'us' as an opportunity.

However, crime leads to more Qi stagnation because the burgled get angry and frustrated.

Sudden Change

Sudden change is Yang. Successful entrepreneurialism; forcing through new government policies; winning the lottery; accident; war; financial calamity: these are Yang-like.

Slow Change

Slow, organic change is Yin. Changes in the law and cultural customs; starvation from insufficiency; steady progress towards an ideal; the building up of your pension or wealth over your lifetime: these are Yin-like.

From all this, what can we learn?

The country you live in is also subject to the interplay of Yin and Yang. Qi represents that interplay as it happens. The change it produces impinges on you as an individual.

How you and your body encounter and react to that change, the different stages of the flow between the political Yin and Yang, produce challenges to which you must adapt or be destroyed by.

How does this chapter help you deal with stress?

Yin Situations

If your stressful situation is stable, meaning that it is a continuing condition which you face daily, then it has the characteristics of a Yin situation.

This might be, for example, the status quo in your life which causes you great tension and frustration but which, in expectations of its long-term benefits, you have tolerated.

Is there a way out of this? The Yin-Yang theory says yes. It may not be exactly what you want but there is a way, and that way is via a Yang process.

If you have understood this chapter, then you will realise that Yang processes involve sudden change, often in the form of surprise, a factor well understood in military circles.

A Yang action might be a question. She or he who asks the questions is temporarily in control. If you have already considerable resources of your own (Yin – which might merely be superior, or at least good, intellectual qualities, or might be assets the withdrawal of which would severely weaken the maintenance of the status quo), then the question may seem obvious to you and may instigate huge changes.

If you lack those Yin resources, you must create them by careful forethought (Yin). This means you must consider all aspects of the situation beforehand, what would be an effective question and what answers or statements might be given to it.

You may need to develop support structures, for example, possible areas of agreement with others who, after your question, will rally to your side. If you know or can guess correctly the likely responses you can think of further questions to counter them.

In other words, you get a debate going the very existence of which may undermine the status quo.

Timing. You must also consider timing. Indeed, perhaps, timing is the most important factor, giving you the potential for surprise. Any very Yin-like situation is actually unstable, requiring more and more resources to maintain it. So surprise, and the right action or question, may de-stabilise it more quickly than you expect.

Yang situations

By their nature, Yang situations are both creative and destructive. They do not last long without changing. For you they can be very unsettling and in extreme situations, may kill you.

So by their very nature, they lead to more stable situations in due course. However, whether you will like the new situation to some extent depends on you.

If you are in that Yang-like situation, you may have more power to change it than you think. Your Yang-like response to it may push it in a positive direction, away from destruction towards creation.

If not, then your response must be Yin like. You must, at least for yourself, try to set up regular, nourishing, supportive systems. Sleep, food, time for yourself, even amongst the mayhem, may allow you to survive it.

If you choose correctly, others will copy you and seeing the sense of your actions, begin to support you. In effect, you start doing what needs to be done – provide a Yin-like solution.

Yang-like situations always have a downside. Yang destroys the status quo. So in any response, think long-term: what good can you create from it?

Summary

The implications of Yin-Yang theory are profound. They directly affect everyday life at all levels. Over the millennia, people spent years of their lives pondering the concepts and writing about them.

If you have grasped the concepts from this small introduction, you may be able to apply them to your life. The idea of Yin and Yang is just as applicable to your country as it is to your body.

Yang processes are quick and often painful, Yin processes slow and inexorable. Yin processes involve long-term endurance, even suffering, while Yang processes are creative, act fast and sometimes destructively.

If Yin processes change too slowly in your country, it dies.

As you grow old, the time comes when your body can no longer repair itself (quick Yang or slow Yin process) and you die.

A political idea will always one day cease to be relevant. How long it resists change depends on its size and strength.

The interplay of Yin and Yang[7] nationally and within your community has a direct effect on your own health. If you take no part in politics you become essentially Yin-like as far as the Yang process of political change is concerned.

Yin-like, your circumstances or days are numbered because when something reaches its most Yin form, it becomes Yang, meaning that a Yang process will change it. In this case that Yang process might be terminal!

From the above you may understand that whereas Yang, given enough Yin, renews itself quickly (as in the morning after a good sleep we feel re-energised), Yin takes ages both to become exhausted and, usually, to renew itself.

Yin deficiency, in one form or another, is a growing problem for many people in the world: water shortage; time exhaustion; living beyond our means. Physically it shows in many modern conditions such as prolonged menopausal problems, continual tiredness and its effects, impoverished foods and the need for nutriceuticals, chronic inflammatory illnesses, conditions associated with aging and so on.

How to prevent and repair Yin deficiency has always been and will always be a lucrative source of income for ingenious innovative Yang energies.

The I Ching, the Book of Change, is an ancient treatise on the myriad ways Yin and Yang interact and gives thousands of examples in theoretical form for us to ponder.

.

What happens when your Qi does not flow in response
to change is the subject of the next chapter.

---

7. My book 'Yang Deficiency - Get Your Fire Burning Again' goes into the political implications of Yang Deficiency in much more detail.

CHAPTER 5

The Four Phases or Five Elements

Getting Stuck in One of the Phases of Life

This idea, of the four phases or five elements, is probably as old a concept in Chinese medicine as Yin and Yang.

This Phase (or Element) system is probably as old a concept in Chinese medicine as Yin and Yang.

For Stress, the Five 'Elements' arranged in a 'Four Phase' diagram can help you understand the good and bad aspects of your situation.

Knowing in which phase you are 'stuck' suggests STRATEGIES TO IMPROVE your situation.

This simple diagram carries a host of meanings.

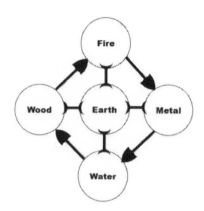

As you see, Fire, Metal, Water and Wood form a daisy-chain round Earth at the Centre.

Read below what each phase means and how they inter-relate with one another.

Each Element[1] or Phase describes part of life

Wood represents morning, spring, starting, making plans, taking chances, teens and twenties: also frustration, storms, anger, many kinds of headache, tensions, cramps, etc.

Fire represents midday, summer, supposedly the fun part of life, recognition, distinction, success, the warmth of friendship, leadership: also loss of control, lack of recognition, manic states, paranoia, hysteria, palpitations and peptic ulcers etc.

·

*Do not take too literally the periods of life described. Some people enjoy a Wood phase into their eighties.
Others retire at 30.*

·

Earth represents steady work and settling down, the people on the bus, fruits of effort, nourishment and family life: also worry, obsession, over-mothering, problems with nourishment and security, digestive problems, phlegm, many kinds of rheumatism and muscle pain etc.

Metal represents afternoon and evening, retirement, autumn, pensions, letting go and making space, careful consideration of all the possibilities, researching to discover

1. This diagram is not the diagram usually used for the Five Elements, for which see appendix 4. I find the diagram I have used in this chapter better when explaining stress.

new ways forward, caring for grandchildren: also regrets, grief, disappointment, partings, skin, lung and large intestine problems, poverty (the result of not saving enough earlier in life), energy loss, weak voice etc.

Water represents night, ends and beginnings, winter, retreating into stillness and contemplation, quietude, adaptability, development of new resources behind the scenes: also fear, back pain, health problems of old age and very early life, memory loss, loss of will-power and the power to renew etc.

Wood, Fire, Metal and Water are a circuit round *Earth*, where each phase arises from the previous one and flows into the next one.

People can get stuck in a phase, leading to Qi stagnation. The problems of Earth, at the centre, often accompany problems of the other four phases.

Earth at the Centre

Fire, Metal, Water and Wood all depend on Earth. They draw nourishment from it and return quality to it, just as leaves change carbon dioxide into oxygen all spring and summer, then are released back to the ground in autumn.

In addition, nearly all the time the plant's roots give and receive nutrients by exchanging them with the soil, usually through soil fungi (mycorrhiza).

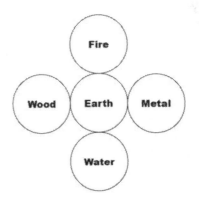

In the same way, one may say that Wood improves through business the efficiency of life. Fire beautifies its surroundings; Metal gives quality; Water, underlying potential for strength.

Some Earth situations over-control the flow of life. Most people know what happens when someone is over-mothered.

When people get stuck in a phase

However, when we get stressed, we get stuck, and often this can relate to one of the phases.

You also see this in people in a phase unsuitable or inappropriate for their stage of life. For example, a child might be considered 'old before his days', meaning that he seems to have missed out on the ir-responsibilities of childhood and gone straight perhaps to the attitudes of Metal.

Some people are stuck in the Fire phase, wanting always to party and experience fun. They find it difficult to take life seriously, to settle down, to save, to be responsible.

Others are stuck in Wood, only wanting to expand and conquer.

Many people at low points in their lives get stuck in Metal or Water, the former unable to let go of past patterns and old memories, the latter unable to bring potential to the seed of life within them.

The classical Jewish mother seems stuck in Earth.

The following explains all this in more depth.

EARTH phase including Spleen and Stomach

The Earth phase shows how your body utilises the Earth and its produce. It is like a pipe, running through you. What is in the pipe remains part of the Earth and returns to it after your body has absorbed the nutrition, the fuel that it needs.

Your car has a similar system, but with two mouths. You

put fuel, petrol or diesel, in one mouth, the opening to the fuel tank. Air comes in through the other mouth, the air intake.

You use the accelerator pedal to control the carburetor, and the fuel and air mix that reaches the cylinders of your engine. In the cylinders it explodes, pushing down the pistons and turning the engine. The faster the engine turns, the more power it generates. You use that power to move the car, generate electricity for the car's lights, heater fan and so on.

The spent fuel is pushed out through the exhaust pipe. At no point is that fuel part of the car, although for a time it is inside as it passes through the fabric of the car. The same goes, in a way, for food in your digestion, which connects with the Earth along the walls of your digestive tract. You are dependent on food to live. You extract what you need and jettison the rest.

Through your skin you also contact the Earth. You wear clothes and shoes through which you remain in contact with the Earth. Those clothes are made of fabrics that come from the Earth and will one day return to it.

Your skin flakes off, and the skin-flakes return to the earth. You discard clothes and old shoes to the waste-bin, the contents of which are recycled through the Earth via landfill, or nowadays through Earth-energy organisations that sell or give them to others.

So the Earth phase is not so much a phase as the centre round which the other Elements circle.

The other elements (Water, Wood, Fire and Metal) represent your life, which would not exist but for the Earth element foundation.

In your body, the earth, as vegetables, meat, fruit and grain is absorbed as food. Those forms of Qi are transformed into blood. Mixed with air, and pumped by your Heart, that blood becomes Blood transported round your body, creating flesh and bone, brain and tendon, nerve and muscle, eye and skin.

The original Earth-like place where you started was your mother's womb: comfortable and free for nine months! Then, pushed out, you were on your own – to live!

In life, your Earth element represents not just nourishment but wherever or whatever you call home. This may be a house but it also represents your community, your family, your society, your friends, your source of income.

All these are your forms of nourishment in one way or another. They keep you in touch with the outside, with the world, with reality.

Literally, they keep you down to earth. You need to be able to rely on them from time to time. Here are some aspects of the Earth phase, good and bad.

Desirable to be able to rely on at times during life:	... that you cannot rely on or that limit your life:
Loving nourishment and nurturing	Comfort foods, baby foods; famine, barrenness; infertility; obesity; emaciation; jealousy, envy; gluttony, greed
Support group, help, security; your safety net; government support or handouts	Prison; the government's or society's action to limit your freedom; gossip
Strong constitution	Weak constitution; lethargy; sloth; attachment; ignorance
Mothering, parenting	Stifled growth, over-mothering
Administration and Development	Disorganisation
Steady work and well-being	Anxiety, obsession, worry – the divided mind
Enabled growth by (organic) multiplication	Disabled growth
Team, employees	Loafers, slackers

Looking at the two columns, you can see on the left the situations in life that you would like to be able to rely on, such as when seeking to grow or when ill.

On the right, are situations or people that you cannot rely on, that limit your potential, that literally take the floor away from under your feet or, in some cases, that tie you down to behaviour patterns that you cannot shake off.

We all need a safe place to be able to rely on. It may be physical, such as a welcoming home or group of friends. It may also be a mental idea, a place to find solace in our thinking.

Stuck in the Earth phase

How do you recognise someone stuck in their Earth phase? These might be people who feel that they just go about their lives while real 'life' goes on round them.

*Of course, someone 'stuck in Earth' may lead a wonderful and fulfilling life, circulating Qi through their outer four phases vigorously in arenas outside work. Miners race pigeons; bank clerks do amateur dramatics. But Qi **must** move or change!*

For example, some mothers devote themselves to nurturing and bringing up their babies and children. Whether this is the high or low point of their lives, they will occasionally look up and notice that former friends have developed careers, made their mark and moved into different circles.

Many people work for a living. The job doesn't excite them but it pays their living costs. It supplies income in exchange for labour. Unless they make efforts to better themselves, they can be stuck in the same or a similar job all their lives. They may be reliable people but lead unexciting lives.

Many Earth people from inclination or from want of effort look with envy on others who through endeavour or good fortune have reached fame, in particular the Fire phase.

However, for different reasons, people trapped by fame in the Fire phase eventually often desire the relative obscurity of ordinary life, signified by the Earth phase. They want to be 'normal' and just live their lives quietly.

Diseases associated with this phase are discussed later in the chapters on Spleen, Stomach and Intestines. Usually, their problems come from digestive tract problems and from worry or anxiety.

Why worry and anxiety? Usually this is because their work or occupation, though vital to others, to their employers and the government never pays enough for them to be able to relax or retire early. They are bound to the wheel of life by necessity. Payday is never early enough. So they worry.

These are everyday worries and anxieties. However, they are shared, to some extent by all the other phases.

Strategies for Earth phase

Because everyone needs a safe place when stressed, mechanisms or therapies to help your Earth phase will be useful to anyone in stress.

The following are examples of Earth-phase enhancing therapies or activities that help nearly everyone who is stressed, though some need practice before they can be used. Others need someone else to administer them. Some are just things you can do on your own that nourish your Earth element.

- Autogenics
- Biofeedback
- Cooking and good food
- Counselling

- Cycling, excluding racing
- Eating out with friends
- Gardening
- Guided imagery/relaxation sessions eg with CDs
- Keeping pets for companionship and to care for
- Massage, gentle, soothing
- Nutrition – the right foods for you can make a huge difference to your health and ability to withstand stress
- Shiatsu
- Storytelling as in being told stories or learning how to tell stories to willing listeners eg children
- Swimming – non-competitive
- Tai Qi
- Team sports that are not played too competitively
- Walking alone to enjoy surroundings or with friends
- Weight training under guidance

WATER phase including Kidney and Bladder

Having considered our foundation, the Earth phase of life, how do we actually go about our lives?

What are the processes or actions that take us from day to day, and how does stress or illness prevent us from moving round the wheel of life?

Start with the beginning, which is also the end, the Water phase. You start as a cell, a seed, germinating into a foetus in the Earth of your mother's womb.

Here you are relatively unconscious. This is the phase when your genes begin to express themselves. Your parents' genes have created you, an entirely new being, unique in creation, for better or worse.

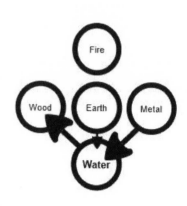

Sometimes you have genes that give you beauty and grace, speed and agility. Some people are disabled. We must all make do.

This is also the phase when you rest, sleep or holiday, when you convalesce or recover from your labours. This is a Yin phase. Processes here usually work slowly, unseen. This is very much the opposite of the Fire phase, see later.

This is winter, night and darkness, a phase of endurance and fears, but also of overcoming fears with renewed determination and new skills that you can use in the next phase of life (Wood).

This phase starts when the previous phase, Metal, lets go. Metal yields the remains of the previous cycle, in the form of savings, seeds, wisdom, teaching, experience and attachments. Those go into the Water phase where they can either be lost or revitalised.

Here are aspects of the Water phase, good and bad.

Desirable to be able to rely on at times during life:	That you cannot rely on or that limit your life:
Rest, sleep, convalesce, recover, holiday, renew	Burnout, lowered immunity, lowered body temperature
Stillness, waiting, patience: also, the power to move on	Paralysis; refusal to shift or change or move
Will-power, determination	Fear, irrationality

Potential, Talents and Powers, Creativity	Dropout(s). Fear of starting anything new
Meditate, concentration	Loss of memory and ability to think, poor concentration
Control and regulate	Pour cold water over every enthusiasm
Resourcefulness	Ruin and bankruptcy

This Water phase is one of endurance but also of potential. Often people stuck here may see only the downside. They are unable to realise that, unless they are close to death or have given up, the cycle of life will eventually take them forward again and they can move on.

That full potential will eventually be realised in the Fire phase, the phase opposite to Water.

In the left column you can see how you may rely on the Water phase to renew and regulate you next cycle. The right column shows how this phase may be wasted or how its failure prevents renewal.

Stuck in the Water phase

How do you recognise someone stuck in the Water phase? This is a time of waiting. It applies at the end of one period or cycle of activity and before the next. You are probably powerless to change this situation, which may be imposed by physical restrictions, such as prison, exhaustion, disease or by legal restrictions on what you can do. You just have to wait. It can also be when you take a sabbatical, a period of time 'out' from work.

You can use this waiting time constructively by learning new skills, by studying for new qualifications or by taking time to consider your priorities, resources and experiences. It may also be a time when you move your location to re-start.

In terms of illness it might be something like post viral syndrome (see the example at the end of this chapter), or the time as you recover from some great stress.

If, from exhaustion, you cannot use this time constructively, the natural emotion is fear, which becomes phobia. Irrational thinking, reduced concentration, weak memory, and impaired immune system are all in part associated with Water.

It is also the phase of no resources and the inability to recover. Diseases of old age and ageing come here, but also those of inability to develop in the womb or after birth, when your body or mind cannot start or restart – or so it seems.

Diseases or exertions which have exhausted your ability to recover come here too, such as post-viral fatigue and diseases of the central nervous system.

Strategies for the Water phase

The following activities are especially helpful for Water phase problems. However, to some extent so too are Metal and Wood phase help strategies, see below. Earth phase strategies help all the phases.

- Alexander technique and spinal exercise (appendix 10)
- Floatation tanks
- Hot stone therapy
- Meditation
- Naps (short sleeps during the day or evening)
- Re-framing (a neuro-linguistic – NLP – thinking process)
- Rest and Sleep
- Learning new skills

- Warm water showers on the head

- Yoga

WOOD phase including Liver and Gallbladder

The Wood phase represents the movement of life as the seed germinates, green shoots appear in Spring, the baby is bornand grows into a teenager, young adult and then towards maturity. It is the phase of advance, expansion and growth.

This can be an exciting time, of executing plans, taking chances, developing businesses and enterprises.

It develops initiative, drive, courage, positive thinking, chutzpah and resourcefulness, assertiveness and a winning culture.

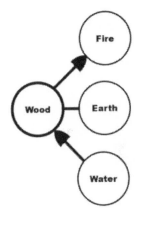

Like all the phases, it can be all-absorbing. Here the absorption is that of being in the driving seat, pushing forward fast. These people are the movers and shakers.

It is also the phase of attraction, of the sexual draw (not the sexual union, which occurs in the next, the Fire phase).

It seems a very desirable phase for many and is occupied by those who want to change things, usually their way. So it is predominantly a yang process.

Below, overleaf, are some aspects of the Wood phase, good and bad.

In the left column you see how this phase takes forward your life process or enterprise. The right column shows how it can go wrong or send you in non-conducive directions.

Desirable, to be able to rely on	That you cannot rely on, or that limit you
Drive and expansion	Aggression, Anger, Rage, Violence
Taking action, taking chances, winning, initiative, enterprise, positive thinking	On edge, 'stressed', overactive, tense, always restarting, never succeeding
Ambition	Frustration
Brokerage, innovation, wheelers and dealers	Always busy, inability to rest or holiday
Attraction	Lust, Repulsion
Freedom fighters	Exhaustion
Decisiveness, courage	Indecisiveness, lack of assertiveness, erratic
Commitment	Indifference

Stuck in the Wood Phase

Because this is such an exciting phase, people stuck in it often do not admit they have a problem!

But if they get stuck in it for long, they will have problems eventually.

Margaret Thatcher

For example, a politician who was clearly stuck in this phase and relished it, was Margaret Thatcher when Prime Minister.

Apparently she was able, for many months at a time, to survive on 4 hours of sleep a night and up until the end of her tenure she looked powerful, in control, in excellent health and as if she was loving every moment.

Because Margaret Thatcher had a very secure home life (Earth) and was also unquestionably leader (Fire), her energies did move on round the cycle. However, she overlooked the Water phase (eg rest) and latterly, probably, the Metal phase (eg succession).

However, after she was ejected from power, she very

quickly lost her concentration and posture and began to look deficient in Blood[2], Qi[3] and Yin[4].

Business Owners

The Sunday Times magazine of 2nd June 2013 (p24) quotes a business owner:

.

"I don't even have time for a relationship. Like women who become obsessed with their children, I think the same is true with your business. I am obsessed with my business and there is no business in the world as interesting as mine."

.

As the Sunday Times goes on to say 'Balance isn't even on their agenda'. They quote someone else: "I wouldn't care for it (ie balance). I wasn't forced to do this – I love every minute of it. For me, everything is tied up in my work."

'Preneurial' Activity

People can occupy this phase even when employed. Corporations who recognise this often do well, encouraging such employees to innovate, create, and generate new profits for them.

Government departments seldom offer the right opportunities for this but they should – though the heavy hand of political expediency usually suffocates them.

Wood Phase problems

Overuse of resources, erratic behaviour, always starting, never

2. See http://www.acupuncture-points.org/blood.html
3. See http://www.acupuncture-points.org/qi.html
4. See http://www.acupuncture-points.org/yin-deficiency.html

finishing – you can imagine the problems inherent in this phase.

Physically, being a Yang phase, energy presses upwards either too much or fails to reach its target, leading to tensions, headaches, migraines, grinding teeth, eye problems, neck and shoulder pain.

They also exhaust their resources, and can fall back into the problems of the Water phase.

The Wood phase contains the Liver and Gallbladder and for the problems these produce, see chapter 8.

Strategies for Wood Phase problems

Often appropriate to Wood phase problems are the following – However! Although Wood phase people crave many of these actions, they should actually often take things much more easily, adopting Earth phase strategies, together with some of those of Water and Fire (see the chapter on Liver and Gallbladder):

- Competing (ball games like tennis, racquets)
- Delegation (a strategy they should rescue from obscurity)
- Diving and driving
- Racing
- Sailing
- Skiing
- Sprinting; interval training
- As you notice, Wood phase people want sports that give the maximum 'burn' for their buck. Their sports are often intense and fast. They need to guard against exhausting themselves through over-straining.

FIRE phase including Heart, Pericardium and Small Intestine

Although to those in it, the Wood phase can seem all-absorbing, most people in the (supposedly-boring) Earth phase want to occupy this, the Fire phase.

This is where the 'fun' starts. Fashion, style, recognition, fame, success, all if possible accompanied by money! This is the period of life when you reach what you dreamed of: love, sexual union, bliss, ecstasy; romantic holidays in the sun.

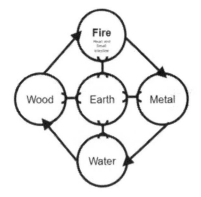

This is what, unconsciously, Wood phase people work towards: to be able to enjoy life without working. (Or so they say! In practice, typically Wood phase people keep working.)

On a deeper level it signifies self-realisation, leadership, power, control, rule, respect; recognition of what is best.

It brings inspiration, creativity, enthusiasm, infectious 'childlike' fun qualities, the need for appreciation: art and music.

See the table for some of the good and bad sides to the Fire Phase.

In the left column you can see the benefits of this phase. The right column lists some of the possible ways this phase can go wrong. When it goes wrong, since it is such an important phase in life, it can deeply affect people, even destroying them, either pushing them into the Metal phase too fast (see below the right-hand column under Metal) or catapulting them into the Water phase. Some just sink back into the Earth phase.

Stuck in the Fire phase

How do you recognise someone stuck in this Fire phase?

Note! People can get stuck in this phase without ever enjoying its benefits. Avarice and envy can make some people so egocentric that they are in effect stuck here. For others, difficulty or an inability to form relationships and friendships also puts them here: they are always searching for attention and love, like actors or small children always in need approval.

Desirable to rely on:	That limit you:
Self-realisation; identity; recognition; differentiation; acknowledgement; pride	Pride, craving for respect, for fame; vanity;narcissism; egocentricity; celebrity culture; identity loss
Style; fashion; glamour; glitz; beauty; stardust; attractiveness	'Bling'; avarice; kitsch; camp; image fixation
Drama; theatre; performance; partying; front of house	Feeling of friendliness; isolation; betrayal; forsaken
Success	Failure; disappointment with life
Inner Joy; a sense of 'grace'; Love	Drug culture; perpetual 'highs'; addiction; burnout; jealousy
Enthusiasm; inspiration; revelation; shaman	Mania; religious fanaticism; hate; self-destruction
Rule; power; splendour; importance; control; delegation	Domination; tyranny, over-control; suspicion; hard to please; wrath; despair; paranoia; failure
Generosity of spirit; prize-giving; praise; reward; friendship	Miserliness; contempt

For others who have enjoyed it, even for a short while, this phase can be addictive. Partying and dancing away the night is great but for some this is not enough; they must take social drugs to enhance and maintain their state of 'bliss' or ecstasy.

Still others like being seen with famous people, in the right places, dressed for effect. With no money shortage, this becomes a perpetual lifestyle.

But that would be a mistake. Each phase should move naturally on to the next. This Fire phase is the proper result after Wood with its effort and enterprise: build an empire and enjoy the recognition. It is the flower that emerges from the seed stored in Water.

To avoid disease you must move on to the next phase before you become addicted. If not, you risk disappointment and psychological effects.

Why? Because once there, you always want more. You crave more and more recognition, more money, more fame, more sun. For safety, the Fire should not be occupied for too long!

Unless you are in control, enjoy the party, but move on. Otherwise you may burn out. And if you are in control for too long? You will become Machiavellian; cunning, suspicious, devious, plotting and plotted against, despotic, autocratic, tyrannical, repressive, cruel.

Fire Phase problems

Addiction to the 'highs' in life becomes addiction to the good life, parties, ecstasy, beauty, youth, romance, medication,cosmetic surgery, drugs: drug addiction, alcoholism, intense depression and self-destruction.

Sometimes there is exploitation of others, particularly of servants, or people cut themselves off from real relationships, lack meaning in their lives and become suspicious, paranoid and suicidal.

For others, risk-taking and adventure become addictions. Religious zealotry and fanaticism are Fire phase manifestations. This is where suicide bombers come from, using fire to annihilate others – Earth – hoping in the process to procure on the one hand fame and on the other salvation, both Fire attributes.

However, just as with other phases, if people enjoy this phase but move on round the cycle, they can enjoy the pleasures of Fire as often as they like, as the cycle returns naturally to it, time and again.

Strategies for the Fire phase

Fire phase problems benefit from Earth phase strategies but they probably enjoy or benefit from activities such as:

- Dancing
- Surfing waves
- Team sports (and the ability to lose gracefully)
- Thrill-seeking (but this often worsens Fire problems)
- Trampolining

You may wonder why Laughter is not included above. The ancient Chinese noticed that too much laughter, by which they meant what we might incline to describe as hysterical giggling or nervous laughter, actually damaged Fire energy.

Of course, natural, unforced laughter is nearly always good, not just for Fire phase types. But there is a slight tendency nowadays to take nothing seriously, to laugh at everything, which comes close to contempt. The Jester played an important part in medieval comedy but he walked a dangerous tightrope!

They can help themselves by using some of the Wood phase strategies and moving their focus on to the next, Metal, phase before they get addicted to Fire! Fortunately, this is often easy.

METAL phase including Lung and Large Intestine

After the Fire come the ashes. Of course, the fruits of summer will have returned to be consumed by Earth, but the essential residue of the Fire leads us to autumn, reflection, retirement, and research.

Metal is the phase of the scientist, the analyst, the logician, the teacher, the reliable older person who carries wisdom and experience: the grandparent or guardian.

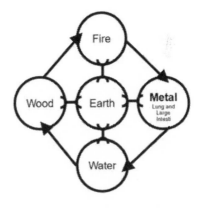

After the fruit or vegetable is eaten, its nuts or seeds fall to earth awaiting winter and the Water phase with their rest and sleep before germinating in the following Wood phase.

If the cycle has been successful, there will be savings, both financial and at home, to tide out retirement; adequate provision for the rainy day.

Here you often find consultants, accountants, book-keepers, doctors, lawyers, intellectual therapists. Here is the experienced mentor. Here is the judge: sitting in judgment on others' efforts. This is he or she who waits and watches: no longer the heart and soul (Fire phase) of the party.

Desirable to rely on	That limit you
Grateful acceptance of the past	Constant grieving over lost or past glory or relationships; the outsider, the alien or scapegoat

Objective judgement and advice, experience takes few chances	Destructive criticism, disdain, disillusion, remorse
Reflection, inspiration, insight	The lone judge and assassin
Wisdom, knowledge, philosophy, theology	Fixed opinions; doubt; perfectionism; 'damaged goods'
Yielding and helping	Cutting off; denial
Seeker after the pure and the best	Stubbornness; dogma
Ceding of power, letting go, giving back, paying forward	Holding on to power, money and position; 'anal retentive'
Environmental awareness and clean-up. Safety	Pouring 'shit' over everyone and everything. Limitation.

Here must people give up, or hand over to others, the reins of power. They can provide the refined essence of their experience by writing 'how to' books and textbooks.

Here they map out plans and goals for the next phase, clean up after the last phase and focus on the essential energy to be needed in the future: the seeds of the past going forward to the next Spring. See the table above for the good and some bad aspects of the Metal phase.

In the left column you see the better qualities of the Metal phase: you see the contrary in the column on the right.

Stuck in the Metal phase

If their Fire phase was a high point, the movement is now downwards. People stuck here cling to the past. They cannot yet yield to the next phase – Water.

They are saddened by and grieve over their lost strength, lost power, lost relationships, lost beauty. Sad people do not breath properly and they do not clear or clean up well; they lack energy. Their rooms contain heaps of accumulated detritus, their lungs are full of phlegm, their souls are cheerless. Their attitudes are often destructive.

The assassin, the solitary killer, often alienated from society is here – quite different from the suicide bomber who wants to destroy society and achieve salvation thereby. The latter blows himself up in the act (Fire); the former kills himself afterwards.

This is, after all, the last phase before winter, before the end, so it is naturally a phase preceding death and leading to death.

However, that death need not be physical. It may be in giving up something of value, or letting something go, or cutting oneself off from harmful influences. If so, the Qi moves on round the cycle, through rest and reconsideration in Water to Wood and growth. Health and the movement and transformation of Qi is preserved.

Metal phase problems

You will read more of these in the chapters on the Lung and Large Intestine Energy organs.

Physically the commonest symptoms are those of poor posture, lack of breathing space and breath, low energy and enervation, exhaustion, skin, respiratory and bowel problems.

People here often feel cut-off from life, or they cut themselves off from it in some way. People who have had no interests outside work all their lives and just stop work to sit and do nothing usually do badly in this phase. In fact, for them early death has been the norm.

As people live longer, for their health they should continue to work if they can. Alternatively, they should find some other occupation to keep their Qi moving round the circle. People stuck in this phase don't allow themselves to enjoy life and often unconsciously – and occasionally consciously – try to stop others enjoying life.

Strategies for the Metal phase

Activities that often help people stuck in the Metal phase include the following, but they can also benefit from any of the strategies for the Earth phase.

They can also still benefit from the warmth of the Fire phase strategies and it helps if they allow themselves to think forward to next, Water phase: this pushes their Qi onwards round the circle.

They definitely need to take exercise and get help with posture! For more on this, see the chapters on Lung and Large Intestine energy organs.

• Alexander technique and spinal work (Appendix 10)

• Aerobics

• Breathing exercises

• Gratitude practising

• Hill-walking

• Indian head massage

• Pilates

• Qigong

• Shiatsu

• Thai massage

• Skipping

• Step dancing

• Weight training – under guidance

Practical Applications of the Five Phase System

The condition someone experiences, such as a disease or

life situation, always fits into this system. Illustrations of how to use this are given throughout the book.

An Example – M.E

Take someone with M.E., (myalgic encephalomyelitis), often much the same as post-viral syndrome. People with this feel stressed in a number of ways. *(This is not to say that all ME sufferers are trapped in the Water phase, of course. It is just an illustration of how such a person, or someone in a similar situation, might look for help.)*

However, their situation is often that of the Water phase: their life has come to a halt. Physically they cannot do what they previously could do and they are often too tired even to think. They just have to rest and wait.

The Water phase represents winter, a time when plants, seeds and bulbs previously planted rest, recover and begin to find life again.

Earth represents their need for immediate *support*.

This may be their home or an institution such as a hospital that provides their day-to-day needs. It may mean that they have to return to their family for a while to be looked after.

The point is that their condition prevents them from caring properly for themselves.

Failing the family home or a hospital, they may need help from their community or from friends.

The Metal phase represents where people trapped in the Water phase will also get help, Metal being the Mother of Water.

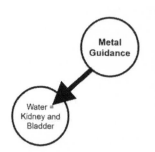

Someone with Metal capabilities will help them understand their situation in life; will provide good advice and the 'steeliness' to continue. Such a person might also provide a belief framework, such as a religious or philosophical idea that inspires them – or money.

The Lung Energy organ (chapter 9), one of the two Metal Energy organs, is Governor of Qi. Its function includes inspiration of Qi via breathing, which emphasises the importance of proper and effective respiration for M.E. sufferers. Here the Lung energy organ (Metal) supports the Kidney energy organ (Water).

Physically, Metal might also represent the savings[5] they have put aside for themselves against just this rainy-day situation, and the kinds of research they need to acquaint themselves with to keep hopeful.

Metal could also be the particular seeds, nuts, herbs, vitamins or minerals they need most: all these are the concentrated forms of life and benefit lingering from the previous cycle.

The Wood phase represents the other side of their Water situation. Wood is what they should be looking towards and Wood represents the next phase as they recover and start 'growing' again.

So, even while they are convalescing in Water it may pay them to consider from Metal the benefits of their life hitherto, to consolidate them, ruminate on them and then, eventually, look towards what they might wish to do when they recover and recommence their new life cycle in Wood.

This could be either a new lifestyle or career, or a

5. **Savings** made during a person's life are a strongly Metal form. They are the residue of earnings, available to support old age or retirement. After death, they pass partly to the state (Earth) in tax and partly to the deceased's inheritors (Water).

renewed effort in or adaptation of their existing capability. People stuck in or moving towards the Water phase often need to learn new skills. For example, ageing people perhaps need to overcome inhibitions and learn how the internet works. If they cannot or will not learn new ways, then they condemn themselves to remaining in the Water phase. Even when unable to do or think much, it pays them to think positively about their future. Wood represents hope!

For some, however, the Wood phase may act another way. It may represent the frustration they feel, and generate in them enough drive or anger for them to achieve recognition and support to change their condition or that of others.

You often see this in people who have suffered a huge trauma, loss or illness that has brought their lives to a halt. They have used it to give them the drive to found a charity or set up a foundation or school or new business. This drive forces their Water phase to move into their Wood phase, which gets the Qi moving round again in their life cycle.

People stuck in the Water phase can often help themselves by moving where they live or work, especially if the previous phase has exhausted their current opportunities.

Further attributes of the Four Phase System

The Four Phase system shows other relationships:
   Fire and Water phases can have a mutually balancing effect:

- Western Medicine is well aware of the urinary system's (Water) potential effect on the heart (Fire).

- To deal with hypertension, diuretics improve urinary function to release fluids, reducing pressure on the heart.

- The energies represented by Fire (including warmth and

laughter) can hugely encourage and inspire people trapped in the Water phase.

A healthy Heart (Fire) helps you take the right course in life and a healthy Mind (housed by the Heart – Fire) can quieten the fears and phobias of Water.

The Small Intestine (Fire) channel supplies the Bladder (Water) channel and important points on the Small Intestine channel govern the spine, the spinal cord and brain, which come under Kidney (Water).

Too much Fire however, is exhausting for people stuck in Water phase. They cannot cope with the partying, the bling, the energy needed to sustain the Fire life. They should also avoid environments and foods that are too heating, which exhausts their Kidney Qi.

Social drugs and now some medicinal drugs use the Fire phase to help people cope with pain and discomfort. They manage, if successful, to put people into a higher state of consciousness. Morphine is used for extreme pain though it appears in many people to send them into an undifferentiated state more akin to the Water phase.

So these drugs mostly seem to work across the Fire-Water cross. Although people are parted from their pain, and are grateful for this, this state is not one they like to occupy indefinitely – and of course like all drugs, whether Fire-like or Water-like, they may have undesirable secondary effects (see chapter 8).

Wood and Metal phases also balance one another.

- Steady breathing (Lungs – Metal) calms the frustrations of Wood.

- But tension (Wood) stops people breathing properly (Metal).

- The energy and drive of Wood can sometimes shake Metal people out of any self-destructive criticism
and disappointment, and encourage them to get moving again.

Looking at the qualities listed for each phase in the relevant tables above, you might think that some attributes could as well be in the next or its preceding phase: you would be right!

For example, Disdain, which I list under Metal, could swap with Contempt (Fire). If you think this, you are well on the way to understanding how the concept works.

Mappiness

As reported in the Sunday Times[6], a recent index of pleasure, from research by the Centre for Economic Performance at the London School of Economics, describes activities and situations that people find pleasurable based on data collected from 20,000 smart-phone users over several years. ('Pleasurable' is not the same as beneficial, of course. Some people find getting drunk pleasurable but it is seldom beneficial.)

One can put these into categories which suggest which might benefit people in different kinds of stress. The table below shows this.

EARTH	WATER	WOOD	FIRE	METAL
Gardening	Fishing	Sport	Intimacy	Exhibitions
Allotments	Meditation	Exercise	Making love	Museums
Talking	Sleeping	Hunting	Theatre	Libraries
Chatting	Resting	Fishing	Dance	Singing
Socialising	Relaxing	Sports	Concerts	Religious activity
Nature Watching	Waiting	Travel	Singing	Reading

6. Sunday Times, 30.6.13 News section, page 12.

Walking	Studying		Performing	Listening
Hiking			Playing with children	Net browsing
Hobbies			Social media	Travel
Pastimes				
Arts				
Crafts				
Childcare				
Housework				
Chores				
DIY				
Administration				
Book-keeping				

The activities listed under Earth will probably benefit everyone, Earth being the universal neutraliser so more activities occur under Earth than under other phases.

Also notice, that activities listed in the phase that follows a given stressed phase may help it too. So for people suffering from Liver Qi stagnation (Wood phase) the activities listed under Fire may also be very beneficial.

However, this depends on the state of energy of the individual. For example, someone in a Water phase, if exhausted and convalescent, would find vigorous Wood activities far too draining. One should not be rigid about this. If you identify your phase but find an activity you benefit from that is however not listed either under it or the following phase or Earth, do not abandon doing what you like just because it is not listed just so! Also, remember that exercise benefits nearly everyone,

though is listed only under Wood in the table.

The table does not show all the activities that were monitored.

NB These categorisations are made by me, not by LSE! Also, commonsense is needed. Not everyone in childcare (Earth) will find it beneficial: some mothers who spend all their time in childcare may want something very different to help with their stress.

Equally, some theologians (Metal) may find too much religious activity wearing. This just reinforces the idea that sometimes it is the activities of the next or preceding phase that you need for health.

A philosophical approach

For the philosophical, from Water through Wood, Qi waxes.

From Fire through Metal Qi wanes.

In Water, Qi is non-differentiated, in Fire it reaches self-realisation.

Psychologically, for health, life must proceed round the wheel of life. It has an order that gives meaning and quality. Any activity, at any stage of life, goes through elements of each of the phases. Order can often reduce stress.

At the start of a project we look forward to its development, thinking that our efforts will culminate in the Fire phase, when actually its culmination is when it gives up its qualities to begin the next cycle, Fire being just a happy chapter in the project's life.

Waxing and self-realisation seem to rush by and we want to hang on to them because they are exciting. Waning and non-differentiation can take forever.

But waxing is balanced by waning, and it is those in the waning side who, if the waxing was successful, enjoy its benefits in tranquillity and wisdom. If not, not: bees have pensions (honeycomb) unlike butterflies.

The Wheel of Life has other suggestions. If we can put some kind of order into our lives, as in going to bed at the same time, or eating regularly with friends, then at least there we have reliability, which helps us to manage our stress in other situations.

Acupuncture has acupuncture points that help smooth the process of Qi in its transformation from one phase to the next. The right points can often help people trapped in a particular phase.

Summary

Recognising your phase gives you additional options for managing stress and getting life moving again.

.

The next chapter explains first how Stagnant Qi can be changed voluntarily, and then what happens if it is forced to stagnate.

CHAPTER 6

What Stagnant Qi Turns Into

Just as Stress – at the right intensity and for an acceptable period of time – can be exciting and invigorating, so Qi Stagnation can be used creatively. Before a rugby match, some teams, for instance the New Zealand 'All Blacks', go through a kind of chanting which promotes a sensation of fullness and power. When the match starts, they release this with forceful action.

.

Following on from the previous chapters: if you have continuing Stagnant Qi, it will eventually force a change.

It will, like cut grass from your lawn, either dry out and blow you away or, if you put it on your compost heap, get hot and cook. It will turn into either 'Wind' or 'Heat'. Or both.

It may push out in unexpected directions as when you overfill your compost bin, it splits open, and the compost bursts out: in effect the Qi goes in the wrong direction.

Think of stagnant Qi as being like air in a balloon. It cannot move; it is constrained. It is under pressure. Air under pressure tries to find a way out. Any weakness will be exploited. Failing that, as you compress a gas more, it gets smaller and hotter.

It takes energy to compress a gas and that compressed gas is a store of energy.

This is similar to hydro-electric power storage, when at times of low demand, the turbines pump water up to a high reservoir.

Then when demand increases beyond the capacity of the water pressure normally turning the turbines, the additional force of the stored water is released to produce extra power.

Stagnating Qi stores power

In fact, stagnant Qi is somewhat like a steam engine. As the Qi is released (cf the pressurised steam begins to do work) that power escapes, transforming into movement, noise, heat and, in living creatures, emotion. From a modern scientific point of view, this confirms the second law of thermodynamics[1].

If unable to escape, Qi stagnation leads to a variety of experiences covered in later chapters, including pain, mental distress and eventually long-term illness. First let us look at ways to release or move that Stagnant Qi power.

How does Chinese medicine deal with Stagnant Qi?

The main techniques used are the following, though some are more effective at moving Qi than others. Some appear under more than one heading:

• Acupuncture: the theory behind classical acupuncture relies partly on a concept of acupuncture channels along which Qi flows. Acupuncture affects this flow of Qi in numerous ways.

---

1. For an enjoyable and lucid account of this, see 'Warmth Disperses and Time Passes, the History of Heat', by Hans Christian von Baeyer, Modern Library, New York 1999.

- It can strengthen the flow, dissipate it, move it to or draw it from other channels.

- Every acupuncture point has a different quality, sometimes indicated by its name.

- Choosing the right points requires knowledge and skill.

- Some points are famous for helping people with stagnant Qi, but there are many more that assist and in certain situations may be better than the famous ones.

The powerhouse that pushes Qi along the channels is in the trunk, the torso. The ancient Chinese had less interest than we do in the actual physical inner workings of the trunk.

.

Although it seems certain that some internal examinations of the body were made, the Chinese developed a workable medicine based round Qi. Western knowledge of anatomy and the workings of the physical organs is much more recent.

.

They were more interested in what they perceived as forms of Qi and how they behaved. So their ideas of the functions of what we call the organs were different.

They looked at the organs from an energetic point of view. This is a point of view that I hope, after reading this book, you will appreciate too.

They called these the Zangfu[2]. I have called them Energy Organs. So you will find reference to the Liver Energy Organ, the Heart Energy Organ and so on, or just Liver, Heart...

In every case where I am talking about the *Energy Organ*, the

2. The zang-fu organs are the functioning units of energy that together create life in the body. Zang organs are yin, fu organs yang. The zang organs are said to be 'solid', the fu organs 'empty', or 'able to contain'. For more, see http://www.acupuncturepoints.org/zang-fu.html

first letter will be capitalised, eg Heart, not heart. When you see 'heart' (small h), I mean the organ itself, as recognised in Western anatomy and physiology[3].

- *Massage*: (the Chinese equivalent of massage), Tuina, using the acupuncture channels to move Qi. This includes acupressure and its Japanese cousin, Shiatsu. These are very different to Western style therapeutic massage. Reiki is not exactly a form of massage but uses the theory of the acupuncture channels to influence Qi. Applied Kinesiology is yet another system, based on acupuncture theory, which moves Qi.

- *Herbs*: the Chinese equivalent of Western pharmacopoeia, based – like acupuncture – on the theory of Chinese medicine. Its formulae have been tried and tested over some 3000 years. A chosen formula for a specific syndrome[4] is adjusted to fit the Qi in individual circumstances.
  Moxa[5]: the application of heat at specific places, usually acupuncture points chosen because of the way the points are known to affect Qi.
  Cupping[6]: a vacuum is created over the skin by means of an inverted cup, drawing the skin and flesh up into the cup. This therapy, which is by no means confined to China, is used in a variety of ways, though mostly to move Blood[7]. Moving Blood in turn helps to move Qi.

- *Meditation*[8]: focusing the mind brings many benefits. As Mind

---

3. It is a bit nonsensical to call it 'Western' medicine or 'Western' pathology, but I use the adjective 'Western' to denote modern medicine as it has developed in the West. The Chinese make good use of it too, of course, and have effortlessly incorporated it into Chinese medicine; a luxury Western medicine has yet to afford itself for Chinese medicine.
4. Syndrome. This is the description of a condition recognised in Chinese medicine. All diseases can be described in terms of these syndromes.
5. See http://www.acupuncture-points.org/moxibustion.html
6. See http://www.acupuncture-points.org/cupping.html
7. Blood. An important concept in Chinese medicine which you will read about throughout the book. See also http://www.acupuncture-points.org/blood.html
8. See http://www.acupuncture-points.org/meditation.html

and body are very closely related in Chinese medicine, the state of one affects that of the other. See appendix 3 for more on this. Helps move Qi. Modern advances now bring us biofeedback and autogenics.

- *(Re-)Education*: teaching people how and what to do for their health. Helps them learn to avoid circumstances that lead to Qi stagnation, and deal better with those they cannot avoid. In modern China the term 'Re-education' covers what in the West we might perceive as being persuasive counselling. (Some in the West might call Re-Education a form of brain-washing but each country has its own culture and mores.)

- *Tai Qi*: a process, sometimes moving, sometimes still, which helps to train the mind and body to move Qi, and strengthens the body to use and store it.

EXERCISE

Using the analogy of the motorway traffic jam described in the Introduction, you might say that exercise is like giving the whole thing a good shake so increasing the speed at which traffic speeds up, leaving the jam behind. It also generates heat, a requirement derived from the Second Law of Thermodynamics, previously mentioned.

- *Qi Gong*: use mainly of Mind and Breath to direct, move and store Qi and Blood.

- *Nutrition*: eating foods that balance the body and maintain its health, and avoiding foods that do the opposite, based on the theory of Chinese medicine. By helping the body to maintain its healthy poise, it becomes less susceptible to Qi stagnation. Some foods also move Qi. As we develop foods formerly unknown to Chinese medicine, they are classified according to their actions on the Energy Organs.

- *Guasha* – Skin scraping: produces a kind of bruise that moves Blood and therefore helps to move Qi.

- *Emotional Freedom Technique* is a modern discovery that uses points on acupuncture channels. Tapping them in a particular way and order often ameliorates Qi stagnation temporarily. See appendix 6.

The impossibility of releasing power without also releasing heat shows how pain and inflammation from Qi Stagnation can be released beneficially. We regard an inefficient engine as being one which dissipates energy (eg heat) without doing (enough) work[9]. Exercise moves Qi but it also releases heat. With this in mind, viewing the above and the following ways of moving Qi, you can assess how directly and well they succeed in easing Qi Stagnation's discomfort.

As individuals, of course, we have also discovered that the following work (some subjects are listed under several different headings):

Physical Ways to deal with Stagnant Qi

- *Exercise* (physical), including dancing, sport, walking, climbing. All force Qi to move round the body, stopping it from stagnating for a while. Often this is enough to release the pressure of Qi stagnation.

- *Thrills, excitement, sex and adrenalin*: increased tension if

9. Steam engines including the boiler seldom reach 10% efficiency. Internal combustion engines (eg cars) seldom exceed 30%. Electric kettles may get to 90%. We are like steam engines, the efficiency of which depends on the difference between the core temperature and the outside or reservoir temperature. So vigorous exercise, if we can do it, produces both more power and more heat, and therefore dissipates more Qi. Somewhat similarly, huge emotional outbursts can be efficient, except that they may cause other problems for us.

released pleasurably usurps and moves our Qi stagnation symptoms. (These are Fire phase activities.)

- *Relaxation*: learning how to relax helps us to lose tension caused by Qi stagnation via Metal-Wood, or Lung-Liver interaction, chapters 5 and 9. However, not so efficient in shedding Qi. Consider biofeedback and autogenics[10].

- *Warm baths*: warm deficient and move stagnant Qi caused by deficiency. See chapters 5, 13 and 15.

- *Essential oils*: bathe our senses and help to dissipate Qi stagnation by relaxing us. Probably mainly work on Lung Qi for its action in balancing Liver Qi. Chapters 5 and 9.

- *Breathing* properly – see appendix 7. Breathing controls Liver Qi to some extent via the 5 Element or Phase system, see chapters 5 and 9.

Attention from others to help Stagnant Qi

- *Talking it over; counselling, psychotherapy*: thinking a different way, adopting a new point of view. Helps us to adapt to the situation causing our Qi to stagnate. (Earth)

- *Convivial company and humour*: take us out of ourselves by circulating Qi through others and back to ourselves. (Fire and Earth – Chapter 5).

- *Massage* skin to skin with a friend: very pleasurable and research is now discovering why[11]. Qi stagnation surrenders to these pleasurable sensations and the attention from a friend helps move Qi between us, thereby neutralising Qi stagnation. (Metal and Earth)

- *Making love*: giving and receiving intimate

10. http://www.atdynamics.co.uk
11. Think that massage feels good? New Scientist 2 Feb 2013 p 15.

attention reinforces self-worth. The process moves and dissipates our Qi, so for Qi stagnation, the more vigorous the better. (Fire)

Using the Mind to clear Stagnant Qi

- *Reflection*: learning to see ourselves from other perspectives. This places our circumstances in a new light enabling us to adjust to our situation better, thereby undermining its power over our Qi. (Metal and Earth)

- *Meditation and prayer*: steadies and focuses the Mind that thereby alters how our Qi responds to stagnation.

Ways to learn to prevent or ameliorate Stagnant Qi

- *Get fit* mentally and physically. Gives you more resilience and ability to absorb stressful situations without becoming stressed or getting Qi stagnation. But being fit also means more mental energy to create ways to adapt to or change the situation causing your stress.

- *Learn how to negotiate*: there are books and courses you can do which increase your ability to deal with stressful circumstances, averting the onset of Qi stagnation.

- *Neurolinguistic Programming – NLP* – teaches you how to behave to increase your ability to understand and influence people.

- *Assertiveness Training* enables you firmly and confidently to express your point of view.

- *Develop Creativity*: learn a language or an art-form (drawing, painting, playing, sculpting) which forces your mind to develop new connections, thereby helping you to think laterally[12] and creatively.

Pleasurable ways to clear Stagnant Qi

- *Biofeedback and Autogenics*: learning how to control the body using biofeedback and mental awareness. Thisis a modern 'improvement' on bodily awareness and reflection, helping us to use our Mind to manage our Qi.

- *Sleep and holidays*: recoup our Qi and Blood, the better to deal with stress and to lessen our susceptibility to Qi stagnation. Holidays also enable us to reflect on our circumstances and make decisions about them.

- *Sexual orgasm*; releases Qi stagnation. However, read Chapter 15 before over-indulging.

Diversionary Ways to Clear Stagnant Qi

- *Supreme experiences* of music, religion or art: move us deeply, replenishing us spiritually. They refine our Qi and give depth to our Blood. (Fire/Metal phase strategies.)

- *Success in another field*: gives us something else to live for, and lessens our Qi stagnation situation by moving it in other directions. This includes creative pursuits. (Success is a Fire phase attribute, so success in another field particularly helps people with Wood phase stress.)

- *Hope, inspiration*: sidelines Qi stagnation and acts like the spiritual equivalent of exercise. (Mostly Fire strategies.)

- *Learning something new*: perhaps a musical instrument or a new language, helps us move and create Qi another way, partly scattering our tensions. Helps move Qi round the 5 Element/Phase system. (Water phase)

- *Humour*: a great way to release Qi stagnation, even if only temporary. It can also make us think about our situation a

12. See also http://www.edwdebono.com/lateral.htm

different way, helping us to see a way through our difficulties. Grounds us in Earth and warms Fire. Hence not always appropriate for some Fire phase excess Heat problems – see chapters 5 and 10 and http://www.acupuncture-points.org/heart-fire.html.

- *Changing* our occupation or circumstances: to distance ourselves from the source of Qi stagnation and give us new challenges. (Mainly Water phase.)

Allopathic ways to clear Stagnant Qi

- *Drugs* both pharmaceutical and social: the Western pharmacopoeia has many drugs aimed at various kinds of Qi stagnation. However, they tend to suppress symptoms and often lead to secondary effects – see chapter 8.

- *Alcohol and tobacco* are widely used to relax. Both move Qi, alcohol by loosening Liver Qi and tobacco by stimulating Lung Qi to descend (because stress often makes Qi ascend and smoking descends it[13].).

NB We rely on the primary effects of drugs, both prescribed and social, for their benefits. Their secondary effects are often damaging or need other drugs to control them. However, we should be grateful for drugs that control extreme states like psychosis or deep depression even if there may be, for example, Chinese formulae that might work quickly or in time. Modern drugs can act very fast.

- Heat or Cold: depending on which diminishes the symptoms. People who get cold when their Qi stagnates benefit from warmth, and vice versa.

---

13. This *descending* action is tobacco's *Primary* effect. Tobacco's *Secondary* effect is *heating* and produces lung diseases of various known kinds. More on this in Chapter 8.

Exercise to clear Stagnant Qi

One of the best ways of dissipating Qi stagnation is exercise. Why? Because it moves Qi, forcing it to 'un-stagnate'. Exercise of the right kind, in the right circumstances can often resolve the early manifestations of Qi stagnation.

There are many forms of exercise that help. Choose what you like or what you know you can continue to do. It can be done on your own, or in company, can be the silent moves of yoga or manic moves of dance. Which form of exercise is probably best for a given syndrome is discussed in the appropriate chapters.

The fitter you are, the more stress you can withstand: like having more resilient, elastic sides to the motorway. (See the motorway analogy in the Introduction.) However, strength on its own does not bestow fitness.

Exhilaration clears Stagnant Qi

Piloting an airplane, even driving a car, can elate, but the release here is more emotional. It is not as effective, long-term, as exercise but it does move Qi. Laughter, too,can often ease out Qi stagnation, if the cause is mild.

Friends.

Social interaction, friends, can help move Qi as well. Here the Qi moved is emotional. Because it is shared, it is easier to bear.

Little bit of technical stuff here, which makes more sense if you have read chapter 5 and appendix 4. From a 5 Element point of view, Qi stagnation, which always includes an element of Liver Qi stagnation in Wood, is 'drawn' off into the Fire Element flow and dissipated in relaxed laughter.

Why do I say 'relaxed' laughter? Because if stagnant Qi turns into

Heat affecting the Heart, the laughter will be far from relaxed and the problem will not be dissipated, but transformed into a more dangerous energy – see below.

When Exercise Fails

Even exercise is not effective when the problem causing the Qi stagnation will not go away. Exercise palliates, but does not cure.

However, exercise helps to get you fit.

Fit people 'contain' their problems with more resilience. Their 'motorway', to use the analogy in the Introduction, is elastic: they can absorb more for a while. Being more elastic, they can bend and stretch more to keep things – Qi – moving.

What if Stagnant Qi cannot be resolved?

Failing easy transformation and dissipation along the above lines, stagnant Qi will ultimately become more destructive, creating excess Yang, the main form of which is Heat followed by Wind.

Heat

In the body, Heat takes many forms but what does it do?

- Heat warms
- Heat dries
- Heated air rises
- Heated air tries to expand
- Heat evaporates liquids

Wind

- Wind moves and shakes, and in extreme situations is terrifying and destructive.

- Prolonged or intense Heat whips up a wind.

- Heat and wind together make for a fireball, destroying everything.

Let us take the attributes of Heat and consider them in turn.

The body tries to minimize damage

First, however, remember that the body tries to keep danger as far from the door as it can. Keeping Qi stagnating, even compressed, is a better option than allowing it to transform into some other form that is more dangerous.

Whilst nobody would dispute that stagnating Qi is both unpleasant and that it can be painful, it is much less dangerous than in some of its other forms.

So when Qi transforms into Wind or Heat, what happens?

As it transforms, the disease process[14], the level at which the body keeps the problem, either becomes more superficial, as in exercise, laughter, sharing a problem, using our powers of communication and mental acuity to deal with the cause of the problem, or using our will-power and decisiveness to walk away from it... or it becomes deeper.

---

14. This idea of the disease process is one that I have taken from homoeopathic theory. It means that as you become more seriously ill, the illness strikes deeper towards the important processes that keep you alive, including the will to live. As it becomes less deep and less serious, it moves away from those deeper more vital processes and towards the surface and the skin. To make an oversimplification, it's better to have a skin problem than a liver problem.

If it becomes deeper, it gets more dangerous.

It ceases to affect just the location where we felt the original discomfort (eg the distension or bloating feeling in, say, your abdomen), but now other areas also. In particular, it starts to attack our Energy Organs (our Zangfu) organs. This 'attack' can take many forms as we shall see.

You may ask, why does stagnant Qi transform into excess Yang forms like Heat and Wind and not into Yin? After all, extreme Yang eventually transforms to Yin and vice versa (chapter 4).

The answer is that the Qi that stagnates is almost always a form of Yang energy. Although Yang and Yin do interchange, they habitually do this only when they reach an excess or extreme[15]. The Yin forms, the Fluids and Blood, do not turn into Yang forms until there is *stasis*, a much more extreme form of stagnation.

Using the motorway jam analogy, stagnation occurs when it all slows down but still perhaps just keeps moving. The equivalent of Stasis might be when the jam becomes permanent, with people living on the motorway, blocking it from being used.

For example take stasis of Blood: it can form varicose veins, which lead to varicose ulcers and inflammation, which is Yang. But Blood does not turn into Yang usually until it reaches this extreme.

Put more graphically, it is one thing to have a bit of compressed air in the system. It is quite another to have a small hurricane or a fire.

So first, consider Qi that turns into Yang excess.

Yang Excess

An example. An idea or thought is very Yang, in that it can easily

15. There is more about this in Chapter 4 (in case you did not read it!)

be changed or altered. As that thought turns into reality, it becomes harder to change.

As illustration of this, I might be a car designer and create a new concept for a car. The more I work on it, the more the details are worked out, the more easy it will be for engineers to tool up for it, and the harder it will be to change the idea without causing a great deal of further work.

Once the factory is tooled up, and production has started, it is very much harder to change it all. Why? The Yang idea is now realised in its Yin form.

But even here, there are some things we can change, and these are the forms that are more Yang.

It is hard to alter the chassis and engine, because these are very Yin: they're made out of steel, forged and moulded, soldered, riveted and formed.

But we can certainly change the colour of the car, the name of the car, the tyres, the seating and lights. (You will notice that these are mostly on the outside of the car, a more Yang location than the inside, such as the inside of the engine.)

Why? Because all these are made so that they can be changed. For example, in winter we might change to winter tyres for better traction. We can often shift the angle of the lights, and if a bulb fails, we can easily replace it. Change the colour? Use a paint-brush!

The harder it is to change something, the more Yin it is and the more slowly it can change: the easier to change, the more Yang. However, following from Chapter 4, when a situation becomes very stable and unchanging, it reaches a point when it can transform, often suddenly, and even a small stimulus, if correctly applied, can topple it.

In contrast, Yang forms are what move the car, (diesel explodes and petrol burns), so expanding a gas that pushes a piston, or electric power that turns a rotor.

Electric power is more Yang than oil, which can make your hands dirty. Electric power just fries you!

Yang in your body takes a number of forms: movement, heat, noise, dryness.

Movement helps to dissipate Qi stagnation

Exercise helps dissipate Qi stagnation.

People who cannot or do not exercise quickly become restless when they have Qi stagnation. Qi feels bursting and distending: very uncomfortable. So you shift around to accommodate the Qi as it tries to find new vents.

In some parts of the body, you can feel or even see it moving.

For example, in the form of abdominal or intestinal gas (one of the forms of 'Wind' see below) you may notice it trying to move along the large intestine. Although this bursting tearing sense of distension or bloating and discomfort can start when the Qi is in the small intestine, it takes a more noticeable form in the large intestine. Here it can bulge, which in thin people you can actually see and touch. When it successfully exits via the anus as gas, it usually gives relief. (Not always! If it does not give relief, the Qi stagnation is already at a somewhat deeper level.)

So Qi stagnation causes movement and makes people fidgety.

.

Typically, Qi escapes by your having a good shout at someone.
Hot Air!

.

For example, if you are flying and your plane is running late, you may not be able to connect with your next plane to take you home or to your next meeting. The more important the plane connection and the tighter the timing, the more your Qi will stagnate. You will find yourself getting tense, restless, tapping your fingers, biting your lips, scratching your ears, taking deep breaths and so on.

The longer the tension goes on the more likely you will feel distension somewhere. It is almost like loading a spring, and when you do land, you will use that stored energy to run for your connection. The trapped Qi may also increase your heart beat, ready for action.

If it cannot be put to good use this way, your Qi stagnation will transform into restless and possibly destructive movement, like air escaping from a balloon.

The weaker the restraint of the walls of the balloon and the greater the pressure of the air inside, the more Wind symptoms you will get.

What does that mean? It means that if you have not learned some form of mental or physical discipline, you will not be able to stop moving, or complaining loudly, even shouting.

One would expect well-trained soldiers, for example, to be able to remain still even in extremely tense situations. The same goes for people who have learned to meditate and for many people who have learned a physical sport.

The opposite goes for untrained people, like children.

What HAPPENS NEXT if Qi stagnation continues?

Wind[16] MOVES and as its pressure builds it become destructive:-

- Chewing your lips becomes biting them until they bleed

- Scratching your ear turns into picking your nose

- Mild scratching becomes tearing until it bleeds

- Playing with fingers becomes biting your fingernails down to the quick

16. In Chinese medicine, this excessive, sometimes destructive, movement is called 'Wind'. There are a number of Chinese medical syndromes of disease with Wind in their name, for example Wind stirred by Heat, Wind stirred by Fire, Invasion by Wind-Heat, and invasion by Wind-Cold. These often affect Liver and Gallbladder Qi for which see chapter 8.

- Tapping the floor becomes kicking the door
- Restlessness becomes angry pacing
- Humming to yourself becomes cursing the cleaner
- Tension becomes rage, breaking things and swearing at the innocent
- Making your point becomes destroying your opponent
- Making haste becomes careless driving and accidents
- Tense boredom becomes solitary masturbation

Heat RISES, ACCELERATES, DRIES and BURNS

In this form, the problem ascends, usually towards the head:

- Gives thirst and a sensation of heat
- Appears often as a rash, often raised and red which may be sore or itch (though itches on their own are more associated with Wind in Chinese medicine)
- Dries skin, but in the presence of Damp[17] gives yellow secretions
- Skin complaints usually appear first on Yang surfaces or channels[18].
- Appears as redness of the skin and complexion
- As it penetrates further gives dry stools and scanty dark urine
- Produces increasingly pungent body odour

17. Damp is the name given to a set of symptoms characterised by stiffness and heaviness. Often caused or worsened by damp weather but there are other causes too. See http://www.acupuncturepoints.org/damp.html
18. Yang surfaces are the upper parts of the body as opposed to the lower parts, the back and sides as opposed to the front, the head and arms more than the legs.

- Pains tend to be burning, as in cystitis, or iritis, or as in stomach ulcer

- Menses are heavy, smelly, and contain dark-red blood

- Leads to mental restlessness, bordering on mania (Heat whips up Wind): impatience and irritation

- Makes your pulse go faster

- Makes your tongue look redder, often with a yellow coating

Become susceptible to HEAT by eating the wrong diet!

- Of course, Heat can come not just from emotional stress but from eating too much of a hot-type diet including too much curry, spicy food, alcohol, red meat, fatty, greasy or deep-fried food.

- If you often eat this kind of diet then you may make yourself more susceptible to Heat from emotional strain.

Infections can cause HEAT

- Heat can also arise from invasion by a bug, as for example when you get very hot with a high fever during an infection, an example of Wind-Heat. Over time, if its cause remains unresolved, Heat becomes...

FIRE

Fire is more dangerous. Heat may be unpleasant, but it is when tinder ignites and your house burns down that it becomes serious.

Fire takes several forms, depending on the Energy Organ, or Energy Organs, most affected. To some extent this depends on the nature of the underlying emotional tension.

- Anger, for example, tends to produce Liver
  Fire (http://www.acupuncture-points.org/liver-
  fire.html) (chapter 8) but can then also, unfortunately, lead
  on to Heart Fire (http://www.acupuncture-points.org/
  heartfire.html) (chapter 10).

The symptoms of Fire in the different Energy Organs
vary somewhat, but include, for nearly all of them:

- Thirst

- Mouth ulcers

- Feeling of heat

- Redness of face

- Red tongue and Fast pulse

- Dark urine

- Restlessness and Agitation tending towards Mania

- Sleep disturbed by dreams

- Bitter taste

- Bleeding, eg of the gums, or nose, or heavy menses

If you look at this list and still wonder why Fire is so serious, it
is because Fire leads to increased pressure in the
system, including the Western medical term hypertension
(though other syndromes in Chinese medicine also produce
this).

Fire can then go on to produce leakages of blood, as in ulcers,
stroke, or *Stasis of Blood*[19] tending to myocardial infarction.

Fire also increases Wind (as anyone who has been in a
bush fire can tell you), leading to manic episodes,
convulsions and epileptic seizures, bodily equivalents of bush
fire.

---

19. See http://www.acupuncture-points.org/blood-stasis.html

If Fire burns up the Yin resources of the body, you may begin to get a condition that for some is like the onset of the Western medical syndrome bipolar disorder.

In this, long periods are spent in a tired, low state, perhaps as the body recovers. These dejected episodes are interspersed by manic episodes that burn it all up again, without sufficient Yin-like control to prevent this recurring.

An analogy may make this clearer. Imagine parched land, covered in sparse, dry vegetation. With even a small spark it burns fiercely: the manic stage. The land then lies barren for a while (the depressed stage), until eventually perhaps after a little rain, small green shoots re-appear. These green shoots of recovery unfortunately lack sufficient moisture to grow to maturity, or if they do, they lack yin-like thickness in their skins (like an orange peel) to resist extreme heat.

So they dry out fast, ready for the next conflagration.

Of course, for most people suffering from simple Qi stagnation, these consequences are a very long way off and never happen. I describe them merely to explain how Chinese medicine understands what it calls energy – Qi – to work and how over time if the build-up of Qi is unable to resolve itself or to move, it can become more serious.

The more dangerous it becomes, the more pressing is the need for medical intervention and the less easy is it for our individual efforts (eg change of diet, taking more exercise) to influence it.

However, Chinese medicine has recognised these syndromes for millennia and learned how to treat them.

Moving Stagnant Qi onwards round the Five Element cycle

As explained in chapters 1 and 5, effective action or treatment for stagnant Qi can also mean helping to move the Qi from the stagnant phase where Qi is trapped on to the next phase in the Five Phase cycle. Choosing the appropriate actions to achieve this can make a huge difference, although sometimes the matter is fairly obvious.

For example, the Fire phase follows the Wood phase. Stagnant Qi in Wood often appears as frustration and anger, tension and either aggression or lack of assertiveness. The Fire phase represents what people in the Wood phase are often aiming towards, Fire meaning laughter, parties, showing off, being seen at one's best, being recognised for achievements and so on.

So, for example, humour – laughter – can defuse anger: from a Five Phase perspective, anger is transformed into laughter.

This particular example also explains why Wood-like characters, often the Type A personality, pushy, hardworking, demanding, action-orientated, like to see and be seen at expensive parties and functions. They like to have their photos taken with successful people to be shown round the world. Here, their Wood energy transforms naturally into the next phase, that of enjoyment, fun and appreciation.

In the same way, people stuck in the Fire phase, with somewhat 'hyper' or 'manic' personalities, benefit from being supported and grounded by their community (Earth) and from wide-open or elevated spaces, such as up mountains, afforded by Metal. If they can learn to teach or write from their experiences they may also be putting their Metal phase to good use, and so move onwards their Qi.

Stagnant Qi, represented by symptoms, is trapped energy. That trapped energy can provide huge benefits. The symptoms may be unpleasant, but they represent our body's best attempt at dealing with its situation. Seen positively, they by no means suggest disaster for us. Rather, they are a source of energy which, if we can release it positively, will help us to greater health and happiness, and frequently in so doing, help our environment and community.

Summary

In this chapter you have read how Qi takes various forms as it continues to stagnate. There is a wide range of methods, ancient and modern, which can help Qi either to cease to stagnate and/or to help it transform into its next natural manifestation, often through our positive action in pushing it forward to the next phase.

The next chapter introduces the main causes of Qi stagnation. After reading it, you should understand more about what sets it off in your life.

CHAPTER 7

General Causes of Qi Stagnation

Certain actions and situations come up repeatedly as causes of stress, which is why we all suffer from them.

Many of them cannot be prevented. As for the symptoms,which ones YOU manifest depend on your susceptibility, which we briefly covered in Chapter 2.

Difference between Causes and Symptoms of Stress

First, it is important to make a distinction. Although sometimes the difference is unclear, in most kinds of stress it is possible to distinguish the originating cause from the subsequent symptom(s).

Some people are not good at evaluating their feelings, emotions and sensory perceptions. If when reading through the following you cannot tell if you have a given sensation or feeling, you may need someone else to help you make sense of it!

In general, I would rate the following as symptoms, though

not all are necessarily caused by Qi stagnation. Most, in time, may lead to it:

- Alcohol – increased consumption
- Back ache
- Bowel movement sudden urging or constipation
- Breathing faster or more shallowly
- Chest feels tight
- Crying
- Depression
- Fatigue and tiredness
- Fears and phobias
- Inability to focus
- Hands and/or feet feel cold
- Headache
- Heart pounding or palpitating
- High blood pressure
- Indigestion
- Insomnia, difficulties with sleep
- Irritability
- Lip chewing
- Muscular tension
- Nail biting
- Neck ache
- Over-eating
- Pain, chronic and temporary

- Perspiration increased

- Pulse rapid

- Restlessness

- Sexual libido reduced

- Skin rash including hives

- Teeth gritting

- Throat feels tight

- Tics and twitches

- Urge to smoke

- Work absences frequent

And there are many others, the above being just examples of symptoms that stressed people suffer. To repeat, many of the above symptoms can have other causes, not necessarily connected with stress. Equally, many of the symptoms listed can themselves cause stress.

Causes

In traditional Chinese medicine, there are two main causes of Qi stagnation. The following list includes the main causes, which were emotions and diet, as well as some others.

A Emotions[1]

The first traditional cause is emotional. Your emotions are natural expressions of your energy. Some feel good, others not. Many cultures, mostly in the West, think it healthy

1. The British surgeon David Le Vay recognised in Hans Selye's work how emotions generated disease. 'Hans Selye and a unitary conception of disease' British Journal for the Philosophy of Science 3 (1952) 157-8..

to express emotions; that they are an expression of our free human spirit, a right not to be denied.

However, as many selfish acts of wanton damage and cruelty have shown, un-tempered emotions can be very destructive.

We now have assertiveness training, showing how to express our point of view without letting emotions overwhelm us.

Other cultures suggest that we regard our emotions as transitory disturbances on the mirror of consciousness – a Zen-Buddhist idea.

I do not think Chinese medicine takes a firm view on this, but during its development over the last 3,000 years many of its practitioners were influenced by Daoism, Buddhism and Confucianism, each of which had objective – but some would say, negative – views on the wanton display of emotions.

Many practitioners nowadays probably align themselves to some extent with these ancient philosophies.

So if you see a practitioner of classical Chinese medicine, whether a herbalist, acupuncturist or other such, there may be a conflict with the 'free expression' model of Western society. This is probably mainly because they tend to notice the adverse health effects of many emotions.

Some practitioners may seem disapproving of patients not used to controlling their emotions.

Whichever camp you follow, there is no doubt that emotions can and do disturb us. In Chinese medicine, emotions disturb the natural flow and expression of Qi.

This is all the more so if they are strong emotions or if an emotional pattern persists over a long period.

The problem is that under stress, either you do not notice the organic effect of your emotion, or you do not attribute the pathology, the dis-ease you later experience, to the emotion preceding it.

Emotions frequently point up underlying weaknesses in

your psyche or physiology. These weaknesses may have been inherited, or acquired through poor upbringing, or have arisen from the ravages of disease or a difficult life.

Growing old, for example, often weakens the body or its ability to fight disease. Without the resilience of youth, emotions sometimes spill out too easily, causing Qi stagnation with its consequent (Chinese medical) syndromes of disease.

.

Growing old happens partly as our Kidney Qi depletes. With less Kidney Qi and less resilience we often become more susceptible to Qi stagnation. Read more in chapter 15.

.

Had that underlying weakness not been present, the emotion might neither have been so overwhelming nor have lead to further pathology.

What emotions are we talking about, and what are their effects?

Emotional stress takes various forms. Each emotion has a different effect on Qi. Depending on that effect, Qi is said to knot up, to scatter, to become depleted, or turn into some other form of Qi. However, its first tendency is to stagnate. We cover this starting in the next chapter, but here we need to understand a little more about how Qi flows round the body, in health and disease.

Flow of Qi in Health

In health, Qi travels around the body along what the Chinese called Channels. It also moves naturally in various directions, doing jobs to maintain health – see also Chapter 1. Here follow three examples of how our Energy Organs behave when healthy. There is much more about them in later chapters, including what happens when their Qi stagnates.

EXAMPLE 1 – LUNGS

For example, when we breathe, Qi is said to descend, particularly as we breath out. That descending function can be used to relax and calm us.

Have you ever been urged to take a few deep breaths before making a decision or taking some action? Those deep breaths provide oxygen for your blood to nourish your brain cells and eyes, enabling a better decision – you hope!

But, and not only from the Chinese perspective, the very act of taking steady deep breaths is calming.

Instead of Qi rushing upwards and outwards, leading to intemperate or impulsive actions that you might later regret, via steady deep breaths your Qi is sent downwards to stabilise your body and mind.

Those calming breaths descend unwanted ascending Qi, as tobacco smokers know well when they smoke to quell tension.

Those who meditate learn this: how to concentrate their minds on the lower abdomen, leading energy downwards. Taking it further, Qi Gong practitioners learn how to move Qi from place to place around their bodies. This mental control or purpose helps it to flow smoothly.

In illness or pain, they learn how to concentrate on a given part of the body, sending Qi there to move and unblock the problem. (What do they feel when Qi arrives? It depends: often it is a feeling of warmth, a glowing sensation. In other cases it can be like pricking a balloon, a feeling of tension being released.)

The Emotion of Grief

The emotion that mainly affects the Lungs is that of loss, separation or grief. A natural response to this is to cry.

.

GRIEF is the emotion traditionally attributed to the Lungs. In excess, or sometimes when it cannot be expressed, it produces an imbalance in the Lung Energy Organ. Sometimes this also affects its partner Energy Organ, the Large Intestine.

.

Great shuddering, heaving sobs help the lungs keep expanding and contracting, but in cultures where to show grief freely is frowned upon, then you may expect disturbances in Lung function to occur arising from Lung Qi stagnation.

Read chapter 9 on Lung Qi stagnation to discover more about what happens then, but each chapter about the Energy Organs describes the main emotions affecting the Energy Organ in question, and the symptoms from its Qi stagnation.

EXAMPLE 2 – STOMACH

The way Qi functions in a healthy Stomach is to descend food, to 'rotten and ripen' it as old Chinese texts put it. Actually, the function goes far beyond this because the thinking that is said to come from the Stomach includes consideration as to the best foods to eat, obtaining, preparing, cooking and displaying them prior to eating. Subsequently it covers chewing food properly and then swallowing it.

Then comes the 'rottening and ripening', the process of digestion. What remains after this is descended further and ultimately evacuated. All these functions come under the Stomach in one way or another, although the Small and Large Intestines and Spleen functions also participate.

If the Stomach Qi fails to descend food, we do not feel hungry, we soon fill up, we lose interest in food and, if Stomach Qi ascends (the old texts say it 'rebels') we become nauseous and may vomit or belch. Connected with this is when Heat in the Stomach ascends, experienced as burping, eructations and heartburn.

Thought processes

There is another function that Stomach Qi governs, that of careful thought and consideration, not just of food but of anything. This is the process of calmly thinking things over, pondering them, meditating on them.

The actual process of deciding comes mainly from the Gall Bladder function, but it is the Stomach Qi that in Chinese medicine gets the facts, puts them in order and mulls over their consequences.

Those with Attention Deficit Hyperactive Disorder (ADHD), often have Stomach Qi that is imbalanced. Calm, considered thought patterns are not their forte.

Poor concentration as in ADHD is often diagnosed in Chinese Medicine as being an apparent Yang excess which is actually due to a real Yin deficiency, usually of Blood.
Having too many things to think about can overwhelm the Stomach Energy Organ, like trying to eat too many things at once.

With ADHD sufferers, eating is often quick after only superficial thought about what to eat. The wrong food choices lead to other consequences that we shall come to, dietary mistakes being another cause of Stagnation of Qi.

ADHD sufferers may have very quick minds but their thinking lacks order and they are easily distracted. Because their Stomach Qi does not properly choose nor digest food, they may suffer from Blood 'deficiency', leading to unreliable memory, short emotional fuses, restlessness and poor sleep patterns.

EXAMPLE 3 – SPLEEN

.

*Over-thinking or worrying are the emotions that upset
the Spleen. These include obsession, working intellectually without
rest and over-concern for others.*

.

In Chinese medicine, the Spleen has a far more important function than in Western medicine.

The Spleen's function is less easy to explain in terms of obvious movement, for instance up or down, although traditionally its action is upwards. Mainly, it 'transforms and transports' food and Blood.

Food 'rottened and ripened' by the descending Stomach Qi is partially turned into blood by the Spleen.

I suppose Western physiologists would say that this was like the action of the intestines in absorbing food into the blood stream, with the action of the liver organ in enriching or detoxifying it, the pancreas in providing insulin to adjust the blood sugar levels and to some extent the kidney actions to regulate the quantity and thickness of the blood.

But it goes further, in that Spleen Qi is said to transport Blood round the body, nourishing flesh and removing excess or degenerated matter.

Of course, the spleen *organ* does not do this: it is stuck under the ribs in the upper left abdomen.

But in Chinese medicine the function of the Spleen (capital S), is to act like a good housekeeper, keeping everything tidy, clean and properly nourished.

Hence the so-called ascending function of Spleen Qi: it takes the Blood and nourishes the outside and upper parts, providing lustre to the skin and cheeks, nourishment for the brain and strength to the muscles. (Chapter 13 is devoted to the Spleen Energy Organ.)

When this Spleen function is disturbed, you get a range of symptoms that can include poor digestion, loose stools, tiredness, breathlessness, tendency to worry, varicose veins, swellings, phlegm, dizziness and nervous exhaustion.

What main emotions lead to Qi stagnation?

The main traditional groups of emotions that lead to Qi stagnation are:

- Anger and frustration
- What we might called hyper-states, eg tending towards mania, or laughing too much, or taking nothing seriously
- Over-thinking, obsession, worry, boredom
- Grief, results of separation or loss
- Fear, terror

We might add others, for instance:

- Envy
- Jealousy
- Over-strain. (Of course, what is over-strain? We can usually take a short period of over-strain, recovering quickly after a rest. Continuing over-strain is a different matter. It wears us down physically whilst keeping us mentally at fever-pitch. This can be lethal, at the least very debilitating. As you grow weaker, from disease, age or travails, you become more susceptible to over-strain.)

B Dietary

The traditional Chinese approach to diet, though sophisticated in its own way, foresaw none of the crazy

excesses, mutations and perversions in modern developed societies. Healthy people from third world countries who move to developed countries and adopt their fast-food and junk food diets soon exhibit the same health problems as those brought up in them.

However, the structure of the basic theory in Chinese medicine seems to accommodate and explain the results of bad diet, from almost wherever it arises.

Some of their dietary ideas are similar to those of other traditional cultures or systems of health, including Ayurveda. The ancient Chinese system we have inherited said that we need to eat foods regularly from each of five 'Element' groups. If we ate this way, we would be nourishing each of our five main Energy Organ systems and they would keep us healthy.

Of course, while the ancient Chinese knew all about famine and starvation, they were not so familiar with constant plenty. Also, their society being based far more in the countryside, people had to work physically to eke out a living. That meant that they moved their Qi and Blood every day through regular physical exertion.

Another point: the Chinese regarded eating as good. Only if you could not or would not eat did they see a problem.

Nowadays, we have learned that over-eating is a major problem, caused by plenty, or at least by plenty of poor quality refined foods, which the ancient Chinese did not have.

So physical work and only occasional feasts of plenty meant that obesity in ancient China was uncommon. Probably to be fat was a sign of wealth, meaning plenty of food and many servants, so no need for exercise.

The way they grouped foods was not in terms of their chemical structure (eg protein, fat, carbohydrate etc.) but in terms of their taste, though other qualities like colour and how the food was prepared were also important.

The five tastes and the Five Elements they related to were: So, they suggested that if you ate foods daily from each taste category you would be feeding each of the Elements and, if the Elements were in balance, so would you be.

Element	Taste
Fire	Bitter
Earth	Sweet
Metal	Pungent
Water	Salty
Wood	Sour

Of course, they assumed you would also have enough (and not an excess) of each of the taste categories to eat. If you ate too much of a given taste, you might damage the workings of the relevant Element.

Nowadays we might also need to say that the foods they used would have been what we might call 'organic', meaning that they grew naturally without the need for inorganic and concentrated artificial fertilisers, preservatives[2], herbicides, fungicides and pesticides[3].

They then categorised foods into one or more each of the Tastes, because although it is easy to recognise that sugar is sweet, what about grains and meat?

Because imbalance arises when you have too little or

2. Chemicals such as phthalates now occur in huge amounts in processed foods, drinks and personal-care products. These chemicals disrupt reproductive processes. (Environ Health Perspect, 2013, 121:473-9)

3. Many pesticides don't work as expected. Even after washing pesticides off fruit, fruit was still found to contain viruses such as the norovirus, a common cause of stomach 'flu. (Int Jnl. Food Microbiology, 2013: 160: 323-8)

too much of a given taste, they eventually categorised all the foods they had.

As anyone who has been to a Chinese restaurant knows, let alone anyone who has spent time in China, many foods eaten there are different to foods in the West.

So they have had to categorise our Western foods too, including our nutritional supplements and medicines, because Western pharmaceutical companies would like even normal healthy people to take medicine regularly, let alone ill people[4].

.

We should also not forget the effect of thirst and hunger on health in general. Both play a major role in
the health of nations. For many countries in the 21st Century, it may become water deficiency, a form of Yin deficiency that leads to all kinds of Qi stagnation.
A deficiency of Yin[5] usually appears as apparent Yang excess: e.g. dryness, heat, anger and aggression.
Farmed food is often days or months old even when marked 'fresh'. Modern soil, depleted by intensive farming, means foods contain less nutritional value than 100 years ago. Probably we should also add sources of Omega 3 oils to our diets. If from fish, marine resources will be another yin reserve we are depleting. All this means people can be hungry even though 'full': more signs of yin deficiency.

.

The Bitter taste

It is not surprising that many medicines taste bitter, because their effect is cooling, and in Chinese Medicine cooling herbs are used to clear Heat from the system, such as in a fever or where there is inflammation.

4. "Middle-aged people will be able to grow old gracefully within a generation by taking a pill which can fight the ageing process, an eminent scientist predicts." Article in Daily Telegraph 29/9/12.
5. For more on Yin Deficiency see http://www.acupuncture-points.org/yin-deficiency.html pr my book on the same subject.

Most people do not like the bitter taste, partly because it is not usually part of our diet and partly because many poisons naturally taste bitter and our genes have given us a natural dislike for them.

Nevertheless, for health we should eat some foods categorised as 'bitter'.

The Sweet Taste

To mitigate the bitter taste we add sugar or sweet-tasting substances (often artificial) to make it palatable.

In developed countries there is a surfeit of the sweet taste in what people eat, but also of the salty taste and, to a somewhat lesser but growing extent, the pungent taste. Food producers have discovered that people will eat more if they enhance the taste rather than if they enhance the quality of the food.

Government laws and consumer demands force them to add nutritional qualities to denatured foods. Bread and breakfast cereals are often enriched with B vitamins, for instance, the flour in them having been refined, originally to make it last longer, but nowadays to assuage the degraded taste-buds of modern consumers.

When we eat too much 'sweet' food, for instance, it weakens our Spleen and Stomach energies, and a common result is that we put on weight. 'Wrong' foods, over-eaten, disturb the proper working of Stomach and Spleen, which allows the build-up of 'fat'. A side-effect is the accumulation of phlegm[6].

Because the Spleen and Stomach energies manage our thinking processes, it can also make us less able to concentrate, making thought[7] more difficult, possibly an influence in producing ADHD. Certainly not being able

---

6. http://www.acupuncture-points.org/phlegm.html
7. Thinking steadily about something, as in 'read, mark, learn and inwardly digest', comes under the Earth element: Spleen and Stomach.

to concentrate or think things through creates the potential for Qi stagnation.

Classification of Drugs

Some years ago many psychoactive drugs were categorised in terms of their actions in Chinese medicine, to show which Energy Organs were susceptible to them.

Too much of a given drug, whatever its other effects or side-effects, can also be seen as unbalancing the Energy Organ system, leading to the potential for Qi stagnation.

Diet is a huge subject. Artificial flavours, concentrated nutriceuticals, refined foods, herbicides, pesticides and modern medicine are creating potentially huge imbalances in the Energy Organ systems of modern man.

Any such imbalance makes us more susceptible to Qi stagnation. Additionally, an adverse reaction to something you have eaten can easily lead to Qi stagnation symptoms. How you react depends also on your state of health at the time. For instance, before a holiday you may be tense and irritable, predisposing your body to react adversely to almost anything you eat.

But a few days later, when you are relaxed and able to take your time to eat in convivial company, you may find that without problems you can eat far more than you could eat normally, including foods that usually upset you.

C Obsession

Obsession traditionally comes mainly under Spleen function but I think it requires its own category because we see it all the time. Whether because of modern medications, or social drugs, or the Internet, our minds become stuck on certain images or ideas.

Where there is such 'stuckness', mental, emotional or physical – or spiritual, if one knows how to define the term –

there will follow disease. But initially this often starts with signs of Qi stagnation.

D Short-circuit

It is a wonderful thing, the Internet. So is the amazing range of ways we can communicate. First we had sign language, then speech, then pigeon post, then the semaphore and written communications. Later we got printing, books, and newspapers.

Then in the space of a bare 100 years we got the telephone, radio, TV, Internet, email, cell-phone, texting, and Skype.

That has lead to instant communications like Twitter, blogs and Facebook. Soon we may wire or incorporate some of these into our brains directly. It will be possible to be in touch with the immense range of information and its flow without opening our eyes, let alone leaving our armchairs[8].

From our armchairs we shall be able to play our games, make our bets, invest and divest, shout and scream, entertain and be entertained.

If someone brings us our food and takes away our faeces, wipes us clean and puts us to bed, we shall be able to live our lives without moving a muscle. We shall not have to speak, or even open our mouths. We shall be purely thinking. In fact, we shall become part computers.

Computers get replaced regularly through hard and software upgrades. So the theory might go.

But we do have bodies that need exercise, work, stretching, movement. None of us can live just mentally. Computer information moves at speeds approaching that of light. Our brain nerve-cells have synapses that allow information to travel either electrically or chemically,

8. 'How to profit from the cyborg era'. Matthew Partridge, MoneyWeek, 5.4.13 and The New Digital Age, Schmidt and Cohen, John Murray 2013

but very much slower than light. Consciously we cannot multitask like computers.

However, we can and do multitask all the time. My heart is beating, my lungs are breathing, my skin is being replaced, my breakfast digested and my kidneys are refining my blood without my being aware of them.

But these are not the conscious thoughts. They came with the equipment, built-in. The little bit of me that thinks consciously is perhaps growing in size and perhaps not – we shall have to see how future generations' brains develop.

Even a few minutes on the Internet apparently begins to rewire how parts of our brains work. The energy required to run our brains may be increasing[9].

If our brains have not been properly trained to cope with this, and the food we eat is not adequate for their needs, the energy will cease to flow smoothly. It will or may stagnate.

The energetic consequence, as we shall see, will be that this stagnant energy turns into either movement or heat. The upside of this is the plethora of ideas leading to benefits for society and money for entrepreneurs.

The downside is that we are not all Einstein and we cannot all make fortunes. Many ideas are barmy, at least for their time. If someone is unfit physically and untrained mentally, the psychic energy will implode, short-circuit and be very destructive, both to the individual and then to society.

The resultant Qi stagnation will lead to 'Wind' and 'Heat'.

Wind – Movement – often appears as hyperactivity; Heat often leads to psychosis or states approaching it.

9. We may or may not be brighter than our ancestors. Gerald Crabtree writing in Trends in Genetics vol 29 p1 says "Someone plucked from 1000 BC and placed in modern society, would be 'among the brightest and most intellectually alive of our colleagues and companions'" as reported in New Scientist 30/3/13.

E Environment

An environment harmful to mental or physical health can lead quickly to many conditions recognised by Chinese medicine, certainly including Qi stagnation.

For example, a working environment where there is bullying or harassment will tend to produce anxiety or fear, emotions already mentioned above. That is your social environment.

Also, we should include your political and economic environment. This is the macro-environment that leads to the micro or social environment you inhabit.

In the long-term, what happens politically affects us all. Different political systems produce very different cultures and living standards. Chapter 4 has already touched on the theory.

But physically, a very cold or airless or hot environment can also lead to symptoms almost indistinguishable from Qi stagnation in those who are susceptible to it.

Cold, for example, causes shivering and tension that stops one reacting smoothly to events. An airless, hot room can quickly make someone who is naturally a 'hot' type of person feel impossibly uncomfortable and irritable: signs of impending or actual Qi stagnation.

Having said this, Chinese medicine purists would probably say that although the result may be what I have described, the process is different (e.g. 'invasion of Cold and or Damp and or Wind blocks the flow of Qi in the channels').

This may or may not then lead to symptoms looking like Qi stagnation along with a bunch of other symptoms. Heat, in particular, is probably more dangerous than cold, because it reduces the difference between the inside and the outside, so making it harder to dispel the trapped energy.

F Trauma

Trauma, such as a bruise, but more seriously a shock (including emotional shock) or accident, often produces what is called Blood Stagnation[10].

Just as Qi stagnation can lead to Blood stagnation, so is the reverse true. The effects of shock and trauma may continue for many years until treated[11].

The residual stagnation in Qi predisposes the individual to more Qi stagnation when the circumstances arise.

G Climatic conditions[12]

For the same reason, the climate can produce Qi stagnation. A 'hot' person goes to a hot country where, unused to the heat, he quickly loses his 'cool' and becomes more susceptible to Qi stagnation, for example.

A 'hot' person has good circulation, wears fewer clothes than others, is often thirsty, likes cold or iced food, is often too hot in bed, and so on. The reverse applies to a 'cold' person.

A cold person goes to a cold climate and, perhaps unused to exercise, does not realise that to keep warm you must either exercise or stay indoors in well-heated accommodation. The latter may be boring, but the former forces your body to work and increases your metabolic rate, which warms you up.

---

10. See http://www.acupuncture-points.org/blood-stasis.html
11. I had a patient who had been injured by an accidental gunshot 30 years before he visited me. He had many symptoms, had received years of counselling and physiotherapy, but said the treatment I gave him, basically to move Qi and Blood, was apparently by far the most effective.
12. See an article 'Weather and Social Behaviour' submitted by Aidan Sammons at http://www.psychlotron.org.uk/resources/environmental/A2_OCR_env_heataggression.pdf

Failing that, he will get cold and grumpy, more susceptible to Qi stagnation.

Likewise, the weather can affect how our bodies and our Qi reacts. Ask any primary school teacher about the effect of thunderstorms on the equilibrium of the pupils[13] (let alone on the dogs and cats).

H Over- or under-activity (also applies to mental activity)

Usually, as you will see later, physical activity is good for Qi stagnation symptoms. Too little or too much physical activity, or the wrong type for you, can however produce Qi stagnation.

Too little exercise can be a major cause of Qi stagnation. Why? Because your body is the result of millions of years of evolution, during which the requirement to sit on its backside all the time was never a satisfactory solution: if they did that, our ancestors got eaten. Your body was made to move, to run, to walk, to bend, stretch, reach and stoop.

It was not made to sit facing a screen for hours on end! All the physical movements mentioned move Qi. Just sitting for too long encourages Qi to stagnate.

Also, lack of exercise means we do not breathe enough for health. We breathe enough to maintain our situation, but not enough to keep our Qi fresh. (The Lungs absorb fresh Qi from the air – a reason for taking at least some of our exercise in fresh, clean air.) So our Qi grows dull and cannot move.

When Qi stagnates, eventually other things begin to stagnate, like Blood, which can be serious as sufferers from Deep Vein Thrombosis caused by extended periods at rest on aircraft or just sitting at a desk now realise.

How much exercise or physical work is too much?

---

13. 'Childhood Fears: Developmental Phase or Specific Phobia?' Jennifer H. Kessler, Behaviour Therapy Centre, Greater Washington.

Physical activity moves Qi, so naturally reduces Qi stagnation. But if you overdo it, exhaust yourself repeatedly especially by

- over-straining or

- over-lifting or

- continuing to work for long after you are already tired or

- do not eat enough for the exercise you take or

- if you are a woman and do not maintain adequate levels of body fat when exercising ... you deplete your Kidney Yang energy and may deplete your Blood energy. For example, female athletes sometimes report reduced menses or even complete absence of them. Over time, this can be serious because the lack of Blood causing the amenorrhoea may also cause weight loss, dizziness, poor sleep and osteoporosis. This form of amenorrhoea often comes about when the athlete does not eat enough for her level of physical output[14].

(Talking of osteoporosis, the right kind of exercise at the right time of life can have a beneficial effect on a woman's likelihood to suffer osteoporosis after her menopause. A Finnish study showed that girls who exercised plenty (but obviously not too much!) before and after the onset of their periods ie in their teens, were less likely to suffer from osteoporosis later on[15][16].

Another study showed that the bone density of high-mileage runners (60-75 miles/week) was lower than that of men who only ran 15-20 miles/week[17].)

Both your Kidney energy and your Blood are resources

14. 'Health Issues for Women Athletes: Exercise- Induced Amenorrhea' Michelle P. Warren Department of Obstetrics and Gynecology and Medicine, Columbia University College of Physicians and Surgeons, New York, New York 10032
15. BMJ. 1999 January 23; 318(7178): 205–206
16. Bearing in mind the conclusions of Chapter 4 on Yin and Yang, one may surmise that, by taking maximum advantage of their Yang growth phase in adolescence, they created more Yin resources for the long term.
17. (MacDougall JD, et al. 1992). (http://www.athleteinme.com/ArticleView.aspx?id=283)

your Liver energy depends upon if it is to work smoothly. Weakening either of them can lead to Liver Yin or Liver Blood deficiency[18], making you more susceptible to Liver Qi stagnation.

(Syndromes like Liver Yin and Liver Blood have very clear meanings in Chinese medicine. I have included them here only to show that practitioners can be very precise. Knowing which syndromes of illness are the matter e.g. Liver Blood deficiency, makes it much easier to decide exactly what would be the best treatment. You can read more about them through the web pages given in the footnote.)

Summary

In this chapter you have read about

- different kinds of Qi stagnation and
- its general causes
- emotions
- diet
- obsession
- environment
- climatic and weather
- shock and trauma
- over- and under-activity

The next chapter is all about Liver Qi stagnation, probably the most common kind, which often occurs with all the other kinds of Qi stagnation. In fact, its symptoms are very like those you have

18. For explanation http://www.acupuncture-points.org/liver-blood-deficiency.html and http://www.acupuncture-points.org/liver-yin-deficiency.html

already read about. From this single syndrome, acupuncturists have made fortunes over the centuries, and deserved to.

CHAPTER 8

Liver/Gallbladder Qi Stagnation

This chapter introduces probably the most common form of Qi stagnation. It turns out to provide the symptoms that often appear with other forms of Qi stagnation too.

What that means is that you often get these symptoms as well as symptoms more specific to your particular makeup.

Essence of Liver and Gallbladder Qi stagnation

Why should you read this chapter?

- First, because in just about all forms of Qi stagnation there is also an element of Liver Qi stagnation.

- Second, if you have ever felt frustrated or angry about progress in any endeavour, you will have encountered some symptoms of Liver Qi Stagnation.

- Third, because if you regularly take medication (painkillers, tranquillisers, anti-inflammatories, antibiotics etc, but also social drugs like alcohol or tobacco) you should know about their Primary and Secondary actions which, over time, may affect you.

In this chapter you will read about:

- The importance of the Gall Bladder in Chinese medicine
- The Gall Bladder Time
- The Gall Bladder Function
- The Liver Time and Function
- Liver Qi Stagnation and how it affects you
- Why Blood Storage by the Liver is significant (and what happens when you do not have enough Blood!)
- Qi Flow reversal
- How and where stagnating Liver Qi presses outwards
- Implications for Circulation and Blood
- What you can do to help yourself
- The difference between Primary and Secondary effects of social drugs and drugs you may be prescribed
- Which treatments help Liver Qi stagnation

Although most of this chapter is about Liver Qi, we need to start with something which in its own way is as important, but often overlooked.

It deals with our courage and ability to make good decisions. But even before that, you need to realise something about the way Chinese medicine looks at life, because it is very different to our outlook in the West.

It is in italics below and perhaps a bit technical, so skip it if you want to. Just remember the page number in case you want to make sense of something later.

Chinese medicine attributes mental and emotional as well as physical qualities to what they call the Zangfu, or what I call the Energy Organs.

Confusingly for Westerners, these bear the same names as the physical organs we know, such as heart, liver, kidney and so on.

For example, the Heart energy organ (capital H) is viewed as far more than the heart. Admittedly, it contains the heart organ but that is just part of it.

Even with someone else's heart organ after surgery to replace your own, you would still have your own Heart Energy Organ, though no doubt it would be changed somewhat because surgery of that nature is highly traumatic. But unless there had been a calamity, you would still be much the same person.

Likewise, you might have your spleen out via a splenoctomy. You can get by without a spleen, though not as well as with it. But your Spleen energy organ (capital S) would continue to function, though again, perhaps less effectively than before.

As you will read in chapter 10, an important function of the Heart (energy organ – capital H) is to house your Mind. In the West, there is some discussion about where the centre of our being resides, but many would put it in the brain and nervous system.

However, the Chinese decided three millennia ago that it was looked after, wherever it was actually situated, by the Heart: 'housed' by the Heart. Similarly, the function of turning one thing into another and moving it round the body (eg of transforming food and transporting Blood and Qi round the body) was looked after by what became known as the Spleen Energy Organ.

Whether by that time they had actually opened up a body and discovered the spleen, let alone its function, is doubtful – though they probably had, but, not having our resources, pursued their Energy-based medicine. Whatever physical organ an Energy Organ was related to, they still needed to understand its energetic function.

Also, if you are familiar with the acupuncture channels, they did not call the channel now associated with the Heart by that name. They called it the 'Hand Shaoyin' channel, (or Hand Lesser Yin channel), and eventually the 'Heart channel of Hand-Shaoyin'.

Similarly, what we call the Spleen channel is actually now called the Spleen channel of Foot-Taiyin (or

Foot Greater Yin). So an Energy Organ covers much more than just its related physical organ. For this reason, an acupuncture channel, (sometimes called a 'meridian') is just one aspect of an Energy Organ, but is, one might say, 'powered' by it.

This book is not about the channels, which is what you think of when you say 'acupuncture', but about the Chinese medical theory of how we are and get ill in certain ways.

GALL BLADDER

Gallbladder Time[1]

From 11pm to 1am the sun stops going lower and starts going upwards in the sky: one day ends, the next begins. The Gallbladder channel itself lies on each side of the body where the front becomes the back.

The Gall bladder Energy is at a kind of knife-edge between one frame of mind and another; between back and front, between past and future, between receiving and defending.

Both between 11pm and 1am and to a lesser extent 12 hours later are times when the Gall Bladder may, if its Qi is stagnating, cause you health problems.

·

These Chinese clock times are less useful if working hours are no longer agricultural, as in the past. From 2008, more people live in cities than rurally but our genes have not yet caught up. This perhaps explains why modern man copes so badly with changing shifts and jet-lag.

1. See the Chinese Clock, Appendix 5

Gallbladder Function

The Gall Bladder 'time' is reflected in the Gallbladder's function which, besides supporting the Liver function of ascending Qi, is *to have the courage to take decisions.*

This is important because all the other Energies depend on this decision-making. (It says this in one of the old texts, 'Chapter 9 of the Simple Questions[2].)

Looking at where it is in the Chinese clock, you can se it is at the opposite point in the clock to the Heart, which houses your underlying purpose and being – your Mind.

As in many parts of TCM, opposites contain aspects of one another. The Heart's action is downwards, the Gallbladder's and Liver's direction is upwards. The Heart, at the centre of the day and of your being (midday), sends the request 'down' to your Gallbladder to make the right decision.

The Gallbladder, at the end of one day and the beginning of the next (i.e. at midnight), with all available resources gathered by the Liver can take the right decision and send it back up to the Heart. It seems odd to suppose that this Gallbladder time, when most of us are asleep, appears to be when we take our decisions.

However, it is not that we take our decisions then, it is then that we may say the Gall Bladder is refreshed as it takes itsturn at running the show. So its ability to take decisions renews then.

Continually taking decisions can be very tiring. It is appropriate that you renew your Gallbladder and Liver energies when you are asleep, so important are they for you when you are awake.

·

We now know that most human growth hormone is released during deep sleep. That many people are in their deepest sleep

2. Huangdi Neigjing Su Wen - a very important Chinese text.

during the Gallbladder time suggests that the Gall Bladder function may be more important than even Chinese medicine suspected.

.

Renewed by sleep, your Gallbladder can help you take healthy decisions the next day. That, of course, assumes the Gallbladder is healthy.

If habitually you go to bed after 1am, it is possible your Gall Bladder Energy function will be less efficient.

Very often people tell me that around 9.30pm –10.30pm they feel tired, they yawn, and realise they should go to bed. But if they ignore the warnings given by the body, they wake up again.

At that point, they feel able to do any number of jobs! For example, they might be able to write some letters, plan a meeting, iron the laundry, prepare a meal, paint a room ...!

If they do this, and finally get to bed when they start feeling really sleepy perhaps at 1am, they will wake at 7 or 8am thenext morning feeling a little under-powered. When they attend meetings, they will not have quite the clear perception they should have had. They will need coffee to produce more alertness. Their ability to take decisions will be below par and the decisions taken may not lead to such effective results.

This is because they did not allow the Qi to renew the Gall-Bladder properly, in sleep.

That first sleep of the night, when during the first 2 hours we sink into the deepest and most dreamless level of sleep, when our brain waves reach their slowest 2 – 3 cycles per second, when most of our human growth hormone is secreted, that is when we renew our Gall Bladder energy.

All the other Energy organs depend on the decision-making ability of the Gall Bladder, as we said, and this time of night is when we renew it.

Have you ever been faced with a problem, or

problems, which you could not solve? Have you tried articulating the problem before you go to sleep, perhaps even writing it down?

Give your sleeping mind the problem and relax into sleep.

In the morning, particularly if you have given the Gallbladder this special boost of deep sleep at the time when it handles the Qi, it will – as it were – awake profoundly refreshed and often produce a solution for you, or a new angle that you can pursue.

This has worked for millions of people and can do so for you.

Of course, many people pray or meditate before going to sleep. During their prayers or meditations they entrust their problems to a greater Self. This is another way of doing it – but you still need a healthy Gall Bladder to help you make or recognise the right decision.

Allowing yourself to sleep deeply at this time, instead of dissipating your energy in a hundred small activities, refreshes your whole Mind.

Besides courage to take decisions the Gallbladder gives you the ability for initiative and enterprise. To be in business as an entrepreneur requires these characteristics. We would all like to have strong Gallbladders! They make us confident and assertive, able to move through life feeling positive.

Good sleep refreshes your body, which benefits from two other functions of the Gallbladder. The first is of storing and secreting bile, an essential function and much the same as in Western medicine. It goes rather further than Western medicine, however, because the bile is a 'pure' substance, said to come fromKidney Qi (technically its actual name is 'Minister Fire', from Ming Men[3]).

In Western medicine bile comes, of course, from the liver. The Chinese derivation from 'Minister Fire' means it provides heat

---

3. For more on Ming Men, see http://www.acupuncturepoints. org/ming-men.html

and Fire for the digestion. This may seem strange. How, you may wonder, do you get Fire from bile?

Not so strange really. If you have ever had the misfortune to be really nauseous, to the point where you have vomited up the contents of your stomach, and are now vomiting up the contents of your intestines, up will come bile. Bile is extremely hard on the throat and mouth – like stomach acids. It is bitter and burning.

For a weak digestion, you can buy Swedish Bitters, made from herbs that are, as the name suggests, bitter. (They often contain Gentian root, a bitter herb.) This bitter taste supplements the presumed deficiency of the bile.

At any rate, from the perspective of Chinese medicine it provides a warming function that improves digestion. Bile, as we now know, breaks fats down into minute sizes that can be absorbed through the walls of your intestines.

Look on bile as being the physical correlation of the mental ability to cut through confusion and reach a decision.

The second function is that it nourishes the sinews with Qi, to help them move and react. That means you remain nimble, able to respond quickly to challenge, versatile and bold.

LIVER and Liver Function

Just above, I said that the Gallbladder's fundamental function was the self-belief to take effective decisions, to be confident and enterprising. The Liver Energy mental function, following right on from the Gallbladder, is *to be able to plan effectively*.

Not just to plan, but to be able to bring all the facts together and marshal them so that the right decisions can be made. Only if properly rested and refreshed can your mind effectively draw on your resources, allow all the possibilities in a given situation to surface, look at all the consequences of given actions and, as it were, see round the corners beyond where you are. For this to work properly, you are better off without the need for drugs like coffee to kick-start your brain.

Good sleep, especially that between 1 and 3am, (the so-called Liver 'times') will have replaced and replenished your resources making you stronger, calmer, more deliberate and clearer in assessing your situation.

Once you have decided on an action, courtesy of your Gall-Bladder function, your Liver can them mobilise the other forces in your body to take the matter forward firmly and without haste.

The Liver sees the big picture and what needs to be done. The opposite time, between 1 and 3pm, that of the Small Intestine, in Chinese medicine is that of taking small decisions, of sorting out the chaff, of putting the nuts and bolts in their respective places ready for action, of checking the oil and windscreen washer liquid levels in your car before you drive.

Also, where there are plans requiring detailed work before the big picture and decision can be taken, the Small Intestine gets the facts and figures straight or assess the moral implications of a decision. All these are small but important: matters for the Small Intestine function. (See chapter 12.)

The Liver also needs the Stomach function (chapter 11) of mulling things over, like 'chewing the cud', and the Spleen function of putting things where they belong. All these actions, plus those of the Small Intestine, are brought together or assembled by the Liver. Then, if the Heart has a clear view of where it is going in life, a healthy Gallbladder can provide the power to decide on action.

So the Liver takes the long view, to decide, with the Gall-Bladder, on how to achieve the objectives set by your Heart.

It cannot do that without the Small Intestine function of ensuring all relevant facts and implications are checked.

The Liver keeps Qi moving smoothly wherever it goes. It does this in two main areas, the chest and abdomen, and the emotions.

In the chest and abdomen, it makes it possible for us to breathe our way out of stressful conditions, to digest our food harmoniously, to move our bowels, for a woman to smooth her menstrual flow, and so on.

Emotionally, it helps emotions to flow so we remain balanced.

How did this view of the action of the Liver came about?

In ancient China, there were various schools of belief and philosophy, notably those that became Daoism, and much later others that became Confucianism and Buddhism.

These had different views on the expression of emotion. These views stemmed from their opinion of what constituted the Mind, which took a different path to that taken in Western philosophy and religion.

Western religion, for instance Christianity, said that we have a soul which departs at death but remains alive, leaving the body behind to decompose. (Western philosophers have held differing views on the properties and actions of the soul, the mind and the emotions, from Plato to Descartes, Berkeley to Hegel.)

That, meaning the Western religious view, meant that each of us has a spirit that to a greater or lesser extent is self-determining. That implies decisions, inaction or an action.

That is more like the Gallbladder function. ('More like' but in no way the same as the 'soul' of religion, of course.)

It can mean anger and force but also logic and objectivity.

In the East, the idea of a separate, self-determining spirit was not promoted. All, everything, is one, or One[4].

If so, allowing emotions to sway us was seen as non-conducive to happiness. So keeping emotions – and Qi – flowing smoothly was paramount for the integrity of the One. *This is more like the function of the Liver.*

Liver and Qi stagnation

Liver Qi stagnation can arise because we entertain the notion that we should always be busy. Always being busy means we fail to stop to reflect, delegate or reconsider. Never stopping dissipates our Qi.
If we run short of Qi, what little we have may stagnate.
Many people revel in running a business or enterprise but if they are unable to stand back (e.g. even on holiday) they risk deficiency of 'Liver Blood' and possibly of 'Liver Yin' – see below. For images of what happens compare pictures of Margaret Thatcher before and after she lost her position as U.K. Prime Minister.

When people talk about 'Qi stagnation', usually they mean 'Liver Qi stagnation'. We all suffer from it and we all mostly recover from it. However, it is a harbinger of many other conditions from which it is less easy to recover.

As you read above, the Liver is the big assembler of plans in life. When everything is going our way, our Qi flows smoothly; mentally we feel good about our actions and ourselves; we expect the best to occur; we look with benevolence on others; our health feels good; we sleep well and our digestion is fine.

We feel little or no tension in our minds or bodies, and any tension is either enjoyable or soon disappears. If we choose to, we can feel grateful for life.

The Liver controls the movement of Qi wherever it occurs in the body. Any stagnation of Qi, from whatever cause, will almost certainly have implications for your Liver Qi.

4. See Appendix 3 for more about the Soul and Emotions.

What that means is that when Qi stagnates in one of the other Energy organs, it will probably also stagnate, to some extent, in your Liver. Liver Qi stagnation symptoms often occur with Qi stagnation symptoms arising from other Energy organs.

Summary of Causes of Liver Qi Stagnation

Many of these were discussed in chapter 7. Briefly:

- Emotional stress, usually from frustration but can be from any emotion. This is probably worse if for cultural reasons people suppress any expression of emotions. However, expressing anger too strongly itself also generates heat that can lead to Qi stagnation, as when a pot boils over and prevents further cooking until the mess has been cleared up.

- Food that is too heating, eaten over a period long enough to generate un-dispersed Liver Heat

.

People with Liver Heat problems, such as from eating and drinking 'too well' in the evening, often wake with indigestion and burning pains between 1am and 3am when Liver Qi is strong. If they already have too much Liver Heat, (perhaps from a history of stress, medications, alcohol or social drugs), they may wake at these times with indigestion even if they have NOT eaten unwisely that evening.

.

- Medication, alcohol, social and hallucinogenic drugs, tobacco etc: all of these can generate Heat

- Trying to do too much, even if enjoyable

24 hour Chinese Clock and the Liver Time and implications for 'Liver storing Blood⁵'

From 1am to 3am is the time of the Liver Energy. This is the time when, still asleep, your body is renewing its get-up-and go and your ability to plan. Liver Energy Organ problems, including from stress, often show up at these times, or twelve hours later.

Normally we are asleep at this hour. Asleep, our bodies renew their strength, and in Chinese medicine, this happens because the Liver has another important function:

Liver stores the Blood

A good supply of well-stored and healthy Liver Blood enables us to be confident, bright-eyed and cheerful, with healthy tendons and joints, giving us bounce and resilience.

That means balance, good complexion and nails, and flexibility both mentally and physically.

During sleep, the Shen – the Mind – is said to rest in the Liver Blood. On awaking in the morning, the Mind has been nourished by the Blood and the Blood has been reinvigorated by the Mind, so we awake refreshed and alert.

Liver Blood Deficiency⁶

What happens when, perhaps because of Liver Qi stagnation, the Liver fails to store the Blood? If Liver Qi is stagnating, this Blood storing process will be interrupted and Liver will neither properly store the Blood nor, through the Blood, be able to rest the Mind.

That means our sleep will be more restless, troubled by dreams or with frequent waking from light sleep.

5. Blood (capital B) is a vital concept in Chinese medicine, almost as important as Qi.
6. See also http://www.acupuncture-points.org/liver-blood-deficiency.html

A *deficiency of Liver Blood* can lead to

- tired eyes, with lack of nutrition to the eye

- scanty periods

- dry skin

- creaking joints

- stiffness or tightness in the sinews

- lack of resilience, all of which leads to

- irritability and moodiness.

It can also lead to Liver Qi stagnation because, if you prefer, the Blood is the oil that lets the Qi flow: no oil, no flow.

We may also find ourselves short of breath or seeming so because the Liver, not filled by plenty of Liver Blood, contracts and tightens. As such it tightens the lungs and our ability to breathe easily and deeply.

This is also because the Lung energy takes over from the Liver at 3am and if Liver Qi is stagnating, so may Lung Qi, giving us a chesty, full or tight sensation and frequent need to sigh or yawn.

The Liver and the Gall Bladder work very closely together in Chinese medicine and if Liver Qi stagnates, it will affect the Gallbladder too, possibly giving –

- headaches (usually one-sided and affecting the eyes)

- neck and head tension

- indecision

- poor self-confidence, and

- pains in our sides or breasts (in women, but perhaps also nowadays in men with large breast tissue)

In other words along the path of the Gallbladder channel[7].

Sometimes cramps too, with less precision in our movements, leading to awkwardness, clumsiness, irritability, and hurt.

12 hours later, between 1pm and 3pm, we may suffer an energy drop and feel unable to concentrate properly. We may also feel impatient when it comes to decisions or dealing with other people.

Since 1pm – 3pm is also the time of the Small Intestine, we may find that our digestion after lunch is less forgiving, that we are more susceptible to sleepiness, and that we have to concentrate more intensively to do things.

We shall also find it more difficult to see the big picture, the long view, the overall concept of what we are doing and we shall feel too tired to think about the small but important matters that underpin big decisions.

Consequently, others will find we are under-performing and harder to deal with because we are prickly and aggressive.

If we are introverted in our personality, we may find we express ourselves even less well or often than usual. We shall not want to meet people and we shall tend to hide away. The idea of going out to parties or public meetings to enjoy ourselves will be even more tiresome than usual. We shall keep to ourselves and cut short telephone conversations. *(Of course, if you are an introvert – not a Chinese medical term – the concept of enjoying a party does not arise.)*

Qi Flow problems from Liver Qi stagnation

Normally, Liver sends clear Qi upwards to enable the mind to think straight and the eyes to see true.

When Liver Qi stagnates, a whole range of

7. The Gall-Bladder channel starts bilaterally beside our eyes, runs to the ears, then over the sides of the head, through each shoulder, down the sides of the chest, trunk and hips, down the sides of the legs to the fourth toes.

unfortunate possibilities open up. First, Qi may not rise properly, leading to one or more of the following:

.

Included here are several examples of Clear Qi not ascending and Turbid Qi not descending.
For example, blurred vision and lack of ideas.

.

- hasty decisions; (because clear Qi does not ascend)

- blurred vision; (because Liver Blood cannot feed the eyes)

- a lack of ideas; (because Blood flow is impeded)

- head and shoulder tension; (because Yang exceeds Yin)

- tired headaches – especially at the vertex; (lack of Qi)

- eye fatigue; (Qi and Blood stagnate so they tire quickly)

- tingling or itchy scalp; (Often from Liver Blood deficiency which enables Wind to develop causing the tingle or itch)

- restlessness; sensation of wind or air in the brain;

- sensation as if the hair was rising, (a bit like after a fright);

- tremors or rhythmic movements for example of the legs or feet (though you will probably want to sit most of the time)

- eyelid tics; (= Wind: Yang rises uncontrolled by Yin)

- mouth tension; (= Yang rises uncontrolled by Yin)

- facial skin tingling (= Wind: Yang rises uncontrolled by Yin) and

- urge to stretch and yawn (Liver Qi impedes Lung Qi).

This urge to stretch or yawn is often marked. It usually comes with a sensation of fullness or tightness in the chest or throat, often described as 'stuffy', bloated or distended.

.

*Many years ago, arising from a job I did not like which had impossible targets to meet, my chest did not feel stuffy so much as **itchy** and **tight**, and I kept taking deep breaths even when I was sitting or supposedly relaxed.*

.

This stuffy or distended feeling can move around so you might feel it first in your chest then later in your abdomen or throat.

Let us hope you do not get all of those symptoms! Getting them all would be unusual. Often you get only one or two of them.

Alternatively, Qi may rise unchecked, too fast, leading to signs of Heat or Wind. These could produce symptoms such as:

- Grinding teeth
- Pounding headaches
- Red eyes
- Red, irritated eyelids, possibly itchy
- Aversion or increased sensitivity to light and heat, noise and pressure
- Temper tantrums, aggressive behaviour
- Tendency to shout at people and talk loudly

*Some of the above symptoms are signs of **Qi turning to Heat**, eg the red eyes, irritated, itchy eyelids and aversion to heat.*

If Liver Qi does not rise up, then it may press ***sideways***: as it stagnates ...

Chest, Head and throat (Some of the following examples are discussed at greater length in the following pages)

- A feeling of bloating or distension
- The head can feel as if it is bursting or pressurized

- Feeling of a lump in the throat that cannot be swallowed
- The chest may feel stuffy or full up, and deep breaths will not clear it.

Abdominal disturbances. The Liver controls movement in the abdomen and this includes movement:

- of the musculature
- of the diaphragm,
- of the intestines,
- of the womb and its blood flow,
- of the urinary system
- of the genitals and
- of food passing through.

Musculature

We do not tend to think about the muscles in our abdomens much unless we want to get a six-pack. Many of us just want less of a bulge there. The abdominal muscles are amongst the most important muscle groups in the body. They lie opposite the lumbar muscles, and together, front and back, these two muscle groups help to hold the body upright, enable it to turn and twist and keep good posture, whether sitting or standing, walking or running, or just holding our position in a jolting bus.

We also have important muscle groups at our sides that traverse the front of the abdomen as well. All of these help keep intact the abdominal wall, behind which lie our intestines, liver, pancreas, spleen, bladder, womb etc.

These muscles help us make just about any move you can think of, including turning over in bed. They all are affected by the Liver and Gallbladder channels, either because their channels penetrate the walls of the abdomen or because the Liver energy has such an important effect on the area in general.

As the Liver is said to be the 'child[8]' of the Kidney, the lumbar muscles, which mainly come under rule of the Kidney Energy Organs, may also be affected. The Mother-Child law can mean problems in the 'mother' deriving from the 'child' or vice versa.

So disturbances and pain in the back can also come from Liver stagnation.

.

I had a patient who came mainly because of loss of libido. He also had various back pains and complained of phlegm and catarrh in his chest and throat. He had seen his doctor and many medical specialists. He was taking testosterone supplements, but disliked their side-effects.

Diagnosing his condition, I realised that all these symptoms went back to a very 'trying' period in his life that had seriously drained his health and mental outlook.

Rather than try to treat his back, his chest and phlegm and his libido as separate factors, I realised that his Liver Qi was still stagnating and was probably the underlying cause. So I just treated his stagnant Liver Qi.

A few days later he returned for a second treatment, dumbfounded. Not only was his libido improving, but his chest and phlegm had almost disappeared, he'd had no back pain, and he was sleeping much better than he had for years. I was surprised by how fast he got better!

.

---

8. For more on this see appendix 4.

Diaphragm

Liver Qi stagnation affecting the diaphragm –

- makes it harder to take deep satisfying breaths
- may cause heart flutters, nausea, hiccups
- can make it harder to keep calm

Intestines:

If Liver Qi stagnation affects the intestines it

- causes cramps
- stops food moving along smoothly
- produces stools that look like sheep droppings – lots of little bits
- causes constipation
- causes pain, often burning (as stagnant Qi transforms to Heat)

Womb and its blood flow

When Liver Qi stagnation affects the womb it –

- leads to tension, mood swings and irritability before the period
- increases desire for sweet or sometimes salty foods, junk foods, usually more so before the period
- can cause cramps in the womb, the abdomen, the back and sometimes the thighs – all are areas traversed by the Liver and Gallbladder channels

- may cause the menstrual bleeding to coagulate, producing clots or a reduction in the normal flow of the menses (because the Liver stores the Blood and when Qi stagnates it partially loses its ability to allow Blood into and out of the store. Blood clots are one sign of Blood stagnation.) (But blood clots have other causes in Chinese medicine as well.)
- makes the periods come too soon or too late
- makes the breasts painful or hot and/or swollen, particularly before the period

Urinary system.

Sometimes Liver Qi stagnation attacks further afield (and tightens up the sphincter muscles) making it difficult to urinate.

Genitals

The Liver channel is one of the acupuncture channels that circulate or travel through or round the genitals. As you have read above, the Liver stores the Blood. If Liver Qi stagnates, moody depression and lack of confidence are reflected in the physical lack of flow of Qi and Blood along, round and through the genitals making it difficult for

- men to get or maintain an erection and
- women to get interested in and enjoy sex. Women may find sex painful or go off it.
- Of course, sex usually has plenty of movement, especially of the pelvis, so sometimes strongly physical sex actually shifts Qi stagnation and makes the woman feel much better about and in herself. A woman may start by being uninterested in

sex unless she realises the eventual benefits. When her Qi stagnation is extreme, however, even strong physical sex may not work and will be repugnant to her. Her partner must be sensitive to her needs.

Food

As mentioned in Chapter 7, irregular eating or a bad diet[9] can produce Liver Qi stagnation. Diet can, however, sometimes also improve Liver Qi stagnation, for which see later in this chapter.

Circulation and Blood

- Because Liver Qi stagnation upsets the storing and supply of Blood to arms and legs, often you feel cold, especially with cold hands, feet or nose (mainly hands).

- The eyes feel tired (because your eyes are nourished by Liver Blood)

- Heavy blood loss from injury, heavy menses, surgery or childbirth, can lead to Liver Blood deficiency which itself can lead to Liver Qi stagnation. Liver Qi stagnation is often connected to Liver Blood deficiency in diagnoses of women suffering from the baby blues, the days (sometimes months) of deep depression after childbirth. Chinese medicine has much to offer here.

What HAPPENS NEXT if you do not resolve Liver Qi stagnation?

These symptoms all arise because of what happens if the Liver Energy organ functions incorrectly and because of the paths of the

9. A bad diet, sometimes described as 'irregular eating habits' in the Chinese literature, covers not just the actual foods eaten but their condition after preparation and before eating, how you eat, whether you rest when eating and how well you chew. Diet is not just food, of course, but water too. See also chapters 11 - 13.

Liver and Gallbladder acupuncture channels. In some cases, the problem has spread to other Energy Organs, for which see the relevant chapters.

The trapped Qi turns to Wind and Heat, and may eventually turn to Fire. Some of the following conditions are recognised by Western medicine:

- headaches and migraines, hypertension
- cystitis and urinary retention
- extreme sensitivity and irritability
- shoulder and neck pain, arthritis
- eye pain or problems, including floaters, blepharitis, thinning, detachment and weakness of the retina, cataract and inflammation
- breathing difficulties, asthma
- digestive problems, ulcers, inflammation
- circulatory problems
- bowel problems such as IBS, diverticulitis, bowel cancer and Crohn's disease
- skin heat and dryness, eczema, psoriasis, allergies
- mental instability
- athlete's foot, especially starting between big toe and second toe or 4th and 5th toes
- menorrhagia, flooding periods, bleeding between periods, dysmenorrhoea,   morning sickness and habitual miscarriage. NB Many of these conditions have other causes in Chinese medicine, not just Qi Stagnation.

Please be aware that when your Qi stagnation has turned into the above conditions, you may or will need professional treatment in addition to whatever you yourself do to relieve, reduce or manage your Qi stagnation.

How to HELP YOURSELF if you have Liver or Gall-Bladder Qi Stagnation

Observations over the centuries by the Chinese culminated in the Five Element System and the Four Phase diagram.

When reading the following, you do not need to understand this system fully but when and if you do study it you will understand why the following applies. Read more about it in Chapter 5 & appendix 4.

For the Wood element, this system of thought suggests what might benefit people with Liver and Gallbladder problems. [For Wood, the main Elements to consider here are the Water (Mother) and Fire (Child) elements – but also Earth, for general support.

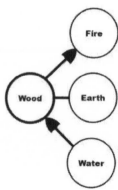

The following uses some of those ideas.

[Most references to the Five Element or Four Phase systems are in square brackets like these, in case you want to skip over them.]

A *First, read again Chapter 7 on 'The General Causes of Qi Stagnation'.*

Why? Because that lists the main causes of Qi stagnation, which obviously you want to avoid if you can.

B Emotions

Learning to recognise the emotions that are making you ill is the first step. This is not always easy, when often you feel that your emotions are justifiable. If so, you are going to be indignant and cross – if that is the right word for it – that the consequences of your justified emotions are illness.

In that case, you probably need to talk to someone about the roots of your anger or frustration – the most common emotions leading to Liver and Gall Bladder Qi stagnation.

If you do not want to talk, you need to go somewhere remote for a few days to consider the matter in depth. [Somewhere remote is the equivalent of falling back on your 'Mother' element, which is Water.]

If you can come to terms with the cause of your emotions, you may be able to see a way forward, even a plan of action. Take no hasty decisions! If you are emotional, hasty decisions might worsen your predicament.

There is no point expecting complete success from treatment unless you deal with the cause. If the cause continues, relief will be temporary. (However, even temporary relief may give you the chance to come to terms with your situation and make the moves you need.)

Talking to someone does not have to mean talking to a counsellor or psychotherapist. You would be surprised how many problems can be helped by

- a skilled massage therapist or

- an acupuncturist or

- a friend, colleague or parent.

Sooner or later, you will have to act, either to improve your situation or to get away from it. Both have a risk, which is why please consider the matter carefully before you act!

[This action of thinking over your situation, discussing it with others and perhaps bringing a new sense of reality to your situation derives from the Earth element. This is the ground, the ongoing basis for your existence. You cannot survive for very long unless your feet remain on the Earth.]

C Doing too much?

Slow down!

Too many projects on the go! Or trying to do everything yourself? You may be enjoying it, and actively pushing them all ahead, but if you are doing too many things you will dissipate your energies. You will either drain your Liver Blood or by pushing your Qi in too many directions it will lose its force and stagnate.

If this is the case, you must reduce your range of activities. If, with your Qi already stagnating, you keep pushing ahead with too many plans and projects, whatever you do to help yourself or whatever treatments you receive will give only temporary relief. Why? Because the moment you get going again, the same problem will recur.

Learn how to say "No!"

Or say to yourself "I don't do that ..."

Then learn how to delegate.

[Strongly Wood types, or those whose Wood energy is not properly regulated, tend to have too many projects on the go. They

benefit from the tempering of Metal (take time, absorb the experience of others) and the belly-laughs, funding and good employees, coming from Earth – their practical resources.]

D Exercise and Motion

By far the most effective way of un-stagnating Liver Qi in the short term is physical movement. Of course, what works for one person may be too much or too little for another.

If you are already in the habit of doing too much (see C. above) then although exercise will help, it should initially be gentle. Otherwise you will use up even more Qi.

However, for most people with Liver Qi stagnation …

… Make the movement –

- strong enough to get you out of breath

- for at least 20 minutes

- daily at least once, preferably more often and

- enjoyable [Why should it be enjoyable? Because things you enjoy are more Fire-like, so doing them takes Qi onward round the cycle from Wood into the Fire phase.]

(If, like me, you do not enjoy exercise, what then? In that case, sorry, but you will just have to find something that you do not like and learn to take pleasure in it, or at least benefit from it. Look on it as an opportunity to try something new which, itself, will move or transform your Qi.)

Your regular exercise might be

- walking to work (fast enough to get out of breath)

- walking home after work (fast enough to get out of breath)

- walking everywhere, including the steps, at work
  (fast enough to get out of breath)

*[Getting out of breath is especially important for Wood Qi
stagnation because in the Four Phase diagram Metal balances
Wood. Breathing fully utilises all of the Lungs. They absorb Qi and
as Governor of the Qi they can push it past even Wood Qi
stagnation. Expanding the lungs also not only stretches the
Gallbladder channel which runs up the sides of the chest but also
forces the diaphragm to move, promoting the Pericardium – Fire.]*

- joining a gym and going regularly [tones Earth]

- seeing an exercise therapist for advice [Water, Earth]

- lifting weights (take good advice on this before you start)

- running (not just jogging: running, preferably
  eventually using what is called the 'interval' training system[10],
  but please not so as to exhaust yourself: do it sensibly,
  resting on days between)

- regular dancing. Most dancing is excellent. [Fire-like activity]

- regular tennis, squash, ball-games … if enjoyed [Fire] …

- with a partner so each encourages the other [Earth]

If you are unable to take these kinds of exercise, try to think of
some form of motion, active not passive, that ideally gets you
out of breath.

For someone old, infirm or disabled, even knitting might help.
It may not get you out of breath, but it is creative and involves
movement of the arms and torso. [An angry knitter can achieve
wonders, if his or her creativity gets recognised, benefiting Fire.]

As people age, their Kidney Qi diminishes (chapter 15) which
makes them more susceptible to Liver Qi stagnation. So get
in the habit of regular exercise when you are young and your

---

10. Interval training means exercise which makes you perform at maximum for short bursts
of up to a minute each up to 8 times in succession, with a slower paced session for up to a
minute each between them. Look up interval training on the web. Work up to 8! Do not
start with it! Get advice if unsure.

toned body will benefit from the habit when you
are old!

Many disabled people can take vigorous exercise, as
the Olympic games have shown. Unable to move as fully as
the non-disabled, they should nevertheless try different
sports and activities to find what suits them.

Why should you get out of breath to move Qi?

Because the Lungs are said to Govern your Qi. (Chapter
9.) Coming to Chinese medicine it can be confusing
because you will hear that while the Lungs govern the Qi, the
Liver controls the smooth flow of Qi, the Kidneys control
the smooth reception of Qi and so on.

What is the difference you might well ask! Well, sorry, that will
have to wait for another book or you can grope around in the
interstices of the Internet for enlightenment.

Exercise should move all of you, not just your legs. Moving or
exercising everything moves more Qi.

If after the exercise you feel better, more relaxed,
steadier, more positive, and sleep better, then almost certainly
you were right! Your problem almost certainly was Qi
stagnation.

*E Social Drugs, Medication and the PRIMARY and SECONDARY
effects of drugs and medication*

*Nearly all social drugs promote the Fire phase – i.e. fun, feel-good,
enjoyment, getting a 'high'. This may seem good, temporarily, if
you have Wood Qi stagnation because it moves you into the next
phase, Fire, child of Wood. There is, however, a downside, which is
that alcohol, for example, as far as the body is concerned, is
generally Heating.*

*Similarly, for Fire Qi stagnation types, social drugs are seldom
conducive to health because they overstimulate Heat and Fire. It is
theoretically arguable, however, that Metal Qi Stagnation types*

might benefit from the Primary effects of Social drugs. However,
why risk it when there are many other options?

.

Alcohol, in very small quantities, eases Liver Qi stagnation. The trouble, as most drinkers know, is that one glass is seldom enough.

Alcohol can be warming or cooling. Chilled white wine is generally thought to be cooling. Red wine is warming. If you are a chilly person, drink red wine in preference to white wine, and if you have good circulation, you will probably prefer white wine anyway. Beer is reckoned to be cooling; spirits warming[11].

However, too much alcohol, whether regarded as cooling or warming, or alcohol taken in even small quantities over a long period of time, will eventually be heating. You may wonder why the warming or cooling effect of alcohol is important. For some people, with unstable constitutions, getting too hot or too cold can happen fast, from what may seem quite small influences (hot or cold food, allergens, drink or surroundings, embarrassment, emotions etc). When they are too hot or too cold, they are already slightly off-balance energy-wise and it is then much easier for their Qi to stagnate.

For example, someone made hot by alcohol may more easily get angry. Someone chilled by food or drink more easily tightens up with tension and shivering.

In both cases, their Qi is under less control and may, if from anger dissipate itself then stagnate, if from cold freeze up and stagnate.

Primary and Secondary Effects

Alcohol's primary effect is nearly always to relax tension but

---

11. For more on hot and cold foods see http://www.acupuncture-points.org/cold-foods.html

its secondary effect is to build up Heat in the system[12], which eventually dries and weakens Yin.

From the secondary effect you get agitation occurring as Liver Yang[13], unconstrained now by Yin (weakened from alcohol's primary effect), rises both to disturb the Mind and to cause the throbbing headache and dry mouth.

These *primary and secondary effects*[14] of medication and drugs apply to *all medication and herbal prescriptions*. In a small way they also apply to food, but good food carries nutritional (i.e. mostly yin-producing) qualities that compensate for any excess yang-boosting effect in the food unless the latter is eaten too much.

Of course, the theory applies to everything you eat! Artificially flavoured food often carries less nutritional benefits. For example, junk foods contain high quantities of salt, sweeteners and spices, which persuade us to eat more of them but which lack real yin-nourishing benefits.

Take Spicy food – If you eat nothing but hot curry, you will imbalance your system and produce signs of internal Heat. That hot curry may have made you sweat and initially have helped your Qi move – that being its primary effect. In Chinese medicine, very pungent food helps to spread Qi, later to dissipate it. That 'dissipation' is partly of Yin.

Then comes the secondary, HEATING, effect often exacerbated by Yin weakness, giving symptoms such as sweating, redness, skin inflammation, itching, spots, strong body-odour, offensive-smelling stools, thirst and irritability.

---

12. You will have read about the long-term effects of this, or anything else that has a heating effect, above under 'What happens Next'.
13. http://www.acupuncture-points.org/liver-yang.html
14. For more on this important subject see http://www.acupuncture-points.org/primary-and-secondary-actions.html

Balance in herbal formulae

Chinese medicine's herbal tradition has produced herbal formulae that always include herbs the energetic effect of which is to balance the primary effects of a formula's main herbs by compensating for their secondary effects.

Western medicine seldom appreciates this and certainly does not seem to apply it.

Many psychiatrists find themselves prescribing additional medication in a somewhat arbitrary fashion, in effect to try to copy what Chinese medicine has been doing for 2500 years.

Whereas Chinese medicine assesses the patient's constitution first and fits the formula to it, Western medicine usually gives the approved drug first and then tries to compensate for its deficiencies or secondary effects.

Lacking an underlying theory, this can easily cause continuing imbalance and even damage.

Can Damage by drugs be explained?

Damage? Take someone who is depressed not from Liver Qi stagnation but from what we shall call Kidney deficiency (actually it is more Kidney Yang deficiency[15]) with a sense of apathy, possibly impotence or decreased libido, tendency to feel cold and probably backache made worse the longer he stands. (More on Kidney deficiency in chapter 15.)

For this individual a prescription for Fluoxetine (also known as Prozac) may start by being very successful. From observations of its actions by experts in Chinese medicine, Fluoxetine's primary effect is to push Kidney Yang upwards, improving the above symptoms but often giving an unpleasant tingling in the mouth.

15. http://www.acupuncture-points.org/kidney-yang-deficiency.html

As such its action seems similar to other individual Kidney Yang tonic herbs in Chinese medicine.

·

Fluoxetine improves these symptoms because they are signs of deficiency eg apathy, coldness, backache tired by standing, as Fluoxetine is a mild Kidney Yang tonic. However, it brings with it extra signs of Yang, the tingling for instance.

·

Taken for too long, however, its secondary effect, having as it were temporarily boosted Kidney Yang (like a turbocharged car) is to begin to exhaust Kidney Yin, the fuel and support.

With less Yin to feed and anchor Yang, the patient becomes anxious and depressed, often similar to the original presenting symptom[16].

Now compare that to someone whose depression derives from Liver Qi stagnation, the subject of this chapter. Not recognising the important difference, the doctor prescribes Prozac, the approved medication. Here, Prozac does the same again, pushing up Yang energy.

However, this patient already has a surfeit of Yang energy, even if it is stagnating: remember that stagnating Qi is actually a form of stored energy, trying to escape.

·

(Reminder! Qi stagnation is like the air in a rubber tyre blown up to high pressure. Although it cannot move (as in some forms of depression), there is an excess of trapped or stagnant Qi: likewise all the pent-up tensions in drivers trapped in a standing traffic wave.)

·

Taking Prozac releases his inhibitions (his stored energy) and he starts behaving like an uncontrollable child, with tantrums and furious interludes that cause all the damage capable of an adult, ending up in court.

16. This explains why many drugs list, among their secondary effects, the very symptom their primary purpose it is to cure.

Another example is Valium (Diazepam). This possesses hypnotic (sleep-inducing), sedative, muscle relaxing and amnestic (makes you forget) properties. Its primary effect is as an anti-anxiety, anti-tension drug.

If Valium is sedative, relaxing and hypnotic, why then, over time, do many people taking it often get muscle cramps, tremors, headaches, dizziness, nervousness, and more anxiety? *These look like signs of Yang excess pushing upwards and outwards: tremor, cramp, dizziness, nervousness: all signs of motion (Yang) out of control.*

Why does it produce many of the very symptoms it was intended to treat? The reason lies in its secondary effect. This, like alcohol in quantity or over time, is drying and Yin-weakening. With less Yin, the Yang of the body presses upwards, producing restlessness and tension again.

.

Moisture is Yin. Water is adaptable (takes the shape of its container) but when heated, it evaporates, so reducing Yin. With less Yin, Yang runs out of control, producing these apparent signs of Yang excess – restlessness and tension.

.

What to do? Your doctor either increases the dose or prescribes something stronger. Or both.

These drugs are sometimes purified extracts of the 'active' ingredients of herbs.

Sometimes? More often they are chemically manufactured copies of the 'active' parts of a herb. By manufacturing –

- only the 'active' part, the other, modifying, parts of the herb are excluded which makes the manufactured drug work faster and more distinctly, being its primary action, but lays it open then to producing stronger secondary consequences;
- the pure drug the manufacturer can patent the medicine;

- the pure drug, the manufacturer does not require
  large quantities of cultivated herbs to produce the
  highly concentrated extract. He just makes it using chemicals
  off the shelf;

- the drug, the manufacturer can justify a good price
  to recover his costs and make a profit, because his
  research, development and testing expenses have been so
  high.

What about other social drugs? Many drugs are relaxing (so drain or disperse the trapped energy of stagnant Qi) as part of their primary effect. Their secondary effect is harmful, over time. Often they weaken Liver Qi's facility for bringing all matters together for decision leading to an aimless life, easily wasted.

.

[In effect, most social drugs, long-term, are heating and enhance Fire, the 'party spirit' or state of ecstasy. This weakens the balancing Water function. Eventually habitual drug-takers become dreamers, trapped in the Fire phase, unable to take effective decisions in their lives, nor to move on. The Heat can also reinforce Liver Heat, leading to anger and violence.].

.

Social drugs, taken over time, often seem to weaken the Gall-Bladder's ability to make effective decisions and the energy to carry things through.

As a result, people become dreamers, reliant on luck and circumstance. Some social drugs make people very hard to treat because either they do not remember or they lie.

It can be as if their minds have grown old and suffer from partial dementia. With Blood and Qi weakened, progress is slow.

Prescribed medication is powerful and directed, and can ameliorate depression, which is often a symptom of Qi stagnation. Very often, the kind of patients who need these drugs develop a weak constitution.

That is to say, they cannot easily stabilise themselves without medication or strong family or institutional support.

·

Family and institutions are Yin-like, stabilising energies. See chapter 4. [Such energies are Earth-like.]

·

As such they lack Yin, and the cause of their Qi stagnation arises from Liver Yang and Heart Yang not being properly steadied by [Earth] Blood, Liver Yin and Heart Yin. This leads to signs of excess Yang upsetting the Mind with panics, tension, tiredness and a depression that can be most profound.

Naturally, doctors have to prescribe medication to calm them.

But like alcohol, the secondary effect of prescribed drugs is often to dry, further weakening Yin and so tending to increase Yang – so over-stimulating Heat and Fire.

·

Prescribed medication for deep levels of depression or psychosis may, initially, control them better than Chinese herbs or acupuncture, which can help the secondary effects. But long-term, the benefits of prescribed medication are less clear-cut.

F Food

What foods help Liver Qi stagnation?

As explained above, you should avoid foods that are heating[17]. For acute Liver Qi stagnation symptoms, these foods to avoid include spicy food, oily food, rich food, alcohol and some raw foods like garlic and strong onions.

Also reduce red meats. However, fresh oily fish is probably all

17. For more about 'Hot' foods, see http://www.acupuncture-points.org/hot-foods.html

right if eaten lightly cooked. Avoid caffeine, which means coffee and chocolate. Avoid roasting and frying to prepare food, though quick-frying of vegetables is usually fine.

.

Caffeine is more strongly contra-indicated than chocolate, which usually contains milk and other oils that are more Yin-like, so balancing the strong Yang effect of its caffeine. Black coffee is much more like pure caffeine.

.

Eat many fresh vegetables of all colours, in salad form or lightly cooked; steaming is best. If there is a single concentrated food that may benefit the liver, it is probably organic Apple Cider Vinegar, because of its sour taste and many nutritional benefits, taken in small quantities. Take one tablespoon of it in warm water on rising.

In general, however, foods that benefit the Liver are those classified as having a sweet taste. Here the adjective sweet does not mean what most people in developed countries understand by the term.

It certainly does not mean sugar, honey, or sweeteners. It does mean a wide range of vegetables, fresh fish, chicken and limited quantities of carbohydrate (low glycaemic index food). All these are good for Blood (relatively Yin), so steadying Qi (relatively Yang).

Eat in Company!

When eating, try to eat with convivial friends. [The aim here is to move your Qi from the Wood phase towards the Fire phase. The Fire phase is where you enjoy life, often with friends. Being with friends stops your Qi from stagnating in the Wood phase.]

The company of friends, their humour and camaraderie, are hugely important in helping you disentangle your Liver Qi stagnation – more about this below.

G Autogenic training promotes awareness [Earth]

This teaches you a way to relax and to use the stress response another way. However, this is not something you can do without training, which makes it less useful in the short-term.

With Qi stagnating, go back to basics

[This is a reference to the Mother-Child law in the Five Element system. The Mother element here is Water. Weakness in Water can lead to Qi stagnation in Wood – see more about this in chapter 15.]

.

Remember that [Square] brackets here means you do not need to read or understand this until (and if) you have read chapter 5 and appendix 4!

.

One of the reasons your Liver Qi stagnates is because you are not grounded enough in your preparations; another is that you are pushing too fast for your available resources (one of which is time, another of which is energy) to keep up.

For continued growth and expansion, you must put in place the necessary resources [- Water. Some of the following examples recognise not just Water as a 'Mother-like resource, but that of Earth and the grandfatherly regulation or guidance of Metal too.]

- An entrepreneur should have the professional advice and support he needs available when he starts, not grabbed in desperation at the last moment before disaster;

- A parent should buy and prepare what is needed for the journey with children before setting off;

- Someone with a good idea but no money will soon feel frustrated if he has no way to develop it in the absence of finance or support;

- An artist will soon get angry with the world if he has no brushes, canvas or paint to pursue his art;

- An author will soon get frustrated unless he does his research before starting his book;

- A speaker will get flustered and embarrassed if hecklers easily dispute his argument;

- Do your homework! Be rested and ready before you start!

If you have done your homework and put the necessary resources in place, you will be in a better position to grab Chance by the single strand of hair on his head as he rushes past.

H Sex

Yes, sex. If you have plenty of Liver Qi but it is stagnating, sex is a great way to dissipate it. Short-term! But please read chapter 15 before you leap into action. Also, the more movement involved, the better – to move the Qi! But please, practise safe sex with consideration for others.

[And if you enjoy sex with another person, you help move your Qi from the Wood phase to the Fire phase, which is nearly always beneficial.]

I Assuming you do not exhaust yourself, be Creative

If your Liver Qi is stagnating, and this is not because you have exhausted your resources, explore lateral, creative thinking. Get others (including employees, acquaintances, customers and family) to help you via the Wisdom of Crowds[18] [so using your Earth resources and, if it is enjoyable, Fire.]

Alternatively, take up some other pursuit, different from

18. The Wisdom of Crowds, James Surowiecki, 2005

your business. It could be an art, or gardening or learning a language, for example.

[Creative art probably promotes Stagnant Wood Qi towards Fire, gardening promotes Earth and a new language gives you a new skill – Water.]

This other recreation will distract your mind from its primary objective and allow beneficial lateral input and relaxation.

Being creative can, however, mean over-use of Qi. Try only one thing at a time!

J Party!

[Fire phase benefits.]

It is no surprise that successful business people like the trappings of success. They worked hard and deserve them. But [from the Five Element system] there is a deeper reason.

Just as children who work hard get prizes and the success of footballers is measured by the size of their transfer fee, hard work and success should culminate in recognition by others. It is a natural need, intrinsically recognised by Chinese medicine.

It moves you from work into play. Enjoy play and recognition. See and be seen. This helps Qi stagnation, particularly Liver Qi stagnation. Find people or circumstances of the right status to reflect your hard work and eventual success.

- Balloons
- Bling!
- Celebrations
- Concerts
- Dances

- Dining at famous restaurants
- Disneyland!
- Festivals
- Fireworks
- Fun! Parties. Give them and go to them.
- Gambling – the odd flutter! Not as a way of life!
- Games (Olympic, Beach, Highland, Village...)
- Holidays, for enjoyment, not recovery [Recovery is more Water phase]
- Invest in beautiful possessions: not (just) for their monetary value but because you like them and want to enrich your surroundings with them.
- Musicals, Plays, Operas
- Performing eg amateur dramatics
- Racing
- Travel

Just remember these are temporary diversions, enjoyable and beneficial, not ends in themselves!

However, we are all different. An introvert will enjoy success in very different ways to an extrovert. The latter wants to be with friends and to throw a celebratory party; the former goes alone or takes just a friend to the local dance or debating society, or on a round-the-world cruise or to the South Pole.

K Humour

[You can help to move Qi on round the Five Phase circuit by

diverting or forwarding your energy from the Wood phase to the Fire phase.]

Humour is particularly beneficial for Liver and Gallbladder because it defuses the frustration, anger, hostility and tensions. Friends or family are usually best, but if not, take humour passively – watch films that make you laugh. [Belly-laughs are Earth, so is farce, though farce is also Fire-like.]

L Neurolinguistic Programming NLP

I rate this as predominantly a skill, [so comes mainly under Water, so particularly beneficial for Wood Qi stagnation, Water being the Mother of Wood.]

NLP can be excellent at helping you change your point of view or adapt it to someone else's viewpoint. It enables you to see your position in a new light. It may also help you in negotiations with those who have been causing your frustration. See a professional.

What treatments help Liver Qi stagnation?

- *Chinese medicine*. Because Chinese medical theory understands Liver Qi stagnation, all of its treatment modalities, including acupuncture, herbal formulae and massage can make a huge difference. Make sure you discuss diet with your practitioner.

Knowing the theory, your practitioner will also be able to help you talk, if you want to, about any emotional or other issues that may be at the root of it.

- *Counselling* For long-term Qi stagnation issues arising

from life situations, you may find Counselling helpful. [Earth and Metal.]

- *Emotional Freedom Technique* is sometimes very successful, if the physical symptoms have not gone too deep. Once learned, you can do this yourself. [Water and Earth.]

- *Breathing* properly can hugely palliate. Read appendix 7 but take lessons. [Metal.]

- *Exercise therapy*. Physiotherapists and sports therapists can advise you. Their encouragement can be incredibly helpful.

- *Tai Qi and Dance* classes. Tai Qi is slow and steady, and hard work. Developed over millennia it aims to move just about all your Qi. However, it takes time to learn and to reap real benefits. Dancing depends on what you like and can be great fun. You meet new people and the activity helps you forget your problems. Moves Qi generally [and benefits Fire].

- *Debt Counselling*

If your problem is financial, face the situation and see a debt counsellor. If your situation is extreme, consider bankruptcy or, in the UK, an Individual Voluntary Arrangement with your creditors (England) or a Trust Deed (Scotland). [Earth]

You may feel ashamed of doing this and if you are an able person, perhaps you should, because your creditors gave you services, goods, money or credit in the belief that you would repay them.

However, digging yourself into an ever-deeper hole saps your strength and may further antagonize creditors. Once you have signed the papers, you will find a huge weight taken off your mind and you can get on with life, and your creditors may get something. You can of course repay them fully later when you make your next fortune.

Long-term, what can you do?

- *Learn Negotiation skills* [Water, Earth.]
- *Get Fit*
- *Consider Assertiveness training* [Water, Wood, Fire]
- Read '*The One Minute Manager*' by Ken Blanchard
- *Buy less and de-clutter* your home and workplace [Metal]
- *Leave work on time* – stop working late
- Learn *good breathing technique* [Metal]
- Do your *homework* [Water]

Summary

In this chapter you have read about

- how Liver and Gall Bladder Qi stagnation arises
- what it is
- what its effects are
- what you can do to help yourself
- what treatments work for it.
- Drug Primary and Secondary effects

.

This chapter has been on the Liver, which controls the FLOW of Qi. The next chapter is on the GOVERNOR of the Qi, the Lungs.

CHAPTER 9

Lung Qi Stagnation

Disappointment, death, loss and separation are often borne privately. It is hard for many people to allow themselves to grieve properly.

Essence of Lung Qi Stagnation

Should you read this chapter? It is a long one!

- Yes, if you have suffered a major disappointment or loss.

- Yes, if are reaching a stage in your life when you either retire, resign, or cease doing something you have done for a long time. This is when you may start looking back on your life up to then, to assess how happy you are with it, without giving much thought to doing anything new.

- Yes, if your experiences are sufficient to benefit others through teaching, writing, counselling, mentoring or advising.

- Yes, if the meaning of your life eludes you and it is important

- Yes, if you tend to hide how you feel about the world and what happens in it and to you.

- Yes, if you feel undervalued, or that you have never received the appreciation or approval you needed
- Yes, if your life is a search for quality or value or balance, without which you feel inadequate
- Yes, if you have respiratory problems
- Yes, if your savings don't cover your outgoings

In this chapter you will read about:

- The function of your Lungs in Chinese medicine
- The proper direction in which Lung Qi should flow
- Why you get Lung Qi stagnation
- Emotional factors
- Diet and Food factors
- Respiratory factors
- Pathogenic factors
- What happens when Lung Qi fails to descend
- Consequences from imbalanced Liver
- Effects on Appetite
- Effect on Spleen Qi
- Effect on Stomach Qi
- Effect on Kidney Qi
- Effect on the diaphragm and the voice
- Lung Qi stagnation
- How to help yourself if you have Lung Qi stagnation
- What happens next if Lung Qi stagnates
- What treatments help Lung Qi stagnation

The Emotions most affecting Lung Qi.

Some of us have been grieving all our lives, without realising it, even since childhood. It affects our energy, our outlook and our health. Here is how.

A new-born baby's first cry tells you its body has taken control. The newborn will depend on its mother for many months to come.

For emotional health, it will depend on its parents, through touch, stroking and their love, before it can achieve a proper sense of self-worth. After that, it will become more confident and outgoing in life.

Without the ability to breathe, obviously the baby dies. With breathing, all things become possible. The inspiration of air triggers all the physiological life functions that enable it to survive outside the womb.

After the Lung Energy Organ breathes life into the system, with Qi now circulating, all the cogs of life that make the body machine work can start turning. (Of course, we know that the body has had nine months in the womb to practise, but unless the Lungs take over at birth, it dies.)

In Chinese medicine, the Lungs regulate all the physiological systems in the body. The Chinese said that this circulating Qi – breath – was a kind of spirit and they called it the 'Corporeal Soul': 'Po' for short.

This word 'spirit' can be a problem for people raised as Christians. In Christianity, the word 'Spirit' can be several things. It can be the Holy Spirit – one manifestation of God. It can also be an individual's soul, the part that transcends death. In Chinese medicine it is neither of these and possibly we should find a better word for it.

In the meantime, however, think of the word 'spirit' in the sense that you might say of an acquaintance that he was in 'high spirits', or on another occasion, 'dispirited'.

It is in that sense that we mean the 'spirit'. There is no implication of spirituality and no intention to confuse it with the Christian concept of 'spirit'.

Function of the Lungs

Once you understand the functions of an Energy Organ, you can often work out what happens when its Qi stagnates. The Lungs were described by the Chinese as being like a Prime Minister, in charge of the whole administration and government of the body. (Compare that to the Heart, which is said to be the Emperor – definitely in first place.)

Those first breaths in life also mean the baby is safely separating from its mother to create a new distinct life. This is a great gain to both: each can begin to grow separately along new paths in life.

But it is also a loss. For the mother, although she still has a baby, it is a different being whereas before birth it and she were as one.

So, often, there is a sense of loss for the mother and this is partly responsible for the after-birth blues. (This is not the only factor. Another, major, factor is Blood stasis[1].)

And it is a loss for the baby. In the womb, everything was provided, a kind of paradise. Now that has gone, it must learn somehow to make its environment provide for it.

Often it does this through crying and laughing. It needs healthy lungs for this. What defines the baby as a separate being is, on the one hand its spirit, on the other its skin, the boundary of its body.

If the spirit has eventually to provide a sense of self-worth, the skin has to provide a proper, attractive definition and a defence. To do that it must be well nourished and flexible. For

---

1. See http://www.acupuncture-points.org/blood-stasis.html

that it needs moisture, and for moisture there has to be the right diet and a system to regulate how food is used.

These themes, inspiration, life and energy, loss, separation, a sense of self-worth, control of moisture and the effective defence of the body are all 'governed' by the Po, the 'spirit' of the Lungs. Its first function is therefore to govern Qi, which gives us our energy, spirit and life, and to look after the process of respiration.

On a more prosaic level, the sense-organ associated with the Lungs is the nose. That must be moist, but not too moist. Through a filter made of hairs and mucus the nose must defend the inside of the body from harmful particles and pathogens and regulate the temperature of the air, hot or cold, before it reaches the lungs.

Lung Qi Flow Direction

The Lungs send Qi downwards to where it is grasped by the Kidneys. This downward sending action is important. We can use it to calm down by breathing slowly and easily. When it fails, we cannot catch our breath.

Some asthmatic people never feel able fully to catch their breath. This is not because they are not breathing, but because the Kidneys (chapter 15) do not 'grasp' the Qi breath sent down. That lead, at least in the past, to some kinds of barrel chested-ness. You do not see this often in developed countries now. That is because steroids and other medications assist the Kidney energy to grasp the Qi, so the barrel-shaped chest, made when people try more and more to take a big breath, does not develop.

What are the functions of the Lungs?

The Lungs govern all the physiological process in the body, or at least the Qi flowing through them, which amounts to almost the same thing. The Lungs also control the blood vessels and generally 'oversee' the acupuncture channels.

- Sometimes structures (for example veins, flesh and muscles) lying under the path of an acupuncture channel lose their elasticity and tone, unlike under other channels.

- Besides being a problem for the channel in question and the Energy Organ which 'powers' that channel, it may be that Lung Qi is also failing along that channel.

- The Po (Lungs) and the Shen (Heart) work together to run the body, nourishing it with Qi (from the Lungs) and Blood (from the Heart).

- The Lungs and the Kidneys rule respiration and the 'Water passages' or moisture levels of the body.

The Lungs have other important functions such as controlling the skin and the space under it between skin and muscles. They also manifest in the body hair (hair on the scalp comes more under the Kidneys). They look after the nose and nasal mucus.

So when Lung Qi stagnates, you may get problems in any of the above areas 'ruled' by the Lungs:

Why should Lung Qi stagnate?

- Emotional factors
- Dietary factors
- Respiratory factors, including lack of exercising the lungs
- Other lifestyle factors

Take these factors in turn.

A Emotional Factors

Typically, those with sensitive or poorly-functioning Lung Qi are not good at dealing with worry, grief, separation and sadness.

They may take many years to adapt to the departure, loss or death of someone or something close. This difficulty may go right back to early separation from the mother at birth or from home, perhaps through death or long illness.

Or it could arise after the arrival of a sibling who draws love away from them, or being forced to go away to school before developing enough confidence in themselves; and a hundred other similar scenarios.

As many now recognise, grief often plays itself out through a range of emotions including anger: indeed, it is been said that grief is a form of unexpressed anger.

But it is not the emotion which causes the stagnation that matters so much, as that it affects mainly the Lungs. Someone with this tendency is less able properly to discharge any emotions, not just the emotion of grief.

Lung Qi stagnation often arises where the notion is held that it is best to be stubborn rather than accede to others. In fact, they often do not really understand boundaries as others do. They can appear distant, hard and unfeeling, cut themselves off, or seem arrogant and unsympathetic.

So someone like this may visit or call a business partner without warning, outside normal business hours. They may or may not mind being rebuffed, but it is their lack of consideration in making the approach that marks them out.

Or they may ring someone and start into the business of the call without the usual courtesies. Or when writing a letter, they may launch into the meat of the matter without enquiring for the well-being of the other, or thanking them for a previous letter. Only when they finish writing might they think, 'Perhaps I should stuff something in to be 'friendly'!'

It is not that they lack underlying emotions and sensitivity. They probably feel as much as others, but showing emotions is difficult. They get blocked or choked up too easily, so they do not let themselves 'go there'.

The ability to play, to enthuse, to fool around, does not come easily. Not that they would not like to, but that to do so might make them lose control of their boundaries.

Maintaining dignity can make them seem stuffy or unfeeling. Sadness is close to grief: like regret but not the same. They can mouth both sadness and regret, but regret is easier because they can say they regret something without having to show much emotion.

It is harder to voice sadness without showing it. It can be done, of course, but people often see through it. Deep sadness over a long period does leave a mark on the voice.

Often the individual does not admit or recognise this. Because the Lungs have the job of bringing Qi into the body, and since Qi is the ultimate source of everything made by the interaction of Yin and Yang, (indeed, you could say that Qi is the embodiment of Yin and Yang), stagnation of Lung Qi is serious!

Sometimes you see people whose voices sound dull and tired, almost old. This could be because of Lung Qi stagnation but it could also arise from Lung Qi deficiency, rather as after a bad chest disease you just lack 'life' and cannot get going.

This deficiency of Lung Qi can itself be a cause of Lung Qi stagnation, just as in a drought rivers cease to flow. Together with the Heart and Liver, the Lungs run the body.

The Heart is thought of in Chinese medicine as being the supreme Emperor, the Throne, but the Lungs are the Prime Minister, the practical, day-to-day boss.

The Liver is more like the General in Chief of the armed forces or police, and in a way it still does the bidding of Heart and Lungs, keeps Qi moving smoothly within the body and brings together all the potential for decisions.

But the Lungs are the Prime Minister[2].

The Lungs and Heart occupy the chest. Together, they are in charge of both Qi (Lungs) and Blood (Heart) the two forms taken by the interplay of Yin and Yang in the body. No Blood, no body. No Qi, no life.

B. Dietary Factors leading to Lung Qi Stagnation

Pharmacological drugs, as prescribed by doctors, were originally often derived from concentrated herbs. Being the concentrated essence of the active part of the herbs, they contained no nutrition. This is still the case, and few doctors are taught nutrition at medical school. Consequently they tend to believe that cure is only possible with the resources they are familiar with – drugs. Lacking nutritional support, patients become totally dependent on their medication which omit the vital Yin-like qualities of food. As they become more Yin-deficient, they manifest increased signs of Yang excess, often causing or increasing Qi stagnation.

Kitchen (or food) medicine is the basis for herbal medicine. Herbal medicine is much more powerful and fast acting than food medicine but it lacks much nutrition.

Obviously, eating the right or the wrong foods makes a huge difference to our health. In undeveloped countries, people have to sow seeds, reap harvests, husband cattle and hunt. There is a close connection between their health and their surroundings.

In developed countries many people do not learn

---

2. It may seem very strange to give a title, even a personality, to Energy Organs like, here, the Lungs. But Chinese is a language very much based on pictograms, and Chinese medicine often uses images to explain things. The words it uses for different forms of disease do the same. For instance Wind, Fire, Cold – each of which conjures up an idea.

the connection between food and health. In fact, for people raised in cities who do not watch television or do so only selectively, the idea that milk comes from cows can be a revelation.

They do not see where the food comes from, and they certainly do not connect different kinds of food with health. So they have lost the 'feel' for kitchen medicine.

Of course, research has shown what happens if you do not eat enough protein, carbohydrate, vitamin C or Omega 3 oil etc..

Hardly a year goes by that a mineral, hitherto dismissed as unnecessary for health, shows by its absence the cause of a disease. At that point a minimum daily requirement of it is decided and promoted.

This leads to people overdosing on nutritional supplements and not eating a balanced diet.

Overdosing with supplements?

• Supplements are concentrated extracts of food.

• Herbs are often concentrated essences of supplement.

• Drugs are often concentrated extracts of herbs[3].

Just as herbs taken for too long can upset your system, so too can drugs and supplements, unless the latter are food-like in that they contain nutrients in the same balance as appear naturally in food.

Of course, supplements have a place but, ideally, we should meet our nutritional needs through a good diet, properly prepared, eaten and digested. Unfortunately that is not possible for many of us because the quality of food has gone down, refining has removed vital nutrients, and storage and cooking deplete them further.

---

3. For example, a modern drug for malaria uses a chemical version of an extract of Artemesia, Wormwood, used in Chinese medicine for malaria.

But the main point is that even if we take supplements, we should try to take them as part of a balanced diet and only increase the amount when there is a clear need for them. For example, active teenagers, weight lifters and athletes need more protein. (So do others! These are just examples.)

C. What foods damage or help the Lungs?

Your Lungs are particularly sensitive to foods with a pungent taste. If you eat nothing pungent, your Lung energy may suffer. If you eat too much pungent tasting food, or too strongly pungent, it could over-stimulate, so damage or deplete your Lung energy.

Highly pungent food makes you sweat, as very hot curry lovers know. Too much unnecessary sweating is weakening and depletes your body of vital nutrients which leave your body through sweat and, to maintain blood balance, urine.

Large amounts of pungent food can give some people diarrhoea. Over time this could lead to malnutrition. Foods with the pungent taste stimulate the Lung Qi and so benefit your metabolism – when taken in the right amounts.

I have patients who as children were raised in countries where hot curries were part of their diet. Their bodies appear to have grown dependent on such pungent food, lacking which they feel under par.

The trouble is that over time, the heat from the hot pungent spices can cause digestive disturbances, burning, tightness and other symptoms that often seem to be like Liver Qi stagnating symptoms.

They also become more susceptible to Liver Qi stagnation because their Lung energy, unless stimulated by highly pungent food, cannot balance the Liver Qi[4].

4. For more about this balancing function between the Energy Organs, see Chapter 5 and Appendix 4.

I have also noticed that people who have taken many social drugs or smoked lots of cigarettes in the past often seen to like highly pungent food. This is as if their bodies grew dependent on Qi stimulation drugs. [Qi stimulating foods can seem Fire-like.]

Anything which stimulates Qi will to some extent be like stimulating Lung Qi and may possibly make Lung Qi more dependent on Qi stimulating foods.

Examples of Pungent taste

Pungent foods and their aromas add acridity, depth, flavour and complexity to a dish. A little goes a long way. Too much can damage. They include:

- Aniseed and Anise
- Basil
- Cardamom
- Chilli pepper
- Chives
- Cloves
- Coriander (especially the seed)
- Cumin
- Cinnamon
- Dill
- Fennel (especially the seed and bulb)
- Fenugreek
- Garlic
- Ginger

- Horseradish
- Kohlrabi
- Mustards
- Nutmeg
- Onion (raw)
- Pepper
- Peppermint
- Radish (especially Daikon)
- Rosemary
- Scallions
- Tarragon
- Thyme
- Wasabi
- Concentrated alcohol, like Brandy, Armagnac, Schnapps and Whisky (although whisky is also strongly Sweet and may in excess adversely affect Spleen energy, see later.)

If the above foods in moderation help Lungs Qi, what about the foods that harm it?

If you consider the idea behind the pungent foods listed above, you can see they are all warming, even heating, and may make you sweat. They help detoxify the system.

Conversely cold (even more so – icy or chilled), raw, greasy (oily, fatty) or dairy foods in excess can exceed the body's ability to metabolise them.

In Chinese medicine terms, cold foods weaken the Spleen energy, leading to Damp and Phlegm. The Spleen may produce phlegm but Chinese medicine has noticed that it often ends up in the Lungs. There is even a saying about this: *'The Spleen makes phlegm but the Lungs store it.'* (Read more about the Spleen in chapter 13.)

Phlegm[5] in the Lungs definitely slows you down. It causes cough and wheeze, tiredness and heaviness. Avoiding raw, cold, fatty, greasy food etc and taking more pungent food – but only for a while! – re-balances your Lungs.

However, I would not want to suggest that only by eating some spices can you cure your wheeze. You should definitely take exercise to make your Lungs work a bit, rest and sleep properly, and have a balanced diet and so on.

D. Pathogenic factors causing Lung Qi stagnation

These 'external pathogenic factors' take the form of coughs, colds, 'flu and other respiratory diseases familiar to Western medicine. See next page for more on this.

.

Various factors injure the Lungs and may sometimes lead to Lung Qi stagnation. These include Dampness, Wind, Cold, Heat and Dryness.

Usually, 'invasion' by these so-called external pathogenic factors leads to other syndromes, like Wind-Cold blocking Lung Qi, but subsequently and sometimes at the same time, you get Lung Qi stagnation.

Alternatively, the invading force exacerbates pre-existing Lung Qi stagnation. Dampness means living or working conditions that are damp, or long exposure to it. This is most hazardous when combined with Wind. Wind is possibly the most dangerous external pathogenic factor because it often combines with other factors like Cold or Heat.

What you get with these are all the signs of what we call a chill or virus: headache, hot and cold shivers, aches, fleeting pains here and there, dislike of cold, sneezing, cough, blocked nose

5. http://www.acupuncture-points.org/yuck-phlegm.html

and so on (these symptoms are what are termed Wind-Heat and Wind-Cold in Chinese medicine[6].)

These forces are said to prevent the Lungs from performing their diffusing function.

.

'Diffusing'? The idea is that the Lungs move Qi throughout the body, chasing away the rubbish and giving it energy. Also they keep it moist, diffusing moisture to where needed.

.

Heat and Cold each, especially when combined with Wind, can quickly disrupt Lung Qi.

Dryness leads to lack of moisture (the Lungs govern the level of moisture in the body) leading to a dry cough, dry skin, dry mouth and throat, dry eyes and inflammation from lack of moisture.

All these factors can make Lung Qi stagnation more likely.

E. Lack of Lung Exercise

One reason elderly people are more susceptible to lung infections is that they cannot exercise so easily.

Many office workers blame air conditioning for respiratory problems when the real reason may be that their underlying susceptibility is from sitting bent over a desk, not enabling their lungs to breathe properly.

As we all discovered the hard way over a century ago, enclosed spaces tend to breed disease in the occupants[7]. Not allowing your lungs to expand properly turns them into enclosed spaces.

Any position that prevents the lungs freely expanding and contracting may lead to greater susceptibility to Lung Qi

6. See http://www.acupuncture-points.org/external-causes-of-disease.html
7. Tuberculosis was greatly feared until the advent of antibiotics before which a vital part of the cure was clean, open mountain air. TB is once again on the increase as the TB bacteria have adapted to resist antibiotics.

problems, including invasion by external pathogenic factors such as Wind or Cold, but also Lung Qi stagnation.

So, if you habitually sit at a desk, make sure your posture is upright, that your knees are if possible slightly lower than, and certainly no higher than your bum. *I suspect that cyclists who bend almost double over drop handle-bars make themselves more susceptible to Lung Qi problems.*

Get up regularly and move around taking deep breaths (both upper chest and diaphragmatic breathing[8].)

.

Yogis say that when the spine collapses, the spirit collapses, so strive for upright posture, head high!

.

Smokers!

Smokers often smoke to clear mild Qi stagnation to which, as smokers, they become very susceptible.

You notice this when you need a quick drag before a telephone call, or before meeting someone new, or half-way through a meal, to help you relax – all pointers to your increased susceptibility to Qi stagnation.

Smoking also dries out your Lungs and damages vital Lung moisture and fluid levels – secondary effects of tobacco[9].

One reason you smoke is that you have become dependent on tobacco, which is a pungent burning herb that makes you
inspire deeply, so making your Lung Qi move properly. Those deep breaths help your Lung Qi descend energy, calming you down and settling your nerves.

To stop smoking, whatever else you do, make sure you learn to take deep breaths without tobacco, to sit properly, to take exercise that opens and stretches your lungs, and to

8. For more on breathing see appendix 7.
9. For more on primary and secondary effects of drugs, see chapter 8.

eat, for a while, a slight increase[10] in more pungent foods to stimulate your Lung Qi.

And when you have stopped, make sure you take extra Vitamins C, B and E for several months. Every cigarette is said to drain you of 30mg of Vitamin C[11], which for many is more than they absorb from daily food. So, you will almost certainly be short of it.

Of course, the decision to stop, and the resolution to carry it through, are also vital to success and to your self-confidence.

Do not try to quit alcohol at the same time. That way lies disaster. Succeed at one thing at a time!

F. Other Lifestyle factors

If you do not smoke, but your parents did when you were growing up, or in the past you frequented places where people smoked a lot, or you have spent some time in places where there was plenty of smoke or heat, such as

- fish-curing factories before Health and Safety features were introduced

- coal-fired boilers or cookers

- kitchens near stoves or ovens

- hot places like laundries

- domestic wood or coal fires

- traffic subject to heavy diesel engine fumes

---

10. But not too much nor for too long. Tobacco is heating. Over time too much pungent food taken to compensate for stopping smoking can deplete your Yin energy, leading to Yin deficiency symptoms, which are made worse by too much hot food. See http://www.acupuncture-points.org/yin-deficiency.html
11. A recommendation from the Institute of Medicine suggests that smokers take at least 35mg more Vitamin C daily than non-smokers.

then your lungs were possibly somewhat damaged by the smoke or heat.

You must make strenuous efforts as you grow older to clear lung disease before it progresses. Be sure to exercise your lungs daily.

Your lungs if in poor shape will affect your Lung energy, making it more susceptible to Lung Qi stagnation. *Be particularly aware of bad posture. It alone can jeopardise your health*.

What happens when Lung Qi does not descend properly?

When Lung Qi stagnates it can have a dramatic and profound effect on the whole system.

First, the direction the Lungs send energy is, in health, downwards. This steady downwards force is vital as it balances the upward moving forces of, for example, the Liver and Spleen.

When Lungs Qi stagnates, other downward Qi-moving energies (these include the Heart, Stomach, Bladder, Small and Large Intestines) must compensate, or make up the difference – if they can.

Why – if they can?

Because when Lung Qi stagnates, there is a tendency for all Qi to stagnate. This is because, as you may have read above, the Lungs ("are said to") dominate or govern Qi. Although the Liver dominates the free flow of Qi, the Lungs dominate Qi itself, so to some extent Lungs and Liver share the job. But if the Lungs stagnate, even the Liver is challenged.

The effect of Lung Qi Stagnation is that no longer does Lung Qi act as an efficient balance to the Liver. (In health, Lungs send Qi down, Liver sends it up.)

A seesaw is fun only if each side is about the same weight as the

other. If one side is much heavier, the lighter side will
remain high in the air while the heavier side is stuck on the ground.
If each end is roughly the same weight, the seesaw
can function as intended.

It is the same with the balance between the Liver and the Lungs. The Lungs are the main counterbalance to the Liver. In good health, the Lungs provide the Liver with the Qi it needs to function, and they can balance the Liver when it sends Qi upwards too much.

Therefore, when Lung Qi stagnates, the tendency is for Liver Qi, and to a lesser extent Spleen Qi, to ascend more easily. That is not good, because imbalance anywhere is not good. What happens then is that besides the symptoms of Liver and Spleen Qi rising (explained in Chapters 8 and 13) you get other imbalances appearing in time.

Consequences from the imbalanced Liver

For the Liver, the consequence is irritability, impatience, haste, and tension. Tension manifests anywhere along the Liver channel but more often than not in the upper part of the body, (shoulders, neck, head and eyes) often as headache.

Tension from the Liver also manifests as tension in the throat and neck (through which the Liver Channel flows) and naso-pharynx.

In the throat, there may be difficulty swallowing or speaking. This does not mean you cannot swallow or speak, just that you may find swallowing more difficult and that your voice is not as smooth as usual.

In extreme conditions, you may find that although one part of you feels or knows you are hungry, when faced with food, you simply cannot eat it. When speaking, you may find the words simply do not come.

This can be because your chest is tight (the Liver Channel, and its associated Gallbladder channel pass through the chest and over its lateral surfaces, respectively). That makes it harder to take a deep breath, so you find yourself sighing, sometimes yawning even when you are not tired, or needing open or cool air to feel comfortable.

Your throat constricts, you find yourself swallowing to moisten and loosen it. You may have the sensation of a lump there too. Curiously, this sense of throat constriction is often actually better from swallowing something solid.

.

Why? Swallowing stimulates another downward directing energy, that of the Stomach. When the Lungs do not send enough Qi down, you compensate sometimes by eating more. Solid food works better than liquid. That is why people who stop smoking often eat more, because the descending function of the Stomach compensates for the loss of the descending Lung function, hitherto dependent on Tobacco for stimulation. However, if they eat more and do not exercise, they put on weight.

Of course, some people don't put on weight, even when they eat more. Lucky them, you say. Perhaps. Often they already lack Yin, and are more nervous, so they burn up faster. Their best bet is gentle weightlifting to encourage muscle growth from the extra food they eat.

.

Because the Liver Qi is not balanced and because Lung Qi is stagnant, your moods are erratic and changeable.

The friendly equilibrium between Lungs and Liver has broken down. Normally the Lungs calm and provide balance, the Liver provides Hope and flexibility. Without this vital interplay, your moods may become paradoxical, even quixotic.

At one moment you have great idealistic expectations, the next you are disappointed, even dejected. You become more sensitive than usual, more touchy. This makes you seem excitable, even hysterical.

Usually in this situation, you will not relish consolation. Consolation, sympathy, a friendly support, means you must

face your emotions, even express them, which may be hard. As your default tendency is to be stubborn, you will tend to cut people off.

The Liver has various other important functions, including storing the Blood. The Gallbladder, the Liver's associated

organ, governs the tendons or sinews.

When Lung Qi is healthy, it stabilises these Liver and Gallbladder functions. When Lung Qi stagnates, both Blood storage and the tendons are at risk. What usually happens is that the Blood (a form of stabilising Yin) fails to stabilise movement (a form of Yang) of the muscles and tendons, giving tremors, cramps and spasms.

Ineffective Blood storage can also lead to dizziness, even fainting.

Another side of deficient Blood storage from Lung qi stagnation is nervousness. Normally the Shen, the Mind, is 'anchored' in the Blood. Without sufficient anchorage, the Mind gets edgy.

Severe loss of Blood can be devastating. It causes symptoms of Shock, potentially a life-threatening condition in which the patient seems to go to pieces. Common symptoms of shock include low blood pressure, faintness, fast, weak pulse, dizziness, shallow breathing, physical and mental weakness and nausea.

With Lung Qi stagnation, there is no actual loss of blood, but the imbalanced energy vectors produce similar, though

milder, symptoms including the fast pulse, the dizziness and weakness. Mentally, as with Shock, there is anxiety and nervousness. So not only is there impatience, there is sensitivity to disturbance and easy excitability with a tendency to tremor and cramp.

Eyes

Liver, by supporting the Blood and because of its channel path, supports good eyesight. When Liver Blood is unregulated because of Lung Qi stagnation, vision can be disturbed or confused, with zigzags, sudden flashes of light, and sensitivity to bright light or glare. Sometimes these lead on to migraine.

Another consequence is weeping, often with acrid tears and symptoms like hay-fever.

Effect on Appetite

Normally the Stomach descends Qi. That means we feel hungry, eat and the food goes down. When Lung Qi stagnates, this descending function in the Stomach can be disturbed. That leads to nausea, vomiting, stomach cramps and peculiar desires and fetishes for food – even for foods that according to Chinese medicine are inappropriate.

However, in the early stages of Lung Qi stagnation, the descending function of the Stomach tries to compensate for the reduced descending of the Lungs. That means that people often feel like eating more, or more often.

Eating satisfies oral needs, and the sensation of food in the belly has a steadying effect. It weighs you down and calms the nervousness and the shortness of breath. Food also provides another source of energy, though this does not immediately compensate in reality, because food has to be digested before the body can use it. Nevertheless, the sensation of food in the belly to some extent compensates for the lack of descending Lung Qi.

Mostly Lung Qi stagnation makes the Stomach want cold food. Why? Because cold food is more Yin and with the descending function ie Yin supporting function of the Lungs partly incapacitated, anything that enhances Yin will help.

Cold is more Yin so is easier to keep down – in this particular situation. (Here you see an 'argument' that demonstrates how Chinese medicine explains, in terms of Yin and Yang, why cold foods are usually desired in this syndrome.)

Note: usually poor digestion caused by Stomach qi deficiency or Stomach Yang deficiency will be better for warm foods, warm being Yang-supporting. That is not usually the situation here with Lung Qi stagnation.

With all that cold food descending to the Stomach, digestion may suffer and that can lead to weight gain. Then you can get a vicious cycle, because the additional weight loads the lungs more, and make exercise harder. Taking less exercise and eating more to calm down is a recipe for obesity.

Effect on Spleen function

Lung and Spleen energies usually work together, in Chinese medicine. There are three ways in which, if Lung Qi is stagnating, Spleen Qi may suffer.

a/ Via the Five Element or Five Phase cycle[12], the Spleen is the 'mother' of the Lungs. The Five Phase cycle energetic shows that if the 'child' (the Lungs) is imbalanced, the tendency will be for the 'mother' to become unbalanced too.

b/ When Lung Qi stagnates, Liver Qi can run riot, and via another aspect of the 5 Phase cycle, the K'o cycle, Liver energy can easily upset the Spleen function.

c/ In the 24 hour Chinese clock, the Qi is passed round from Organ to Organ every two hours.

The Lung pairs with the Large Intestine to form the Metal phase, and the Stomach pairs with the Spleen to be the Earth phase. (This pairing, observed and theorised about in antiquity, helps predict how a paired organ will respond during illness of its 'partner'.)

12. For more on the 5 Phase or Element cycle, see Appendix 4.

Stagnant Lung Qi can lead to overcompensation by its partner, the Large Intestine, with cramps and spasms in the organ itself, constipation or loose stools, and along the pathway of the Large Intestine channel.

Element	Energy Organ	Time
Metal	Lung	3-5am
Metal	Large Intestine	5-7am
Earth	Stomach	7-9am
Earth	Spleen	9-11am

The primary surface channel of the Large Intestine starts on each forefinger and ends beside the nose, theoretically on the opposite side to the forefinger at its start[13].

Qi from the Lungs 'transfers' to the Large Intestine at 5am and flows up to the nose. From there at 7am it 'hands over' to the Stomach channel under the eye. The Stomach channel flows down the neck, chest, abdomen, thighs and legs to the 2nd and 3rd toes.

At 9am Qi transfers to the Spleen where it begins on the medial side of the Large toenail.

This close correlation between Metal and Earth energies means that Stagnation in the Lungs can set off a chain reaction in Large Intestine, Stomach and Spleen, all of which can be disturbed by unruly Liver via the K'o cycle (appendix 4) interference. The upshot is that when Lung Qi stagnates, many of the Stomach and Spleen functions may also be disturbed.

If Lung Qi stagnates, some of these Spleen functions suffer:

---

13. That's the theory. However, I have come across quite a few people where the channel does not cross over to the other side of the nose. Unfortunately, either I have not seen enough of them or I am not observant enough to be able to say what difference this makes, if any.

- Compromised transformation: can lead to nasal phlegm and loose stools.

- Lack of Blood leads to anaemia-like symptoms including shortness of breath and dizziness, palpitations and tiredness.

- Phlegm build-up often starts in the Lungs, with nasal, throat and lung catarrh and blockage of easy breathing.

- In the Lungs, phlegm compounds Lung Stagnation by leading to Lung Qi deficiency, with chronic coughing, chilliness, shortness of breath, and more heaviness in the chest.

.

All the above technical detail may seem a little overwhelming but it shows the sophistication of Chinese medical theory and its ability to explain very real symptoms.

.

Effect on Stomach Qi

As we have seen, Lung Qi stagnation can be to some extent compensated for by the Stomach energy: often we find ourselves eating more, even if we know the food does us little good. Stomach Qi descending may replace the lack of Lung Qi descending for a while.

The Lung and Stomach channels traverse similar areas of the chest externally via their Sinew channels and the Stomach primary channel[14].

It is partly through these that Lung Qi stagnation produces the characteristic heavy, stuffy or oppressed feeling in the
chest.

But the Stomach channels also penetrate the breasts, the mammae. The sense of breast swelling or distension many women feel pre-menstrually can come from many sources,

14. Every primary acupuncture channel, like the Lung channel, also has other secondary channels: eg sinew, connecting, divergent.

notably Liver-Gallbladder Qi stagnation pushing 'sideways' onto them, but also from Lung Qi stagnation working through Stomach sinew and primary channels.

If Lung Qi stagnation is the culprit, it would occur with other symptoms of Lung Qi stagnation, (eg depression, breathlessness and sighing) and pulse and tongue qualities – see below.

Effect on Kidney Qi

Lung Qi stagnation has an effect on all Energy Organs. In the 5 Element and 4 Phase cycles, Lungs are the mother of Kidneys so one would expect an effect on Kidney function.

This does happen, but usually only after a long time or in old age. The reason is that Kidney function is very resilient: our Kidney energy controls the growth and phases of life – it is our ultimate resource and the phase of ends and beginnings.

Usually only after prolonged and debilitating illness, or as we grow older, does Kidney energy begin to weaken, so although Lung Qi stagnation theoretically may cause, for example, urinary dysfunction, it seldom happens.

Having said that, sadly we see a growing number of children who survive birth but have what you might call a deficient Kidney energy from early on.

It is good that they survive birth but not so good that they are lumbered with deficient Kidney Qi from birth.

Although there are other factors, one of the 'causes' of ADHD may be weakened Kidney function. In other words, their inherited genes are deficient.

Effect on Diaphragm and Voice

The Lung sinew channel spreads over the diaphragm and the floating ribs nearby. The sinew channels are often overlooked by acupuncturists but in this case the connection with the diaphragm is important.

Our upper ribs expand the upper lungs on breathing in, but the lower part of the lungs is actually controlled more by the diaphragm: any classical singer will tell you how important the diaphragm is in controlling the voice.

Lung Qi stagnation works in two ways on the breathing and voice. It can lose effective control of both the upper ribs and the diaphragm. This means the voice, for example, may be unreliable in volume and steadiness. What that means is that your voice may be louder or softer than you meant it to be and that you cannot keep it modulated properly: your voice carries a tremor. This is a little like when you get old and your voice quavers.

The tremor noticeable in the voices of some old people comes partly from deficiency in Lung Qi and partly from Kidney Qi deficiency. The opposite is the paralysed voice, where you can hardly whisper, let alone speak. For the lungs, it means breathing is disturbed and does not flow. You see this in the shaking, sobbing motions of someone overcome by grief, anger or disappointment, as they weep.

Lung Qi stagnation prevents full expansion and contraction of the lungs. Overcome by grief they may be, or just controlling their emotions, but you see people taking much smaller breaths than they need, periodically compensating with huge sighs.

My observation is that the upper lungs are more susceptible to grief and crying, the lower part ie the diaphragm is more affected by deep sadness.

Effect on the Lungs themselves

We have talked about what happens with Lung Qi stagnation in terms of other Energy Organs. Now let us consider what happens as a result of the inner world of the Lungs stagnating.

People with Lung energy stagnation protect themselves in various ways.

The Lungs and Large Intestine energy organs are classified as Metal according to the Five Phase or Five Element system, a major system of thought in Chinese medicine coming down from antiquity[15]. [In Metal, the cycle wanes.]

As people age, looking back on how they have behaved and their life experiences can often be seen as a kind of refining process, both on themselves and on those around them. They bring, or have the potential to bring, quality to the lives of others.

This quality could be in terms of art, music, manners, social intercourse. It could also be in terms of political or business sense or technique. They tend to want to do things the right way. Perhaps they have a moralising tendency.

Of course, the down side is that they can be critical. They can cut you dead, cut you off, or withdraw completely.

Cut-off has benefits!

Such actions can seem bizarre and impossible to justify to others, and it is not that they will not lose by cutting people, but withdrawing means they preserve their own rights and standards.

They would rather be free to live the way they want than have to live a way that is uncomfortable to them.

You can only go so far with these types. Often charming and helpful on the surface, if you push them too far, they will cut loose. Someone you thought was a dependable friend will exercise his individual right to freedom as a priority over your needs and requests for help or what you see as the mutual benefits of friendship.

So, they bring high standards, but can cut you off. It is an odd combination. They seem sociable and accommodating, but only so long as their own energy is not overdrawn. This is where the underlying process of being Governor of the Qi comes in, because, (depending on their physique and health of course) they only have limited supplies of Qi.

If they see too much Qi is demanded of them, they cut

15. See Appendix 4.

off. This cut off is often the first sign of Lung Qi stagnation. They get huffy or irritable. This is not anger: more like a touchiness, with a sense of frustration. Since it is the Lungs we are discussing, there will be a tendency to sigh, weep or sob (probably in private).

If they do not do that, they may just become incommunicado for a while.

Worry and Depression

As mentioned above, the Lungs and Spleen share many energetic functions in the provision of Qi and Blood to the body.

In Chinese medicine, Lungs are associated with grief, as from the loss of someone or something, and Spleen is more associated with worry and obsessive or over-thinking.

But Lung Qi stagnation brings a tendency to worry, and whether it arises from the Lungs themselves or from the Spleen hardly matters. With Qi stagnating, being so low brings a kind of depression.

This depression often hurts most between 3am and 5am when they wake and then cannot sleep. This is also a very 'private' time, which you would not know about unless you lived with them – and not necessarily even then.

If they do wake then, they will be low in Qi and low in spirits. Any mental worries that during the day hardly trouble them will be exaggerated at this time. Fortunately, if they can remain in bed they may be able to make up for this in part between 7am and 11am[16].

Yawning and Shortness of Breath

Not just that, but physically they may become short of breath. This can be because of an infection (invasion by an 'external pathogenic factor' to give it its proper title) or because of overstrain, of pushing themselves too far, or of too much being demanded of them. So they sigh and yawn.

16. 7am to 11am are the times of the Earth element, the Spleen and Stomach Energy Organs, which support – are the 'Mother' - of Metal and Lung Qi.

Literally, their Lungs cannot provide enough Qi. Lung Qi deficiency fairly easily turns into Lungs Qi stagnation.

Worse, the Qi does not flow through the Lungs properly, leading to shortness of breath, tiredness, and cough. Phlegm
may collect and be hard to hawk. The voice may suffer, tremble, grow weak, or need to be forced.

There are many little pointers to Qi stagnation, once you know how to recognize them. In the case of the Lungs, the arrival of phlegm in the nose soon after eating points both to Lung and Spleen deficiency, possibly arising from Lung Qi or Spleen Qi stagnation. This phlegm is a kind of turbid Qi, failing to descend.

They may wonder if life is worth it. They may feel like walking out from partners of leaving their job or calling.

Twelve hours later, between 3 and 5pm, they may also feel tired. Or they may find they do not know what they want, except not this!

Meantime, they can lose their sense of smell. The voice becomes hoarse, the nose blocks, and when speaking to people they run out of puff, so either speak more quietly or, if they start loud, soon need to take a breath to keep going.

They may sigh or yawn a lot. They may like their upper back rubbed or want to press it against an edge or corner, to massage out knots and kinks there. The nose may feel blocked up. Surreptitiously they may pick it.

This phlegm, or sensation of nasal phlegm or blockage, which may occur also in the throat , comes from the Lungs
not being able to maintain the free flow of Qi through the nose and from Spleen Qi (being compromised by Lung Qi
deficiency or stagnation) not able to transform food properly.

By the way, that phlegm, arising from foods or eating habits that do not suit the constitution, appears first in the nose, but later on it starts to accumulate in the lungs.

Depending on circumstances, 'later on' may mean almost immediately or up to several hours or even a day later.

If the latter, you will not associate the phlegm build-up with the food you ate the day before, unless it was the only food you ate, of course.

Tongue

Often there is a slight swelling along the sides of the tongue towards the front at the level of the chest area in the tongue.

Pulse

With Lung Qi Stagnation there is usually only a small change only in the pulse. It makes the right-hand front (distal) position, that of the Lungs, slightly tight. Of course, if Lung Qi stagnation has caused changes in other Energy Organs like the Spleen for example, then there will be changes in that pulse too. If Lung Qi is deficient, the Lung pulse is usually smaller or weaker.

What HAPPENS NEXT if Lung Qi stagnation is not resolved?

The conditions already mentioned grow worse and diseases recognised by Western medicine may appear. For example:

- Respiratory problems develop: ongoing cough, bronchiectasis, asthma

- Depression grows stronger, often around 4am

- Many thoughts of mortality

- Tendency to cut-off from society, eventually leading to a form of paranoia

- Skin problems: eczema

- Nasal problems eg sinusitis

- Facial pain, often misdiagnosed as toothache

- Weak digestion, constipation and bowel problems

What YOU can do about Lung Qi stagnation ...

[Observations over the centuries by the Chinese culminated in what we call the Five Element or Phase system. See chapter 5 and appendix 4. When reading the following you do not need to understand this system fully but when and if you do study it you will understand why the following applies.

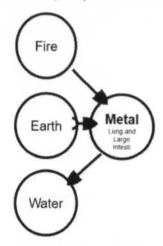

For the Metal element, this system of thought suggests what might benefit people with Lung and Large Intestine problems. For Metal, the main Elements to consider here are Fire (Metal's Mother), Earth and Water (Metal's child). The following uses some of those ideas. Most references to the Five Element system in this section are in square brackets in case you want to skip over them.]

If you are suffering a loss or disappointment, it is natural to have some Lung Qi stagnation. You are not suffering from some grievous malady and though life may seem unbearable, your reaction is normal. Given time, you will overcome your loss and life will move you on.

If, however, you seem to be stuck with symptoms of Lung Qi stagnation like those described in the pages above, then you have a number of options.

A Support – to exchange Qi.

[These supportive structures are mostly Earth-like, Earth being the Mother of Metal in the Five Element system and the support of all the other Elements in the 4 Phase system.]

- Support: [Earth] Although you may not find it easy to seek its support, [because if you have strong Metallic traits you will tend to cut yourself off from it] your community, or an individual within it, almost certainly has considerable experience of dealing with the situation you face. Opening yourself to that support may be your first step to feeling better. Look for support groups of like-minded sufferers.

- Your community may be your family, your social network, personal friends or even colleagues at work. You may find that someone with whom you have previously had difficulty may show a different and more sympathetic side to his or her personality when asked for help.

- Food and Nutrition are vital [Earth]. You may be feeling less energetic than normal. When you are feeling without value, without meaning in life, forsaken, you need to feed yourself with good, basic, simple food. Do not worry about getting exactly the right energy for what you eat, or exactly the right nutritional supplements! Just eat food. Having said that, avoid foods that are full of artificial substances, and seek out simple, 'farmhouse-style' food, unrefined, with adequate protein, vegetables and fruit: not too many grains or potatoes. Avoid junk food!

- Counselling. [Earth] This need not be professional,
  just sharing your concerns with a friend.

- Sometimes, however, you have nobody with whom you want
  to share your problems. In that case, see a professional
  counsellor. Talking it over may help you explore your options
  more clearly.

- If possible, develop a safe place [Earth] in your home
  that becomes your zone. If such a place is impossible,
  make it a time of day that is yours, for yourself, to relax in.
  Even if your time there is limited, retreating to this place can
  help stabilise you. In this space you can play music, do a
  gentle breathing exercise, do a shoulder stand ... It's up to
  you!

B Moving your Qi [To benefit your Metal]

*While Tai Chi and Qigong can take ages to learn properly, you may
be able to find someone to teach you a fitness Qigong called Eight
Section Brocade. This is fairly easy to learn. If you cannot find a
teacher, look it up on the internet.*

- Take Exercise: by which I mean vigorous exercise that gets
  you breathing deeply and heavily for at least 30
  minutes, 5 days a week. This is really important because it
  will move your stagnant Qi and give you hope. If you are able
  to climb hills or mountains, or run or walk in parks or
  forests, you may also find you get a different perspective on
  life. Ideally, the exercise should allow your lungs to open as
  fully as possible, (so cycling with low-slung handlebars or any
  form of exercise which prevents full lung expansion is not so
  good).

- Hill-walking is good, not just for the exercise and air but also
  for the different perspective on life that it gives. Indeed, any

exercise that takes you into high places may be good – if the air is clean, of course. [Hill-walking particularly benefits Metal.]

- Check your Posture: be sure to sit and stand upright, allowing the lungs to expand easily as you breathe. However, with Lung Energy deficiency and stagnation you have a problem, because your Lung Qi is stagnating you will feel tired, with a tendency to feel sorry for yourself, if not outright depressed. People who feel tired or depressed typically adopt a matching posture with shoulders slumped, back stooped and head lowered. If you try that posture while reading this you will realise that it compresses your lungs.

- That means Qi cannot flow through them and they cannot govern Qi. So make a definite effort to improve your posture to enable your lungs to breathe fully.

- If sitting on a chair, ensure that your bum is no lower and if possible a little higher than your knees, with your feet flat on the floor, so that maintaining a natural arch in your lumbar spine is easy. This arch helps you keep your upper back straight, your shoulders back and your head up.

- Read appendix 10 and do the spine exercise described.

- Consider taking Alexander technique lessons.

- If using a computer it helps to have the screen marginally lower than your eyes so that you do not look down on it too much.

- Check your Breathing. Even if you cannot exercise, spend time every day doing breathing exercises. In the Yoga tradition, there are powerful breathing exercises that both test and exercise your lungs and others which aim to balance the two sides of the body and mind.

- These exercises do not require that you adopt any special positions (asanas) to do them: you can do them sitting in a chair or, for some of them, lying in bed. However, it is usually better to be upright when doing them.

- Some of the more vigorous Yoga breathing exercises are quite tiring and can even make you dizzy. This is because they force you to take in more oxygen than you need, so you can get a bit 'high'. (Too much Qi arrives for your Lungs to be able to descend it, to be technical.)

- However, doing just plain deep breathing can help, if you do it for five minutes several times a day. (Five minutes is a long time if you are not used to it – trust me! Work up to it gradually.)

- You can breathe using your diaphragm or using the upper lungs. Diaphragm breathing pushes your belly in and out. Upper lung breathing raises and lowers your chest, and is what you do when you are out of breath but often not otherwise, so if you have Lung Qi problems, make sure you do not ignore it.

- Get into the right posture – see above – and start panting, as if you would having just climbed a hill, using the upper lungs mainly. Start off with just a few seconds and work up to a minute or two. Then do the diaphragm breathing for several minutes. And repeat all this several times a day or at breaks.

- Enjoy Laughter: [Laughter stimulates Fire, which is the Mother of Metal in the Four Phase system explained in chapter 5.] We all know laughing is good for you! Allowing yourself to laugh has a mechanical effect on your lungs and diaphragm, forcing them to expand and contract, making their Qi flow. Does it matter what you laugh at? It probably does, so aim for books and films or movies where the stories are not too hurtful to others. Slap-up comedy from

Buster Keaton never seems to hurt anyone, so perhaps start there. Or, if you have not already done so, watch Les Vacances de M.Hulot with Jacques Tati.

- Take up Singing: join a choir, sing in the bath, join in when others sing. Singing allows you to learn to move your Lung qi again. If you do it with others, you may find the company beneficial. [Fire and Metal.]

- Start Dancing. You move rhythmically, you breathe deeply, you get out of breath. What could be better? Do it with others, if possible. [Fire and Metal.]

- Eat the Right Food: In the short-term, spicy food helps the lungs 'breathe' better. But do not neglect all the food groups and do not become addicted to sweet, fatty or creamy foods, junk foods or junk tastes as these weaken your Spleen energy, further weakening your Lung Qi [qv the Mother-child law in the 5-Element cycle: Earth.] Food is important also because you use it to prevent food stagnation. (What is food stagnation? Ever been constipated? That is one form.)

- Foods that help to keep your bowels moving include most green vegetables and to a lesser extent, some root vegetables. Fibre in grains also helps, unless you are sensitive to grains in which case their fibre may not help. (When your Qi is stagnating, you become more sensitive to foods that you can otherwise tolerate.) Why do not you want to get constipated? Well, quite apart from its unpleasant sensation, it stops your Large Intestine energy working or flowing properly. Because your Large Intestine energy organ partners with your Lung energy organ, any problem with one can spill over to the other. And if your Lung Qi is already stagnating, you certainly do not want to worsen it by getting constipated.

- One extra item! Add nuts and seeds to your daily

food intake. Eat as wide a range of these as you can buy, except peanuts. (Sorry, farmers! Peanuts may be too heating!) Take a handful every day – unless you have nut sensitivities, of course. *Nuts and seeds represent the refined and concentrated essence left over at the end of a cycle so are very beneficial for Metal deficiency.*
Likewise; concentrated nutritional supplements.

- Look for Inspiration: if you can, look to religion or philosophy to help you see yourself from a greater perspective. Listen to people who help, such as priests. Visit the places where others have found meaning – these may be churches or mosques, temples or monasteries, libraries, and art or science museums. [Metal]

- Inspiration may come from a new philosophy, or ideas about religion or metaphysics, or the wonders of astronomy, or from travellers' tales: anything that opens your mind to different perspectives.

- Some people find prayer or meditation[17] helpful.

- Learn to count your Blessings. This is an old, old way to help you recognise how you compare with others. (Blessings? Whatever has been good or beneficial for you.)

- Surround yourself with uplifting art or possessions. However, there is a catch: for everything you acquire or buy to improve your home, you must throw or give away (or sell) at least two items you already possess. [Metal]

- Clean out and tidy your home and workplace. [Metal people tend to hoard stuff. This stuff collects dust and blocks thinking. The dust invades their lungs and the garbage prevents them from moving on.] Get rid of stuff!

17. Read about meditation using your breath at http://www.acupuncture-points.org/meditation.html

[How does disposing of stuff benefit you? It symbolizes the Metal phase process of making space and clearing the dregs. It also moves Qi round the Five Element cycle, in this case from you to the Water phase where it remains until life finds new purposes for it. The main thing is it forces Qi to move on round the cycle.]

- What cannot be repaired, throw out. What can be repaired, learn how to repair and enjoy the process.

- Put stuff in boxes. If you have not looked in the box during two years, dispose of the box (without looking inside it!)

- Get into the habit of decreasing your possessions and willingly giving up some status, rights or positions.

- Your skin and your nose provide important ways to help yourself. [Skin and nose are Metal sense organs.]

- For your skin, as mentioned, make sure you eat a healthy diet that contains no bad foods. And why not enjoy a relaxing full-body massage, with good-quality oils that nourish your biggest sense organ – your skin, ruled by your Lungs? And remember the benefits of natural sunlight!

- For your nose, visit gardens and parks, botanical gardens included, to view and smell their wonderful plants, tree barks and flowers. Buy flowers (so long as you are not sensitive to their fragrances) to provide colour and real fragrances for your home. Before you drink or eat anything, take time to savour its odour.

- Enjoy the pleasure of a warm wet flannel on your face as you lie back for a few moments

- Make sure you eat the right mixture of Omega 3 and 6 oils for your skin to benefit, and drink plenty of clean water.

- Eat plenty of foods containing Vitamin C.

C Considering how to move your Qi on round the Four Phase diagram [this concerns the Water element].

- As you work through the Qi stagnation in your Lungs or Large Intestine Energy Organs, you will find some newphase of life unrolling, if you care to look for it. Keep an open mind for it, but do not necessarily accept the firstthing that comes along.

- Next phase of life activities do not always come from where you expect.

- Make a Will (Not that you are going to die! Just that it helps you think constructively about yourself and your future and about what you can hand on.)

- Discarding possessions and decreasing your range of activities means that in your next cycle, you have time and space to concentrate more on something you already do or, alternatively, to start something new.

- Think what you can do that will benefit others, including your own family and friends.

- What about Work? Grieving people often throw themselves into work[18]. What 'work' is best for grieving Metal people? Whilst to some extent any work is better than none because it moves Qi, for Metal Qi stagnation people, the best activities are probably symbolised by the Water Element. This means learning new skills, attending evening classes to explore knowledge and the world, and supporting people at either the end or the beginning of life. It could also include any activity that ends one phase of life for people and starts another. On a prosaic level it includes planting seeds, on another it means learning or presenting kernels of truth. These kinds of activity nourish the emotional processes that

18. Some thoughts about stress and the work situation. Richard S Lazarus in Levi (ed.) Society stress and Disease iv Working Life 54-8

move the trapped Metal Qi onward into the next (Water) phase.

- Mindfulness [a mainly Earth meditation system is often particularly good for grieving Metal people.] This form of meditation teaches you how to watch thoughts as they flit across your consciousness, but not to be attached to them. However, there is much more to it than just that! There are many resources and books to help you learn 'mindfulness' meditation. Search the internet.

- Enjoy the de-stressing benefits of standing under a warm shower as it plays on your head. (The Japanese love this!) This works because the warmth helps stimulate Yang and Qi, and the downward movement of the water helps the Lung Qi descending function.

What Treatments Help Lung Qi?

- *Acupuncture and Chinese herbal medicine* are good. Go to someone who allows you to open up in your own time, who does not push you, but knows how to use acupuncture to help you release your emotions. But also someone who understands when you just need treatment to help, and does not insist or try to make you 'let loose'. Acupuncture has many points that can free your Qi. Chinese herbal medicine can also help as it uses the same theory as acupuncture.

- *Emotional Freedom Technique* uses acupuncture channel points and can sometimes help old emotional habit patterns release their grip on you.

- *Massage* [Earth and Metal] can allow you to come to terms with your life without needing to talk about it much, or not until you are ready. Any form of hands-on treatment that moves Qi may be helpful. Some, like Shiatsu and Reiki, have a clear understanding of how Qi behaves, but there are many other kinds that do not explain their theory in terms of Qi but do in effect make use of it.

- *Homoeopathy* is rather out of fashion these days, at least in the UK, but I have found it very powerful when done right. The theory behind homoeopathy is sophisticated and comprehensive and it is not a do-it-yourself process. See a professional who can identify the homoeopathic remedy that you need. [Metal] *Homoeopathy is one of the most Yang forms of treatment that exists. Hence it is strongly Qi-like, as compared with herbal and nutritional treatments which are more Blood based. As Governor of Qi, Lung Qi (Metal) usually responds quickly to the correct homoeopathic remedy.*

- *Nutrition* A good nutritionist may spot deficiencies and recommend compensating nutrients. However, once you are improving or have got better, go back to a balanced, normal diet and stop taking the extra supplementation, or do so only as part of your diet. [Earth]

- Supplements are concentrated foods and over time can act like medicines unless really needed. Would you continue to take medicines long after you were better? Probably not! But some supplements are made from concentrated foods and contain all the nutrients in the proportions found in the original foods: these may benefit you. [Earth and Metal]

- *NLP* Where your thinking is dominated by 'shoulds' or 'musts', (as in 'I must go to the gym' or 'I should be at work early' or 'I must help more people') [these being Metal constructs] counselling and particularly NLP may help you shake off thought patterns that keep you stressed. However, see a professional.

Summary

This chapter has been a long one. Why? Because this book is about Qi stagnation and the Governor of Qi is, according to Chinese medicine, the Lung Energy Organ. So when Lung Qi stagnates, it has big implications for all the other Energy Organs.

Some Lung Qi stagnation symptoms are, in effect, what happens to other Energy Organs when Lung Qi stagnates. That is why you will see some of the symptoms described in this chapter turning up in other chapters.

However, you should now have a good idea –

- of how your Lung Qi works through your system

- what it does

- what happens when it stagnates or becomes deficient

- what you can do to help yourself and

- what treatments may help.

Treatments you receive will work much better if you adopt some of the do-it-yourself suggestions.

The next chapter is on the Heart, which 'houses' your Mind.

CHAPTER 10

Heart Qi Stagnation

In Chinese medicine, there are all sorts of conditions affecting the Heart, as well as those more serious ones that Western medicine recognises.

.

The Chinese view is altogether a broader and more philosophical position, but immensely practical too.

Essence of Heart Qi Stagnation

Should you read this chapter?

- Perhaps, if you have trouble expressing your joy of life
- Perhaps, if you have difficulty joining in when others are enjoying themselves
- Perhaps, if you feel unrecognised for your efforts; cast aside
- Perhaps, if you are anxious about maintaining your position
- Perhaps, if you have problems in making or keeping companionable friendships
- Perhaps, if you are always on edge for the next adrenalin rush

- Perhaps, if you have palpitations – sudden pounding in your chest as if your heart is out of phase
- Perhaps, if your friends say you tend to be over-excitable or sometimes a bit manic

Spotting a problem early can prevent it becoming more serious. Chinese medicine has its own ways of recognising this.
What's in this chapter?

- Functions of the Heart in Chinese medicine
- How the Heart governs your Blood
- Your Blood, your Heart and SHOCK
- The Vital connection between your Heart and your MIND
- The connection between your Heart and JOY
- FIRE and HEAT and how they damage your Heart
- The Chinese Clock time for your Heart
- The Heart's direction of energy flow
- What happens when Heart Qi stagnates
  o Physically
  o Mentally
  o Emotionally
- The Causes of Heart Qi stagnation
- What may happen if Heart Qi stagnation is not resolved
- What YOU can do about Heart Qi Stagnation
- What treatments help it best

The Functions of the Heart – Introduction to the Heart Energy Organ

Traditionally, in Chinese medicine, the Heart is the residence of the Shen – the Mind. The Shen is like the Emperor or King of a country.

Like an Emperor[1] the Heart is said to take no direct role in affairs of state, which are run by his ministers, but he (could be a she, of course) represents the State at its highest level, he is the individual to whom the people owe allegiance and it is their desires, acting through him, that the ministers enact.

If he is troubled, the people are troubled and if the people are troubled, he is troubled. He acts for and is supported by his people. Of course, the concept of the Heart and its function was developed over time but in many ways seems similar to that of the current constitutional British Monarchy.

Possibly some Mafia leaders and Drug Barons work the same way, never actually being seen to do anything themselves but acting just through servants. However, they don't have comparable 'subjects', unless you count those who are terrified of them.

The current British Queen under the UK constitution has very few direct powers, but represents the UK wherever she travels, at home or abroad. Those who wish to become citizens of the UK, together with members of Parliament, the Police, Armed Forces and many other public servants on taking office have to swear an oath of allegiance to the monarch.

Whatever the political slant of their government, British people would overwhelmingly support and fight (and some would walk through fire!) for their Queen, but probably not for their Prime Minister.

There is far more excitement and importance attached to a visit from the Queen than from the Prime Minister or a member of the British Cabinet.

The British Queen meets her Prime Minister regularly, usually on a Wednesday evening for a private discussion.

1. In China, it was an Emperor or Empress.

The Queen visits her subjects on over 300 occasions every year. After 60 years of this she probably has as good a

feeling for what her people think as anyone. One presumes that she puts this to her Prime Minister. Equally, she was crowned Queen of a Commonwealth of Nations and has not forgotten it, as apparently some of her ministers have noticed.

If you have read chapter 4 on Yin, Yang and Life, you will realise that the people of a country are what give it value and continuity. They are Yin – at least most of the time. During an election they become Yang for the brief period during which they can decide who governs them, but otherwise they are Yin.

In your body, your Qi pervades it all, but Qi has many forms, and one of the most important forms is that of Blood. As any surgeon knows, loss of too much blood is terminal for the patient. It is with and through the blood that the body feeds, cleans, detoxifies and mends itself. The blood is pumped round by the heart.. Without that pump, death ensues. So pump and blood work together.

In Chinese Medicine, other Energy Organs (like the Lungs, Liver, Spleen etc) manage the body and various emotions, but the Heart "governs" the Blood and the blood vessels.

So the similarity with the British Monarch extends even here, where the people (the Blood) are represented by the Monarch (housed by the Heart) who appoints a Prime Minister (the Lungs and other Energy Organs) to form a government to run the country.

The other similarity is that the British Monarch continues indefinitely whatever the Government may be like. (In the UK there is an election every five years unless one has been called before.) Likewise, your Heart and Blood continue – until death – whatever else goes on.

This continuing unchanging[2] presence of the Monarchy is considered a strength in British politics.

A Heart Governs the Blood [3]

In Chinese medicine, the Heart has an important role in making Blood. In fact only after the red liquid (blood) having picked up oxygen from the lungs, has passed through the heart and been given motion, is it considered to be Blood. Until that point, it is merely a red liquid, occupying space.

As in Western medicine, a poor supply of Blood signifies a lowered health level, with less ability to think, (because the brain needs blood), to heal, to mend injuries, to menstruate. It also means poorer circulation, especially to the hands.

Blood, your Heart, and SHOCK

If you have ever seen someone seriously haemorrhaging, perhaps from a wound, you will recognise the signs of shock. As the quantity of blood depletes, the heart pumps faster and more violently to preserve blood vessel pressure. The individual goes white and dizzy, sweats, palpitates, panics, and eventually loses consciousness.

(By the way, just compare that to the symptoms of deficiency of Qi, which also has weakness and tiredness, lowered spirits and vitality, but not necessarily pallor. Qi deficiency is not going to kill. Blood loss can.)

Eventually, if too much blood is lost and transfusion is not possible, the heart fails. At that point, dying starts.

Heavy Blood loss and Heart failure both lead to death. The

2. Unchanging in the sense of the office of Monarch. Clearly, when a Monarch dies, new allegiances are formed to the new Monarch, but the Monarchy itself, representing the people, continues immediately to the next in-line to the throne.
3. Read much more about the Chinese concept of Blood at
   http://www.acupuncture-points.org/blood.html

ancient Chinese made much of this connection between Heart, Blood and life.

B Heart Houses the Mind ('Shen')

In the West we think the Mind is in the brain. The Eastern concept is slightly different. By the Mind (the word used is 'Shen') they meant the spirit, in the sense of the spirited-ness of the individual, his vigour, the personality as manifest.

They did not mean how clever you were, or your Soul. So the concept of Shen – Mind – is more like the consciousness of the individual, which of course includes the emotional state.

If there is plenty of Blood and the Heart is vigorous, then so will be the individual, with a definite personality, effective memory and perceptive thinking.

If Blood is deficient, then the individual will have a weaker personality, poor memory, clouded thinking and probably will not be happy or confident.

The Blood, governed by the Heart, is where the personality resides. As mentioned above, you can see the personality of someone in shock, say from blood loss, 'going to pieces'.

Chinese medicine has given considerable thought to the connection between Heart and Shen and I do not pretend that what you have read is a full discussion but it is enough for us to see the consequences if Heart Qi stagnates.

C Joy, the emotion of the Heart

A healthy Heart enables joy e.g. joyousness. This word 'joy' is easy to misinterpret. When one of the Energy Organs, in this case the Heart, is out of balance, the emotion connected to that Energy Organ misfires. In this case, that means that simple joy is not possible.

·

*To understand what the Chinese meant by Joy being
a dangerous emotion just try telling your children at bedtime that
tomorrow you're taking them to Disneyworld, and see if they sleep!*

·

Instead, the individual becomes hysterical and manic, although sometimes it goes the other way, with the complete inability to enjoy anything.

It also means that if the emotion, in this case, joy, is too extreme, it disturbs the Heart. Over-excitement (another form of 'joy') often severely disturbs sleep in children, for example. People who are hyper, too keyed up, also manifest excess of 'joy', with restlessness and anxiety.

·

*Joy, in its 'bad' sense of being over-excited, and wanting to be
like that all the time, keys people up but drains their Heart Qi. It
weakens Heart Yin and Blood so they cannot sleep.
Then they need prescribed medication to help them sleep, and
may need intensive therapy to come off
social drugs.*

·

Nowadays, we see a lot of excess of joy. People rush from party to party. They crave constant excitement; the adrenaline junkie searches for the next thrill, the drug fix, the horror movie at midnight. They crave constant laughter, continuous contact and gossip of the twitter-sphere, Facebook and blog.

If you recognise this in yourself, then your Heart energy is under strain. What you are doing may be very pleasurable and great fun, but it will eventually over-stimulate and imbalance your Heart energy.

Similarly shock, which stimulates the Heart to beat faster.

Sometimes patients are diagnosed as having too much

Fire because they display joviality in excess, or laugh too often, inappropriately or too loudly.

D Heat, Fire and the Heart

The Heart is in the Fire element or phase. (See appendix 4 and chapter 5.)

.

> *If mania is one form of Fire 'evil' (internally generated), climatic heat like that of a hot desert is another,*
> *(externally generated).*

.

The excitement, mania, restlessness and so on just discussed are signs of the Mind being over-stimulated by Qi stagnation turning to Heat.

As you may have read in earlier chapters, when Qi stagnation disturbs an Energy Organ, Wind and Heat are often created. With the Heart, these can 'attack' upwards, disturbing its functions. One form of Fire is Heat, and the Heart is said to hate Heat, for example climatic heat, e.g. a hot desert, intense heat in summer: also the heat of a sauna if you stay there too long, or working too close and too long next to an open oven or furnace. These may, in susceptible individuals, create Heat in the Heart[4].

E Other Heart functions

The Heart has a direct relation with the tongue, taste and speech. For example, stuttering relates in part to the Heart. Tongue pain (especially at the tip), tongue ulcers, frequent sticking out of the tongue, serious biting of the tongue, loss of taste, extreme dryness, strong bitter taste all suggest the Heart Energy Organ may be out of balance. The

---

4. Read more about Heart Fire at http://www.acupuncturepoints.org/heart-fire.html

Heart also controls sweating. Sweat is a body fluid and its source is your Blood. When the Heart's control of Blood fails, as in shock, you may not just feel dizzy but find yourself sweating profusely.

Sweating is also regulated by the Lungs which are said to open and close the pores.

Excess perspiration can debilitate the Heart.

Heart time

The Heart Energy takes the strain between 11am and 1pm. Like all the Energy organs it has a number of functions besides that of running its associated channel. This time of day is at the top of the day, the most Yang part of it, when the sun reaches the zenith.

Weakness at this time of day sometimes suggests Heart or Blood deficiency. This weakness or tiredness can include sleepiness, even narcolepsy.

Which direction does Heart send Qi?

The Heart's physiological function is to **descend** energy. When we help someone who is anxious to calm down we talk soothingly, reassuringly, and we tell him he will be OK: we want him to calm down. If our comforting words do calm him his Heart can continue to send Qi downwards.

If sleep is difficult it may be because the 'Heart cannot *descend* the Mind to rest in the Blood'.

If my heart slows down as I relax it speeds up when I panic. When Heart energy travels the wrong way, we get anxious, panicky, nervous, frightened. We find sleep difficult or impossible, and we may feel nauseous. As Heart Qi ascends, you get what people describe as 'My heart in my mouth!'

Women suffering from Heart energy ascending rather than descending find that their menstrual cycles are delayed or even stopped[5]. Female athletes sometimes stop

5. There is another reason for this, in fact several. As regards the Heart, because it controls or governs Blood, a disturbed Heart may be unable to send menstrual blood downwards

having periods, or have much shorter periods, partly because the heartbeat is so often raised or is raised so intensively. (However, there are many other reasons in Chinese medicine for amenorrhoea, the lack of monthly periods.)

I grew up on a dairy farm and we always made sure to keep our cows very comfortable with their lives. If they were happy and undisturbed, milk production remained high. Allowing our cows to canter instead of walk, in other words over-exciting them, disturbed their milk production.

Natural female Yin functions such as making milk, monthly menstrual periods and carrying a foetus can be perturbed by the heartbeat going too fast, as when the Shen is disturbed.

What happens when Heart Qi stagnates?

When Heart Qi stagnates, the symptoms common to all forms of Qi stagnation occur, but with the addition of symptoms arising specifically from pathology of the Heart energy. These common symptoms (common, that is, to all kinds of Qi stagnation) usually include:

- A distending or bloating sensation somewhere in the trunk, but with Heart Qi stagnation, this occurs in the chest much more than in the abdomen

- The feeling may move its location around in the chest

- Low spirits, negative outlook

- Impatience or irritability

- Mood swings

at the appropriate time. Of course, some sportswomen, and others, do not eat enough for their needs so their bodies do not make sufficient blood for regular periods. However, if insufficient blood were the problem they would probably have other symptoms, like coldness and faintness.

- Deep sighs and deep breaths even when inactive
- Yawning even when not tired and frequent attempts to 'catch the breath' even when there is no other sign of difficulty breathing. Faster breathing.
- Pulse: often wiry
- Tongue may be a little red on the sides

In addition there are other Heart Qi stagnation symptoms:

The Heart channel, although it starts in the heart organ, has branches descending to the small intestine; rising upwards through the chest and neck to the face and eye; entering the chest and lungs; and extending along the insides of the arms to the small fingernails. With Heart Qi stagnation, pain may occur along these paths.

In the Chest the distending or pressure feeling can range from fullness with inability to catch the breath, to a sense of pressure around the heart organ. This comes with a desire for air, for openness and for open spaces; dislike of crowded areas; an element of claustrophobia; aversion to tight clothes or pressure over the chest. (Read more about this below.)

This full, bloated, pressing or distending sensation is often felt along the path of the Heart channels, as in the neck and face. In the neck or throat it can feel like a lump. This pressure or distension in the chest is accompanied by:

- Palpitations. By 'palpitations' is meant the physical sensation of the heart beating, often faster or more strongly than usual. This sensation is not the same as feeling one's pulse and realising that it is running fast. This sensation is actually felt in the chest and neck, and it is alarming. It can feel like a thumping, a fluttering, or a weakness. It may or may not be fast. People become self-conscious and frightened.

- Shortness of Breath is common – unable to get quite enough oxygen, because the heart organ is not pumping it round properly

- Perspiration is common. Suddenly you feel damp. This can be felt on the chest, the neck, under the arms or on the upper back: sometimes on the face or head. It may be hot or cold sweat. This perspiration does not come from exertion (though exertion makes it worse) or from heat (though heat makes it worse). It occurs unexpectedly and is often embarrassing.

- Weakness is common; sudden tiredness; desire to sit down; desire not to be bothered by others' concerns; need others to give you help and reassurance. Weakness comes in the form of lethargy or a sheer failing in vitality in your limbs. They lack the power to carry you, to exert yourself fully, to lift things, to walk far, to write or type much. You find that you need frequent rests or breaks from activity. This weakness is particularly noticeable if you also have Lung Qi deficiency.

- Mentally, in addition to the above there is a form or restlessness, of insecurity and fear. This means you cannot concentrate on anything for long, you become self-centred, unable to empathise with others, and anxious about the health of people on whom you might have to depend. If you enquire about their health, it is because you seek to reassure yourself that in your need they will be able and willing to help you. You become impatient and short with them.

- Thoughts of your own mortality. Depending on your personality, you may let everyone know, or no one. – If the former, you will probably quickly contact your doctor for treatment and all your friends will be very aware of your problems.

– If the latter, even you closest friend of partner may
not know, as you wrestle alone with your inner
demons. Because demons they can become, and as demons
they exacerbate your situation, compounding your fear
and anxiety.

- Sleep. These demons, these alarming thoughts and worries
that interfere with work and relationships, certainly affect
you in other ways. For example, you may find it hard to get
to sleep, worrying yourself into sleep only after hours of
tossing around, listening to the turmoil in your chest. When
you do sleep, it is restless and light, full of frightening
dreams and nightmares from which you wake suddenly,
covered in perspiration. In the morning you are tired and un-
refreshed: wrung-out.

- Depression. If you see a doctor, whatever other diagnosis he
makes, he will realise you are depressed and anxious.

- Your throat may feel blocked by something. Swallowing does
not clear it and it interferes with speech. Singing sometimes
helps but you are not inclined to sing. Eating can be
impossible when your throat feels blocked.

- In addition, your stomach can feel full, un-receptive to
the idea of food. Remember that Heart Qi should descend so
if there is Heart Qi stagnation it may instead 'attack'
upwards, meaning it blocks the movement of Qi in the chest,
throat, face and head. That is one reason why swallowing
can be difficult.

- Because your 'rebellious' Heart pushes your Qi
upwards towards the head, you will feel better sitting than
lying. If you lie down, you will want to lie with your head
and upper chest raised. This works because gravity helps to
counteract the upwards pressure from Heart Qi and Blood.

Conversely, stooping, or putting your head low or between your knees, makes it worse.

- Coldness: even if you already have poor circulation, you will notice a difference. You will feel even colder and find it very difficult to warm yourself. If you normally get warm by taking a hot bath, you will find that the heat makes your palpitations worse, may make you sweat more than is comfortable and may weaken you further. Your hands and feet (mainly hands) will feel cold even when otherwise you feel warm. You may find your small or middle fingers are particularly cold.

- Your Appetite suffers. This are several reasons for this in Chinese medicine. One is that because the Heart channel descends to the Small Intestine, when Heart Qi stagnates, this natural descending function ceases to work properly and your intestines do not make room for food. You may even feel slight nausea.

- Your complexion also changes colour. Normally, on its own, Heart Qi stagnation merely makes you paler, but if it worsens your lips may be slightly blue or purple, especially in cold weather. Mild activity does not change this. (Why? Because Heart Qi stagnation is now leading on to Blood stagnation, meaning blood circulates more slowly and so the oxygen in it gets used up before it completes the circuit. Hence blue lips.)

- Pulse: because Heart Qi is so important[6], when it stagnates, all your pulses are affected and usually they become weaker or empty. However, the Heart pulse itself, in the left distal position, may be slightly over-flowing, like a wave that tries to reach too far, lacking power in its full stretch. So, in general your pulses are probably wiry and

6. It may seem a bit fatuous to say that Heart Qi is so important, because Qi stagnation can be important wherever it occurs. But if your Heart Qi stops flowing, you may die.

weak or empty, except in the left distal position, when the pulse may be over-flowing.

CAUSES of Heart Qi Stagnation

Heart Qi is affected by all emotions, but particularly those of

- Betrayal,
- Separation,
- Over-extension of one's powers,
- Disappointment,
- Shame and Grief.
- I think that lack of recognition over a long period of time may also cause it; also, inappropriate levels of recognition, e.g. too much, may set it up that the individual becomes more susceptible when recognition ceases or is withdrawn.

In a way, the default mental image Heart people carry with them is that of perfection; they often believe, deep down, that they are or should be perfect. From this position you can see why shame, betrayal, lack of recognition and pushing oneself too much can be problems for them. Betrayal takes many forms. One thinks of the stories of betrayal in classical fiction of course, but it can also occur in what seem much milder situations, especially if they keep recurring or persist over a long period of time.

For example, when you have to be responsible for something over which you have no real control, and for which you receive criticism when problems arise.

The emotions arising from this, in effect from power being misused and responsibility for it delegated to someone unable to put things right leads not only to betrayal but all the other destructive emotions that come in its wake, including desire for revenge, vindictiveness, mortification, rage and sorrow, not to mention a sense of hopelessness. Shame affects the Heart. Shame is often hidden: we put on a brave face. For example, when someone goes to prison, whether rightfully found guilty or not, he or she enters a different world where all have been found guilty.

So there is no extra guilt: everyone is equal. Learning to cope in this new environment can be a challenge, and not everyone manages it successfully.

The bigger, ongoing shame is that of the family. This has lost part of itself and may lose friends, home or possessions, but despite the disgrace must hold together and carry on. When the family visits the prisoner, they're cheerful and smiling: he or she must not know how they feel because they worry for him more than for themselves. Yet they may need help. All these emotions can stagnate Heart Qi.

Disappointment and grief affect other organs too, notably the Lungs, but they weaken and disrupt the flow of Heart Qi as well.

Betrayal also manifests in separation. The earliest separation is that from the womb, and this first separation, if immediately followed by satisfactory contact with mother (e.g. from bodily contact and breast-feeding) gives a healthy stimulus to the Heart.

The Heart channel sends a link down to the Small Intestine, in effect to the umbilicus, through which until its birth the baby has fed. By taking that point of nutrition up to the mouth, the baby learns how to start to adapt to the outside world.

If, of course, it cannot be breast fed, as we now know, the baby is slightly more likely to suffer from health problems later in life[7]. From the point of view of the Heart Qi mechanism one might expect the non-breastfed child to be a little more susceptible to Heart Qi stagnation, other things being equal.

7. Rev Obstet Gynecol. 2009 Fall; 2(4): 222–231

Loss of close personal relationships is a major cause of Heart Qi stagnation. So is loss of prized or highly valued property and fear of loss. Loss of money or possessions or income can also injure Heart Qi, as many stories show[8][9].

·

*Loss and separation also affect the **Lung Energy Organ** See chapter 9.*

·

Now we have identity theft too, surely just as great a risk for Heart health.

Later in life, there are many ways in which separation produces Heart Qi stagnation, including parting from family, from partners, through broken relationships, divorce and death, including the deaths of pets.

Conversely, good relationships with close partners (and pets!), especially with mutual physical touching and holding, enormously improve Heart Qi.

I mentioned lack of recognition by others as being a cause of Heart Qi stagnation. By this I mean when someone has striven to please or impress someone else and has achieved all targets but still receives no recognition.

This can be very 'disheartening', and the first sign of potential illness may be some Heart Qi stagnation. Heart Qi can also stagnate because of stagnation in other Energy Organs, notably of Lung (chapter 9) and Liver (chapter 8). Pre-existing Heart Qi deficiency can bring it on, simply because without enough Qi, the pump cannot thrust so Heart Qi stagnates.

It is also common for Liver Qi stagnation to turn to Heat and this Heat to be transmitted to the Heart, in which case

8. "Sheriff Leon Lott is proud to partner with the American Heart Association and Carolina Records & Information Management to provide an opportunity for citizens to learn how to keep their financial health and heart health in a state of well-being." Newsvine article Mon May 21, 2012.

9. Suicides in Greece rose by 17% in 2009 from 2007 and unofficial 2010 data quoted in parliament mention a 25% rise compared with 2009. The Lancet, Volume 378, Issue 9801, Pages 1457 - 1458, 22 October 2011

the Heart Qi symptoms will be worse, with more palpitations, more mental restlessness, thirst and insomnia.

What HAPPENS NEXT when Heart Qi stagnation is not resolved?

Heat in the Heart leads on to a range of potentially serious mental problems too.

Heart Blood stasis and Heart Vessel obstruction are the most common conditions to which Heart Qi stagnation leads. If Heart Qi is not pumping Blood around properly, given extra problems Heart Blood may actually stop – Heart Blood stasis[10]. Then you have a heart attack.

Those 'extra problems' might include emotional adversity over a longer period, and what are called Heart Blood deficiency (not enough blood to pump) or Heart Yang deficiency (not enough heat to keep things warm).

Mentally, as Heart Qi stagnation is prolonged and turns into other syndromes, there is increased instability, leading sometimes to (Western) medically recognised conditions such as:

- Mental Ill health (often Heart Yin not balancing Heart Yang)
- Manic-depression: bipolar condition (often from Heart Qi not being balanced by Kidney Qi)
- Circulatory problems (often Heart Yang deficiency or Blood stasis)
- Myocardial infarction – heart attack (Often Blood stasis)
- Stroke (Wind rushes upwards, blocking channels)
- Ulcers and inflammation in your small intestine (Heart Fire transmits to its partner Yang organ, the Small Intestine)

10. See also http://www.acupuncture-points.org/heart-bloodstagnation. html

What can YOU do about Heart Qi Stagnation?

[Observations over the centuries by the Chinese culminated in what we call the Five Element or Phase system.

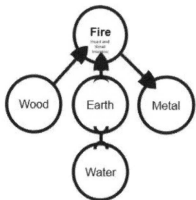

When reading the following you do not need to understand this system fully but when and if you do study it you will understand why the following applies. Read more about it in appendix 4 and chapter 5.

For the Fire element, this system of thought suggests what might benefit people with Heart and Small Intestine Energy Organ problems. All the other Elements are important – Water, Wood, Metal and Earth. The following uses some of those ideas. Most references to the Five Element or Four phase system in this section are in square brackets in case you want to skip over them.]

A Avoid influences that dampen your spirits

[This idea derives from the way sometimes the Water element can douse the Fire element. Water is directly opposite Fire and should balance it as water controls a fire. But too much Water appearing perhaps as terror or fear can douse the Fire.]

If there is someone or some activity that regularly dampens your pleasure in living or your enjoyment of work or play, then you must work out how to avoid him or it.

It could also be a fearful situation in which you find yourself regularly, or something you have to do that always fills you with dread. This might be someone who holds the power of life and death over you, as in a rather remote boss who can sack you or make life very difficult for you without ever appearing in person. [Water people, for Fire, can represent beginnings and endings.]

Remember that your symptoms, though often unpleasant, are signs of trapped energy – *YOUR trapped energy working at full power to encourage you to make changes.*

B Start thinking about why you have Heart Qi Stagnation

[The Wood element is the Mother element for Fire so that means …] … your Heart Qi may be stagnating because you have not paid sufficient attention to what happened to set it off. This may have been a situation of anger or frustration or of plans not thoroughly worked through.

Unless you can come to terms with why you have this syndrome, whatever you do to help yourself and whatever treatment you receive, the benefits will be only temporary.

Of course, temporary benefits are better than none! However, do not be surprised if those you seek help from want you to explore why you need their help. They want you to get – or behave – better, not just temporarily, but for good.

C Regulating Fire in your life

Fire in your personality gives you warmth and the enjoyment of pleasure in good company. You do not have to be entertaining or funny or over-generous to show this. It comes naturally as an inner vibrancy and kindness.

When Heart Qi stagnates, as you will have read, this steady warmth is lacking; you have too much or too little.

In general, however, surrounding yourself with bright colours, flowers, warm-hearted people and company, allowing yourself to enjoy sunlight regularly, owning things or investments you take pleasure in and which others can enjoy: all these will help your Heart Qi manifest better.

In contrast, owning things that might give pleasure to others but hiding them away to keep just for your own enjoyment – these are activities that show your Fire energy may not be flowing as it should.

If you recognise this in yourself, then you may be able to do something about it.

D Movement

Nearly all forms of Qi stagnation benefit from movement, not least Heart Qi stagnation and the problems to which it may lead[11].

Why? Because physical movement helps Qi to move along the channels: like when your car breaks down and you get a friend in another car to pull yours along until by engaging a gear you force your car's engine to turn, starting the engine[12].

However, with Heart Qi stagnation, and the weakness it brings, only gradually commence strenuous activity. Instead, start by gentle walking or dancing, slow running, swimming, yoga or Tai Qi. Avoid highly competitive sports to begin with.

Dancing[13] is particularly good for Heart Qi

---

11. Recent research supports this, showing that exercise is as effective as drugs for treating common diseases like heart failure and stroke. BMJ 2013;347:f5577
12. Do not try this is in cars with automatic gears! Probably better to use jump-start leads. But even jump-start leads use Qi in the form of power from another battery to turn your car's engine.
13. American Heart Association's Scientific Sessions 2006, Chicago, Nov. 12-15, 2006

stagnation. Preferably dance with others, and ideally with a partner, such as in ballroom dancing, where your Qi learns to move with that of your partner. The motion back and forth benefits your Qi by both giving and receiving, each of you acting in consideration of the other.

Any exercise that entails laughter is good. So easy ball games (where you play for neither money nor honour, but for fun) are good.

E Laughter

Then find people with whom you can laugh, not in anger or vindictiveness but from the belly[14]. Ideally, your laughter should not be too intellectual; not too witty.

Think of the pleasure of laughing at farce: this is the kind of laughter that gently shakes you, that uses all the abdomen and chest and takes you out of yourself.

This laughter is another form of movement. Belly laughing is particularly good as it moves the diaphragm and the diaphragm is the muscle of the Pericardium Energy Organ[15].

The Pericardium surrounds and assists the heart, so moving the Pericardium's muscle helps move Qi in the Pericardium enabling it better to assist the Heart. (See also chapter 16.)

F Breathing

Take lessons in breathing. Your Lung Energy Organ shares your chest with your Heart. They have a major influence on one another. About the only organ that you can control with your

---

14. [Being from the belly, this kind of laughter derives partly from the abdomen and the Earth phase, Earth being the Mother of Metal and the Lungs being Metal. Also, each element is rooted in Earth so belly laughing helps ground Fire.]
15. branch of the Pericardium 'muscle' channel is said to enter at the axilla, then disperse inside the chest and finally converge at the diaphragm.

mind – at least to some extent – is your lung. For example, at will, you can breathe fast or slow, deep or shallow. Read appendix 7.

Learn to breathe slowly and rhythmically to calm yourself.

G Meditation and Prayer help to calm your mind.

Calming your mind means that you learn to calm your Shen – your Mind (capital M). As the Heart is said to 'house' your Mind, and your Mind is like the Emperor at the centre of your being, a calm Mind has huge influence on the other Energy Organs and on your Heart and heart.

It helps if you have done it before! If you are just starting as a result of Heart Qi stagnation, learning to meditate will not be easy, so concentrate on the other methods mentioned here first. But even a few minutes of counting your breaths[16], a classic process leading to meditation, will be helpful. You may or may not be religious, but whatever your views, at its best religion has been a huge inspiration and support for people in adversity for thousands of years. As you age, your body will take longer to repair itself and you will not have the energy you had when younger. You may find that religious sources and people can be a boon for your well-being[17].

H Concerning your Diet and Food

Do not over-eat. Small amounts regularly are all you can and should take. Make meals easy to digest: reduce the amount, particularly of high protein, heavy meats and fatty food.

16. http://www.acupuncture-points.org/meditation.html
17. Qi in its universal context is expressed as everything that exists, on all levels. Whether you believe Qi is God's Holy Spirit or the assemblage of all manifestations of energy, for your health your Qi MUST flow. Anything which helps it flow more smoothly will increase your likelihood of enjoying better health.

Take food warm, not iced or cold. Why? Because eating food warm assists the digestion, helping Stomach Qi. As you regain health you will not need to worry so much about the temperature of the food you eat.

What foods should you eat? Apart from avoiding excessive protein, refined carbohydrates and fatty food you should eat a broad range of foods. (So protein is good, natural fats from animal and vegetables sources are good, and olive oil is excellent to help you feel full.)

Traditionally the Bitter taste suits the Heart. Many poisonous plants are bitter as a warning not to eat them. However, the more one's Fire Element energy is lacking or out of balance, the more you will tend to like (or sometimes, hate) it, whether as strong coffee, dark chocolate, or quinine tonic. It is better to eat the bitter taste by eating foods in the Brassica family, chicory, watercress, and some almonds as these contain other nutrients and are not so concentrated.

Make sure you eat plenty of fresh food, newly cooked, avoiding artificial additives. Include oily fish in your diet several times a week, failing which take advice on what to eat to replace the essential fats oily fish provide.

The view from traditional Chinese medicine is that you should eat foods from all the five food taste groupings (read chapter 13), including the bitter taste (see above).

- *Chew Well*
  Whatever you eat, chew it well.
  (Why? Because chewing strongly exercises branches of the Stomach, Small Intestine and Gall-bladder channels in the jaw, readying their connected Energy organs for action.) Chewing, from a Western perspective, of course breaks food into smaller and more easily digestible chunks. Chewing also slows you down, and Heart Qi stagnation nearly always comes with a sense of time running

away from you. Chew slower and live longer! Chewing helps you recover control over time, and the time taken to chew also gives you time to relax and reflect. Convivial company helps you view problems differently. Avoid foods and drugs that over-stimulate, including caffeine. Short-term, coffee makes you feel better. But some hours later you may feel more tired than before. Avoid it.

I Rest

If your Heart Qi is stagnating, you will often feel tired. Get plenty of rest, lying in the sun if you can. (Observe sensible precautions about sun-burning of course!)

You may find that warmth on your upper back between your shoulder-blades will be especially pleasurable and beneficial.

Absorption of Vitamin D through sensible skin exposure to the sun has many benefits1, not least for circulation and Heart Energy organ.

J Massage

Get yourself massaged by someone skilled. Relax into it to the point of sleep if you can. [This attention by another human is like Earth nourishing your Fire Element.]

K Company of a pet (if no human available!)

If you cannot enjoy the company of another human, and you are able to, get a pet – preferably the kind that enjoys your stroking it.

But please, if you get a pet, do so responsibly. Make sure you have the resources to care for and feed it, the time to exercise and spend with it and the money to pay for professional help should it fall ill.

And if life suddenly improves for you and you no longer need it, take care when passing it on to another owner, that you do so responsibly and for the benefit of both the new owner and the pet. [The pet can nourish your Fire Element.]

L Sleep

First, do not eat much before bedtime. Eating too much then will disrupt your digestion and your sleep. Do not take alcohol before you sleep for the same reason. It may help you get to sleep, but the sleep you get is not as valuable.

Be wary of taking drugs unless you really cannot sleep, and even then, be very careful. It is very easy to start medication and then become dependent on it.

M Singing

Singing is good. It teaches you to breathe properly, the music transports you and the company enlivens you. [Singing uses Metal energy via the Lungs to move Qi, and together with the community benefits of Fire and Earth it warms and anchors your Shen.]

N Share your trouble with someone else.

Talk about it, either to a professional counsellor or to a friend. Seek help, if you can, to manage the situation. If the trigger was death or sudden loss or divorce, allow yourself to go through the grieving process that society allows for: there are deep psychological reasons why they work.

O Autogenics

A powerful way to learn how to recognise your stress responses and use them another way. However, this has to be learned so is not a short-term measure. Learn it in a group [Fire].

P Return to Life

It is better to allow your body and soul to move on by proper adaptation: movement,   friendship,   laughter, remembrance – opening the heart to new experience. These allow your Qi to move and mingle with that of others, so reducing its stagnation.

Q Giving to your Community

[This action helps move your Qi round the Five Phase system from Fire to Earth and Metal.]

Giving means not just financially, if that is an option, but more importantly, by working physically with your community to help and strengthen it.

Your community may be any of the following, or similar:

- your family
- your neighbours
- local charities or voluntary associations
- social groups through work
- volunteering to help in hospitals or hospices
- your religious community if you have one
- your hobbies, crafts or interest groups
- your political links if you have them

What does 'giving' mean? To move your Heart Qi should involve physical participation, actively promoting the activities of the community. Acting alone, remotely from your home, and instructing or paying for people to do what you tell them, is not the same as actually doing things yourself!

Let me repeat that! If you sit at home, or remotely from the action, perhaps participating just by telephone – well! It is better than nothing, but you will get more benefit, and your community will gain more, if you do it yourself in person.

Find out how you can

- give lifts to older people (if you have a car) or
- participate in works outings or
- help organize meetings in person or
- push trolleys around in a hospital or
- clean up the local river or
- take or join people on countryside walks
- help out in charity shops
- or similar...

Only then will you become a part of your community and part of its support group [represented by the Earth element.]

But also, you now know why charity organizers love big events, such as Comic Relief or Charity Balls, because when people are in their Fire phase, they are more open to making donations.

[Being seen to give like this, in a big event, gives recognition [Fire] and moves Qi from Fire onto the next phase, Metal. The donation made also returns resources to Earth which helps to ground any over-exuberant Fire.]

What help can you get – what TREATMENTS may help?

- Acupuncture and Chinese medicine have been treating the symptoms of Heart Qi Stagnation for thousands of years. They can often really help.

- Counselling and psychological help from someone experienced and able to help you adapt to circumstances.

- EFT Emotional Freedom Technique can be learned. You may find it ameliorates the worst of the panics. See appendix 6.

- Learn Tai Qi, including 'Touching Hands'.

- Massage, of various kinds, helps ground you.

If you have enough money, a much-respected treatment, though one with only temporary benefits, is retail therapy!

Your doctor can do tests and recommend treatment, depending on the health system of your country. Be aware that he or she may have little knowledge of alternative systems of health and may denigrate them.

Summary

In this chapter, you have read about your Heart Energy Organ and how, when it stagnates, it affects your mind and outlook and can, if unresolved, lead to long-term and serious problems.

.

The next chapter covers the Stomach Energy Organ. It has many close relationships with the Heart.

Stomach Qi Stagnation

How can something stagnate in your stomach?

All too easily is the answer. From eating too much to worrying too much, from not being able to swallow an idea to a piece of fish, it is here!

When you have read this chapter, read Chapter 13 on the Spleen.

Essence of Stomach Qi Stagnation

Read this chapter if:

- You are a worrier or have many anxieties
- You are expected to feed or care for others
- You sit (e.g.at a desk) for long periods when working, whether or not you use a computer
- You weigh too much or too little for supposed 'health'
- You sometimes feel that you cannot take 'any more'

Stomach function

The Stomach's function has to do with absorption and digestion[1]: processing, including idea processing[2].

In Chinese medicine it takes energy downwards. When this function is disturbed, energy either fails to descend or flows upwards.

When it flows upwards instead of downwards, physically we feel nauseous, we lose our appetite, we retch, burp or vomit.

In terms of mental activity, when the Stomach functions poorly, we cannot think straight, we 'cannot take it' any more, and we may come out with a whole range of crazy, half-baked ideas that probably do us no credit.

Someone with good Stomach energy is reliable, steady, prepared. Her arguments are well thought through, properly considered and articulated. Her thoughts are supported by dependable evidence, arranged in logical and accessible form.

In other words, she has brought all her facts and ideas together, assembled them and thought them through. Then she has presented them in a way that is useful to the world.

In food terms, she has thought about the food she needs, gathered, prepared and cooked it properly, presented it attractively and then chewed it well in sensible bite sizes. After that she has taken the time to digest it. Her body can then absorb it easily and make best use of it.

Common symptoms of Qi Stagnation

When Stomach Qi stagnates, the symptoms common to all forms of Qi stagnation happen, with the addition of symptoms arising specifically from pathology of the Stomach

---

1. The classical texts describe it as 'rottening and ripening'.
2. The Stomach channel is one of the few channels that link directly to the brain (the others being the Bladder, Governor and Motility (Qiao) channels.

energy. The symptoms that are common to all forms of Qi stagnation include:

- A distending or bloating sensation often somewhere in the trunk
  ?That feeling may move its location around within the body

- Low spirits, negative outlook

- Impatience or irritability

- Mood swings

- Deep breaths even when inactive

- Yawning even when not tired

- Frequent attempts to 'catch the breath' even when there is no other sign of difficulty breathing

- Pulse that is 'wiry'[3]

- Tongue may be a little red on the sides

Additional symptoms deriving from this being Stomach Qi stagnation:

- Pulse is wiry especially in the middle right position.

- Tongue. May be slightly red on the sides or in the centre.
  As the condition worsens, bringing additional syndromes, these signs will grow stronger.

.

Pulse and Tongue qualities, diagnosed by an acupuncturist, can often produce a wealth of additional information about your health. Learning how to do it takes time.

.

The following Stomach Qi stagnation symptoms often occur, though some of them arise because Stomach Qi

3. http://www.acupuncture-points.org/pulse-diagnosis.html

stagnation turns to Heat. Many relate to the Stomach channel pathway.

Stomach area

- Distension: particularly felt in upper abdomen, chest or throat. Pain – bursting, expanding, stretching. Some people experience this more as a tense, contracted feeling or as a lump they cannot shift. This lump is a form of Qi and will come and go.

- Pains: sudden, twisting, jerking, spasmodic. The upper abdomen can feel bruised and sore, though this feeling can spread elsewhere in the abdomen. Food may seem to be lying like a weight in the epigastrium.

- Burping, nausea, belching, eructations, vomiting. Using the motorway 'standing wave' analogy, Qi starts going back up the motorway, (burping) and pressing out (hiccups).

- Hunger – surprisingly – but you may dislike eating.

- Appetite: varies between aversion to all food and great hunger.

- Hiccups from eating too much, or too fast, or from eating something too cold or too fatty or from drinking drinks that are too cold or too hot. Hiccups can occur while eating if given sudden, disturbing, news.

- Often you become sensitive to strong odours or food smells.

- You loosen clothes: aversion to tight clothing.

Mental symptoms

- Worry, irritability, impatience and disgust.

Physical symptoms

- Headache: can cause pain over the forehead above the eyes, especially if your bowel movements suffer because of over-eating.

- Cramps in legs (calves and soles), or your limbs go to sleep.

- Gait unsteady. Joints crack, especially the knee joint.

- Yawning from lack of nutrition (even if you are eating supposedly healthily, you can get this symptom because your Stomach Qi is not absorbing nutrients from what you eat) and tiredness, earlier than normal in the evening.

- Sleep: tendency to wake up very early (because your Blood is not fully nourished and cannot retain your sleeping Mind – your Shen – as it sleeps) and then be unable to get back to sleep again.
  If you get up in the night, you get cold faster than you expect, and that coldness may prevent further sleep. (Take a warm drink and a hot water bottle or warmed wheat bag back to bed, to warm your abdomen and legs). Sleep is disturbed by restless anxious dreams. You may snore or talk in your sleep.

- If you feel too hot in bed, as you may, uncovering will quickly make you cold and overall you may prefer to be too warm.

- Eyes: blepharitis, inflammation, pus, conjunctivitis. Some photophobia – aversion to very bright light, such as sunlight.

·

The blepharitis and inflammation come from Heat in your Stomach, probably from either over-worrying over a long period, or from eating foods too heating for your Stomach Qi to deal with, causing Qi stagnation turning to Heat and ascending to the

> *upper end of the Stomach channel near your eye.*
> *The photophobia occurs because your Blood is*
> *undernourished. Turbid Qi fails to descend, causing pus, and Clear*
> *Qi fails to ascend, causing photophobia.*
>
> .

- Ears: Eustachian tubes may block. Ears may itch.

- Nose: may block with phlegm or run with watery mucus. May dry out, causing the urge to pick at it. Can be very sensitive to odours. Sometimes bleeds during sleep or on first rising in the morning. Sneezing. (The phlegm occurs because your Stomach and Spleen energies cannot metabolise your food, leaving phlegm as a by-product. Soon after eating something creamy for
example, you may find your nose feels more moist or stuffed up.)

- Face: red cheeks, or yellow or pallor round the nose, mouth and under the eyes, depending on your constitution. May have blocked nose or sinuses.

- Cheeks under eyes are puffy in the morning. Eyes may water very easily or in cold wind. Some pain or swelling in the infra-orbital area.

• .

> *(The redness comes from Heat in your Stomach, usually from a*
> *diet that is too Heating. Such a diet contains what Chinese*
> *medicine calls 'hot foods[A]. These produce signs of Heat.)*
>
> .

What can we say about the kinds of people who are very susceptible to this?

a/ People with cold constitutions, ie poor circulation, may like warmth on the stomach. As Stomach Qi stagnation develops, it

---

4. http://www.acupuncture-points.org/hot-foods.html

often produces Heat in the Stomach, in which case, although the individual may

be cold, he will not like heat or pressure over the upper abdomen. People with poor circulation often eat more than their stomachs can handle. They do this because from the food they eat their bodies do not quickly generate enough heat to warm them up, so they keep eating. The same happens if they eat cold or raw foods, which require Stomach Yang in the form of warmth to digest them. Lacking that warmth, the benefits of eating are slower to arrive, so they continue to eat, even when they are full.

b/ People who work hard but take little exercise, and use food and drink to relax. If they take exercise, it is not regular: this is the weekend jogger or once-a-week footballer: the skier who does not get fit before skiing. This is also the type who works (too) hard during the week then eats an enormous curry with lots of beer on Friday night. Or just drinks lots of beer on an empty stomach.

(This is a common situation, affecting men and women. Their work schedule makes them already prone to Liver Qi stagnation. This 'attacks' the Stomach and Spleen energies. By the end of the working week they are tired and a bit under-nourished so they over-eat or drink. Their Stomach Qi is not ready for this and quickly rebels. See also 'food accumulation' below.)

c/ People who over-eat (and over-drink) leading to food accumulation[5], which can cause Stomach Qi stagnation.

Stomach Qi Stagnation prevents the movement of nutrients into the body, so the individual gets cold and is sensitive to cold weather and air. (Of course, even people with good circulation can get symptoms of Stomach Qi stagnation by taking too much alcohol on an empty stomach.)

In frail people, the lack of nutrition caused by food accumulation can make them tremble and even faint.

5. Food Accumulation is also a common syndrome in babies who are overfed or are fed too frequently. See also http://www.acupuncture-points.org/food-retention.html

- Time: in acute Stomach Qi stagnation, the condition is worse soon after eating, and often early in the morning.

  (Weakness or tiredness after eating is usually a sign of deficient Stomach Qi, particularly deficient Stomach Yang Qi. But if there is Stomach Qi stagnation, the Stomach Qi cannot work effectively, so you may get tiredness after eating anyway.)

- <[6] Cold: people with Stomach Qi stagnation usually like warmth, except possibly over the stomach itself.

- < Mental work or concentration makes them worse. In fact, they cannot concentrate at all on work, or indeed on much else. For example, watching a film takes concentration, which is tiring.

Conversely, disturbed sleep, either from interference or from discomfort, makes them much worse. Sometimes, if they have had a bad night's sleep, they find that they can sleep much better between 7am and 11am, the Chinese Clock[7] times for the Stomach. This helps them recover some of their lost sleep.

Aetiology – Why do you get Stomach Qi Stagnation?

A/ Emotions: worry over a period can disrupt the Stomach energy. This can be from work, financial or relationship issues, or from concerns over the welfare of others. This disrupts the normal flow of energy in the Spleen and Stomach, leading to Qi stagnation. Why should it attack the Stomach rather than one of the other Energy Organs? This is because each of the Energy Organs is disturbed by its 'own' emotion or thought.

---

6. '<' means is 'made worse by' whatever follows the symbol. So < cold means that the condition is made worse by exposure to cold conditions or, here, cold food.
7. Read more about the Chinese Clock in Appendix 5.

For example, the Liver is disturbed most by Anger and Frustration – see chapter 8, though these disturb other Energy Organs too. Fear affects the Kidneys (chapter 15), Grief mainly the Lungs (chapter 9). Worry and over-thinking mostly affect the Stomach and Spleen[8] (this chapter and chapter 13).

The worry can be a single big worry, or a host of small worries, signifying a 'worrying' type of personality, who would be someone more prone to Stomach qi stagnation. Some very empathetic individuals have similar problems.

Often people in the healing professions who have a deeply caring attitude to their patients suffer from either Stomach Qi stagnation or Intestines Qi stagnation (chapter 12).

Any kind of frustration or anger that cannot be relieved causes Liver Qi stagnation. Liver Qi stagnation easily 'transmits' itself to the Stomach and Spleen energies, disrupting the way they work.

If Liver Qi stagnation is the cause, the taste in the mouth is more likely to be acidic, burning or sour. If the work they do puts them under constant stress, it keeps them in a constant state of worry, sometimes concealed from others.

The old description for this (health-)worrying type was *hypochondriacal*, because the pains they get are not confined to the epigastrium but can spread under the ribs i.e. into the whole hypochondria. This word 'hypochondria and its derivations come from hypo- = under and chondros = ribs so means the area inferior to the ribs.

Subsequent centuries adjusted the meaning of hypochondriacal to mean worry and exaggeration of symptoms arising when there was no Western medically recognised reason for them[9].

8. These observations have come down to us from antiquity and were written about in the classic books on Chinese medicine, for example, the Huang di Neijing, the date of which goes back much more than 2000 years.

As you can see, the Chinese perception of Stomach Qi stagnation would include hypochondriasis in many ways, starting with 'over-worrying'. This hypochondria or over-worrying can start long before medical symptoms arise.

In one sense Chinese medicine does not give hypochondriasis any more validity than Western medicine, because the actual medical condition may not exist. In another sense it fully justifies it because Chinese medicine regards it as treatable, not least because mental and physical conditions are seen as being derived from the same source[10].

If that source, in this case the Stomach, can be corrected, both mental and physical conditions will improve.

B/ Shock and disappointment can also trigger Stomach Qi stagnation. You notice this when, during a meal, you get bad news and find you cannot eat any more.

C/ Irregular dietary habits: this covers a multitude of situations! The most common is that of someone who perhaps has a sedentary lifestyle, (someone who takes insufficient exercise, or does take exercise but also spends considerable amounts of time at a desk, or lying or sitting) who eats more than necessary or more than is needed at the time.

Over time, continuous snacking blocks the tubes!

In adults this does not show up quickly, but in babies it can happen quite fast, when a baby is fed to stop it crying. The health of babies and small children is a major subject in Chinese medicine. The main idea is that babies, in particular, have inexperienced digestions and weak lungs because neither stomach nor lungs were needed in the womb.

There is a saying that diseases of babies are in either stomach or lungs.

9. In due course the word 'hypochondriacal' came to mean anyone who worried too much about his health.
10. See appendix 3 for more on this important idea.

Babies fed like this may, in effect, be always eating. The narrowness of their tubes and the inexperience of their digestions leads them to suffer from what is called 'accumulation' of food, blocking them up. There are several specific acupuncture treatments for this, but the parents often need to be what in China they call 're-educated'!

It also covers those who

- eat on the go, or

- work at the same time as eating, or

- eat while exercising or walking or driving somewhere.
  This kind of individual may not be fat at all. Indeed they may look thin and active, but their activity is mostly on their work, which is where, one might say from nervous energy, they burn the calories. This kind of person often lacks empathy, or is impatient with others who do not move at his or her pace. They easily get irritable.

This irritability leads to Liver Qi stagnation, which then also causes Stomach Qi stagnation.

It covers individuals who like experimenting with new dishes – and overeat, or take food that is inappropriate for their needs. As a result, their food is not properly digested. Over-eating is definitely a cause of Stomach Qi stagnation, for example after banquets and big meals at major festivals.

As you grow older and your circulation and digestion deteriorate, you become more susceptible to Stomach Qi stagnation.

The solution? Learn to chew more carefully, taking longer before swallowing each mouthful. Sweet tasting food and food that quickly becomes sweet when chewed is greatly desired by those with Stomach Qi problems. On its own, it is definitely not good for them. Better is a diet with all the tastes.

This gives your stomach more time to digest and forces

a more leisurely approach to eating. It makes your stomach send 'full' symptoms earlier to your brain. (There is even a Slow Food movement – see http://www.slowfood.com)

D/ Alcohol and social drugs are another cause. The individual who works hard but takes little exercise 'self-medicates' to relax. A small amount of alcohol is known to help people relax[11].

The trouble is that at the end of the working day or week, people are not inclined to limit themselves to one small drink.

Alcohol interferes with the body's ability to absorb nutrients from food. If large amounts are drunk, they fill the stomach and reduce the appetite. If the individual does then eat, they over-fill themselves, with the consequences set out above.

Sometimes there is a craving for spicy or sour food, both of which, in small quantities, may help: spicy because it can help disperse phlegm and moves the channels, including the bowels; sour, because it stimulates peristalsis.

What HAPPENS NEXT if Stomach Qi stagnation is not resolved?

Stomach Qi stagnation can lead to various other syndromes, some of which have already been mentioned. These move into the realm of Western medically recognised conditions:

- Liver Qi stagnation: griping bowels, colic, symptoms of irritable bowel syndrome, flatulence, difficult bowel movements, which often seem to start but reverses direction, with inactive peristalsis and much straining.

- Piles.

11. Almost two-thirds of people rely on alcohol to relax in the evenings, the charity Drinkaware has warned. BBC News 6 July 2012

- Stomach Heat: great thirst and continual hunger, often for cold foods and drinks. This causes constipation. Heartburn.

- Toothache. Mouth ulcers. Fetid breath. Sinusitis.

- Stomach Fire: here they get burning pains, stomach ulcers, acidic risings and irritability that is much more overt. Cold milky drinks often temporarily ameliorate pains. They become habitual users of antacids. Taste is sometimes not just acidic, but bitter. Gums swell, get abscesses and may bleed with onset of gingivitis: painful sinusitis; inflamed eyes and blepharitis[12].

Why does this affect the gums? Partly because the acupuncture channels of the Stomach pass through them, but also because the Stomach Energy Organ rules much of what happens in the mouth, including tongue ulcers and toothache.

This Stomach Fire can spread to other parts, causing heat in the:

- Intestines, with smelly, hot, urgent diarrhoea.

- Heart: Fire attacking here can bring palpitations, particularly when lying down. In effect, Stomach Qi stagnation is causing the onset of Heart qi syndromes.

- Phlegm: this accumulates in the throat, then may spread to the lungs. Often it is hardly noticeable, or not attributed to the diet, but appears as a slightly blocked nose or extra mucus in the throat. Can appear as lumps in the breasts. If in the nose, the individual wants to blow the nose or pick it. If in the throat, he has to clear his throat before and often while speaking. Sipping warm drinks helps to dissipate this, but only temporarily.

- Blood stasis: in the stomach Blood Stasis[13] means

12. For more, see http://www.acupuncture-points.org/stomach-fire.html

a continued pain, often stabbing in nature, much worse for pressure, with reduced digestive power. This Blood stasis can extend to varicose veins in other places along the Stomach and Spleen channels, for instance in the thighs and, below the knees just medial and lateral to the shinbone.

Self-Treatment (not all kinds of which are always recommended, however)

1. Not recommended but can help in the short-term:

- Antacids and cold milky drinks help if there are signs of Heat or Fire.

- The commonest self-treatment is caffeine, in the form of strong coffee, immediately after the meal. This often works well when taken only occasionally, as after a banquet or festival meal. If caffeine becomes habitual, it ceases to be effective, and the symptoms will return unless the coffee is taken stronger and stronger. By that time, the coffee may actually be upsetting the Liver Qi, leading to Liver Qi stagnation which itself can spread to Stomach Qi stagnation, creating a vicious circle. Caffeine does have a stimulating effect on the ventral nerve in small occasional quantities. It wakes you up and moves the intestines and bowels. Unfortunately, it also depletes Kidney energy: this eventually has a weakening effect and leads to another situation. Here, if an habitual user then stops taking coffee, he will get strong headaches and head tension, caused by Liver Yang rising, unconstrained by Kidney qi because Kidney Qi, which in health controls Liver Yang, has been weakened by overuse of caffeine. Young people do not usually notice much effect from drinking plenty of coffee. They have lots of Kidney Qi and freely squander it. Only later

13. For more on Blood Stasis see http://www.bloodstasis.com

does a deficit build up, when they realise they simply cannot take so much caffeine. You can assess the health of your Kidney Qi by seeing how soon you realise you must not drink too much coffee, assuming coffee temporarily makes you feel better. If no matter how much coffee you drink you notice no change in your alertness, then probably your Kidneys have given up the fight and their – and your – health age[14] – is greater than you might want to admit.

2. Warm drinks often help, except when there is vomiting and strong nausea. In many cases, ginger tea can help, ginger being a Spleen tonic. Helping the Spleen helps the Stomach, its partner.

Use ginger tea made from a slice of ginger root if possible. Dried ginger powder can be too heating.

If you dislike ginger, try fennel or mint tea. They do not work in quite the same way but they often help.

3. Rest helps. Preferably take your mind off your worries and do something else. Listen to music or the radio (stories or plays). For a few days, do not listen or watch the news: it is usually upsetting! Do not underestimate the power of rest, during the day! 25 minutes of dreaming can have a rejuvenating effect on your Stomach and general Qi, your mood and outlook.

4. Meditating can help it you know how. But when your Stomach Qi is stagnating, mustering the energy and resolve to meditate properly is difficult.

5. Keeping warm helps.

6. Discharges help: e.g. vomiting and bowel movements. Bowel movements are not always easy, because this condition often comes with constipation. But clearing

---

14. There are many health age calculators on the Internet, e.g. http://www.sonnyradio.com/realage.htm

the tubes with a good vomit often ameliorates[15], (not that I recommend it).

7. Read Chapter 13 for more ways to help yourself.

What forms of Treatment might help?

Because these concepts of Qi stagnation, Heat and Fire derive from Chinese medicine, most helpful can be

- Chinese Herbs if you can swallow them. But if your Stomach Qi is stagnating, this may be difficult – their smell and taste can make you nauseous.

- Acupuncture has been used for millennia and can be very effective. There are many strategies an experienced acupuncturist can deploy. Acupuncture has many points that move Stomach Qi and food accumulation.

- Cupping moves Blood and Qi.

- Moxibustion warms acupuncture points to help Qi.

- Shiatsu massage, which is a Japanese development inspired originally by Chinese medicine, often works well.

- Bowen technique helps many.

- Nutrition: Chinese medicine has a major interest in and knowledge of the energetic effects of food. Knowing which foods are more likely to lead to Stomach Qi stagnation and which may ameliorate or help it can make a huge difference to whether you get it or not.

If you have been undernourished for some time you may need advice on the nutritional values of the foods you eat, but I would still advise you to see someone knowledgeable about

---

15. This fact is known to bulimics who eat hugely then vomit it up. Apparently the Roman Emperor Caesar also did this after banquets according to Cicero's Progetto Ovidio "vomere post cenam te velle dixisses" – the desire to vomit after dinner.

Chinese medicine first. Stomach Qi stagnation often follows worry, obsession, anxiety and over-thinking. If you have work or home experiences that are giving you this syndrome, consider also:

- Counselling
- Assertiveness training. Assertiveness training is great for people with Stomach Qi stagnation. It helps them recognise their rights and needs. For the same reason ...
- Learn Negotiating Skills
- Read 'The One Minute Manager' by Ken Blanchard. This may help you work out what to do, whom to speak to, and how to do it.
- Read 'Slow Food Nation: Why Our Food Should Be Good, Clean, and Fair', Rizzoli
- Read 'Thinking, Fast and Slow' by Daniel Kahneman ... but not so much reading that makes you worry!
- Learn to relax using breathing and meditation (see appendix)
- Learn to meditate[16] Learn how not to worry, or at least, how to control your thinking, regulating your Qi.
- Take up something creative but different from work: eg a musical instrument, or gardening, or keep-fit classes, or choir singing. This helps to change the Qi stagnation you suffer from by moving it in another way.
- Do not be tempted to do too much voluntary, caring work. You do this, in a way, already. Doing more might further drain or block your Stomach Qi.

---

16. See our website http://www.acupuncture-points.org/meditation.html

- As soon as you can get around, do not forget the benefits of exercise, extolled elsewhere in this book!

.

Please also read chapter 13, on the Spleen Energy organ, which you will find covers some of this ground but takes it further.

CHAPTER 12

Intestines Qi Stagnation

This chapter tells you how pain and discomfort in your lower abdomen often comes from Qi stagnation affecting your lower tubes!
Of course, Qi stagnation also affects your mouth, throat, chest and stomach but this chapter is specifically about the part of your gastro-intestinal system below your stomach.

.

Essence

Have you ever found you get pain in your abdomen from embarrassment? Or that you find yourself passing wind when you are upset or anxious? Or that you have to rush to the toilet after a stressful meeting?

Or perhaps you get constipated when you go somewhere new, like a foreign country, or a new office? Or you get burning pains in your abdomen in stressful situations?

All these are examples of what happens when Qi stagnation affects your Intestines. With this form of Qi stagnation, you push the 'Wind' and 'Heat' downwards to where they can play havoc.

But there is much more to it than that, so read on!
In this chapter you will read about:

- The functions of the Small and Large Intestines

- The direction they should send energy

- The common symptoms of Qi stagnation plus

- The symptoms for Small Intestine Qi stagnation

- The symptoms for Large Intestine Qi stagnation

- Why you get these symptoms – the Aetiology

- What YOU can do to help yourself

- Self-treatment

- Treatment from others that works

As in Western medicine, in Chinese medicine you have two intestines, the Small Intestine and the Large Intestine.

Small Intestine

The Small Intestine organ keeps the Qi in the Qi circuit[1] moving between 1pm and 3pm. This is the opposite time to that of the Liver Energy Organ, with which the Small Intestine works closely. Both sets of times can be when Small Intestine problems are more obvious.

The function of the Small Intestine is to 'separate the pure from the impure'.

Food, after it is absorbed through the walls of the small intestine organ is transformed and transported by the Spleen – see chapter 13. What the Small Intestine does not absorb it sends on to the Large intestine.

The Small Intestine sends energy *down*.

As with the Large Intestine, if Qi stagnation affects the

1. See also Appendix 5.

Small Intestine, energy may fail to descend, and may even ascend.

The Small Intestine when working as intended also has a calming effect, like the Heart channel. But whereas the Heart energy organ calms the Mind – chapter 10 – the Small Intestine channel is often used for clearing Heat.

You might not think there was a connection between the calming effect of the Heart and the Heat-clearing effect of the Small Intestine, but in Chinese medicine Qi takes many forms. Heat is one form of Yang energy and it can disrupt the Mind (ruled by the Heart).

·

People often tell me that if they have eaten a very spicy evening meal, for example with chilli in it, they will wake between 1 and 3am feeling slightly anxious and possibly in a mild panic. This suggests the Heat has transmitted to their Heart. 1am – 3am is the time 12 hours from the Small Intestine time when it should be resting.

·

There is a close working relationship between the Heart and the Small Intestine so that excess Heat and Yang arising in the Heart can sometimes be cleared by draining Heat from the Small Intestine.

This is a bit like a couple, one of whom gets very upset and emotional over the news, whilst the other is good at calming him (or might be her, of course) down. In the case of the Heart and Small Intestine, it is the Heart that gets upset and the Small Intestine energy organ that dissipates the Heat.

That Heat might not be emotional in origin. It could have arisen from an itch making the owner frenzied and emotional. Either way, the Small Intestine Energy Organ can help.

·

You also often see this 'Heat' affecting the Mind in babies with eczema, made frantic by the itch. So Heat generated in the Small Intestine can go the opposite way and 'harass' the Heart.

Common symptoms of Qi Stagnation

When Qi in the Small Intestines stagnates, the symptoms common to all forms of Qi stagnation can happen, but with the addition of symptoms arising from pathology of the Small Intestines' energy.

These common symptoms (ie common to all kinds of Qi stagnation, though you do not necessarily get all of them occurring at the same time) include:

- A distending or bloating sensation somewhere in the trunk. If the stagnating Qi is in the Intestines, the sensation will nearly always be in the abdomen. The feeling may move its location within the body. For example, you might find it is worse perhaps on the right side, but transfers to the left.

- Low spirits, negative outlook, depression

- Impatience or irritability

- Mood swings

- Deep sighs

- Deep breaths even when inactive

- Yawning even when not tired

- Frequent attempts to 'catch your breath' even when there is no other sign of difficulty breathing.

- Pulse: wiry

- Tongue may be a little red on the sides

Pulse and Tongue qualities, diagnosed by an acupuncturist, can often produce a wealth of additional information about your health. Learning how to do it takes time.

.

As we said, there are two forms of Intestine: Large and Small. In health, both descend Qi. When this Qi stagnates, it may fail to descend, leading to abdominal distension or instead it may ascend. (Actually it can both descend and ascend at the same time.)

After a period of time stagnating, Qi here can turn into another form, as when friction creates heat.

Small Intestine additional Qi stagnation symptoms

Staying first with the Small Intestine, in addition to this sense of distension or bloating, stretching or bursting, there will often be pain.

This Small Intestine Qi stagnation pain is usually *twisting* or *griping*.

Because there is a close relationship with the Bladder channel, this pain can extend to the back and from the Bladder's relationship with the Kidney channel, to the testicles.

You also get:

- With stagnant Qi trying to ascend: rumbling, borborygmi (noises), flatulence. If flatus (wind) escapes, it helps only temporarily.

- Dislike of pressure on the abdomen. You prefer loose clothing, and want to remove anything tight or restrictive.

- A sense of uncertainty about retention of stools.

- Pulse: depending on how chronic the condition is, may be

wiry and deep. The Small Intestine pulse (left wrist, distal, superficial) may be thin.

- Tongue: tongue coating is usually white

Aetiology of Small Intestine Qi stagnation

The two main causes of this condition are *bad dietary habits* and *emotional strain.*

1/ **Diet**: The Small Intestine is paired with the Heart. The Heart and the Small Intestine are both Fire organs. Too much Heat generated within the body can injure them, sometimes causing Qi stagnation.

Heating foods[2] include red meat, spicy, rich, fatty or oily foods and many junk foods.

But so can eating too much Cold food. Eating too much cold or raw food disturbs both the Spleen transforming function and the Small Intestine separating function.

This means that food does not get sorted, meaning that 'clean' nourishment fails to be extracted properly from the 'dirty' dregs which are normally sent onwards to the Large Intestine.

Unable to sort the food, unable to descend it further, the food sits around causing distension, abdominal noises and often pain. If the cause of this is cold[3] food, the pain is *twisting* and *griping*, even *stabbing*.

2/ **Emotional strain** causing Small Intestine Qi stagnation is really the same as that causing Liver Qi stagnation. If Liver Qi stagnation (chapter 8) is the cause, it may itself be the cause

---

2. For more on heating-type foods see http://www.acupuncture-points.org/hot-foods.html
3. Pain takes many forms. As examples: burning; cramping; bursting; drawing, pulsating. If pain is stabbing, twisting or griping it is usually diagnosed as being caused by Cold. Classifying pain is very helpful in Chinese medicine because it helps you diagnose the problem (eg from Heat, from Cold, Damp, Dryness etc). If pain is rightly diagnosed your Chinese medicine practitioner or acupuncturist knows how to treat it.

of Small Intestine Qi Stagnation. See the Mother-Child law in appendix 4.

- The difference, if there is one, is that the Liver does not distinguish between different kinds of strain. The Small Intestine type of strain comes mainly from being unable to distinguish right and wrong;

- to decide between the best and the next best way to do something; or

- to discriminate between a choice of moral dilemmas;

- to think through the logic of a situation and

- to assess the consequences of that action.

Sometimes it comes down to a crisis of conscience.

Just as the abdomen dislikes pressure, so the individual will not like being pressurised, and can become acutely sensitive to social strain or criticism.

If so, the energy may transform into Small Intestine Heat. This may transmit to the Heart, causing intemperate, sometimes even manic, behaviour. These forms of behaviour indicate Heart Fire.

It can also affect the Liver, causing angry outburst and actions that you later regret. (See Mother-Child law in appendix 4.)

'Heat' from the Internet

From what I have read, a fair amount of vituperation expressed on the Internet betrays weakness in the Small Intestine 'sorting' function. There are signs of frustration and anger, suggesting that the individuals concerned have Liver Qi stagnation too.

This form of Heat, and failure of the Qi to descend, can also lead to constipation (dry stools, difficult to evacuate, because if caused by Heat they dry out).

It may also cause nausea and vomiting as the Qi in its

struggle not to stagnate escapes upwards. You could say that the vituperation is another form of vomit. Uncontrolled, it tends to lead to further syndromes such as Liver Yang excess[4] type headaches and confusion, and many kinds of tension.

Pain then becomes acute and severe. Stagnant Qi has now ascended to the Stomach, preventing it from descending and reversing its flow, causing nausea and vomiting.

Little bit of technical stuff.

Still, you may find it interesting, especially if it affects YOU! There is another condition called 'Small Intestine Deficiency from Cold'.

Sometimes, if people habitually eat too much food, (too much that is for the Yang energy they have available) or if their Yang energy is unstable, or as they grow old their Yang energy diminishes, and especially if they eat too much cold or raw food, their Small Intestine energy may become deficient.

This leads to the inability to separate the 'clean' from the 'dirty' dregs, so although un-separated clean and dirty dregs still wash around inside, the descending function remains in place.

Lack of control of bowel function may then follow, but often it fails and though they have loose stools, they cannot move them. So, although constipated, their stools are soft or loose.

This comes with a sense of abdominal weakness, or deficiency, which feels better for warmth and pressure, for warm drinks and gentle massage. You sometimes see this in older people. Here there is plenty of urine and probably diarrhoea. If it is diarrhoea, it will be loose, with little odour and possibly bits of food in it.

Cold in the Small Intestine

Because food is not being absorbed properly due to lack of sufficient internal Yang heat, there will be a lack of Blood, and the patient will feel cold.

This is not Small Intestine Qi stagnation, but it is a bit like it. Other symptoms of Blood and Yang deficiency might include

---

4. See http://www.acupuncture-points.org/liver-yang.html

poor concentration, memory lapses, dizziness on exertion and poor skin quality.

I have also noticed this condition in thin people (usually it is thin people but occasionally not) who take lots of exercise but do not wear enough, particularly over their legs or lower abdomen.

Although they may be eating warm foods, they are leaking Yang energy from their lower abdomen and extremities, and this depletes their Kidney Yang energy. It is worse in cold weather.

As the Small Intestine derives its Yang energy from Kidney Yang, loss of the latter leads to depletion of the former. Here the deficiency feels better for warmth and pressure, the opposite of Small Intestine Qi stagnation.

There is another category of people who may suffer from Cold in the Small Intestine symptoms.

This is that of young women who wear too little for fashionable reasons, even in winter. Although the young mostly have plenty of Kidney Qi, it can be depleted by too frequent exposure to cold. This happens when they do not wear enough in cold weather.

Such young women (though of course it applies even more so to older women) then get 'cold in the abdomen', causing Blood Stasis[5], with painful periods and heavy blood-clotting.

Even young men who decide to wear too little for the prevailing conditions may lose Kidney Yang over time. They may not notice much until later in life, when their circulation will be impaired. It probably will not be possible to repair this fully. (Even with excellent Chinese medicine!)

I work in a cool climate and see more problems from over-exposure to Cold than from over-exposure to Heat.

However, acupuncturists working in Hot climates see more patients than I do who suffer from exposure to Heat. This can affect the workings of the Energy Organs just as much as Cold.

5. http://www.acupuncture-points.org/blood-stasis.html

Large Intestine

Between 5 and 7am[6], the Large Intestine Qi takes the 'strain'. In a country, this might be the time when the streets are cleaned, the rubbish removed, air and other filters replaced and the power stations re-sourced.

If the rubbish men strike, garbage builds up, rodents multiply, disease tiptoes closer. We cannot do without this important function for long. We need our garbage disposal in the same way as we need our bowel movements.

The Large Intestine sends energy down. What that means is that when Qi stagnation affects the Large Intestine, energy will not go downwards so easily and may even ascend. Read what that means below.

This is also the last stop on the journey of food through the digestive tract, the final process in sending it down, after extracting nourishment.

The contents are still fluid, as the job of the large intestine is to absorb liquid to dry the stools ready for storage until defecation[7].

This process of absorbing liquid is very important and relates to the Lung's function of managing the moisture in the body and on the skin[8]. If the Large Intestine absorbs too much, the stools will be too dry and become hard to eject, causing constipation.

If the constipation is severe it can interfere with breathing.

If too little liquid is absorbed, then you get diarrhoea, hard to control, and the Lungs will not receive enough moisture so cannot moisturise your skin.

Often dry skin, itchy skin, inflammation on the skin, (i.e. eczema, dermatitis) are treated in Chinese medicine

6. Refers to the Chinese Clock, Appendix 5.
7. It also absorbs some vitamins and salts at this stage.
8. The Lungs (chapter 8) and the Large Intestine Energy Organs work together as a pair, part of the Metal element – see appendix 4.

including acupuncture by draining Heat from the Large Intestine. There are acupuncture treatments for this, also herbs, and other suggestions which if followed can greatly relieve these problems, assuming Dryness or Heat syndromes in Chinese medicine have caused them.

If Lung Qi is weak, say after prolonged disease, or in the elderly, the Qi of the Large Intestines may also be weak, This is because the Large Intestine is paired with the Lungs from which it gets its Qi, so expelling stools will be difficult, even if they are loose[9].

Symptoms of Qi stagnation in the Large Intestine:

- Constipation

- Abdominal distension

- Pain that can be felt over various parts of the large intestine organ, though it often concentrates on one side or the other. It can be stretching, drawing, distending, even burning.

- Several Western medicine diseases, like Irritable Bowel Syndrome MAY be diagnosed in TCM as this form of Qi stagnation. In time, they can lead to other, additional, syndromes.

- Pain may be better for gentle pressure or warmth

- Stools are made up of small pieces, often compacted like sheep stools

- Itch or irritation around your nose, with extra mucus which, when it dries, makes you want to pick your nose (Turbid Qi fails to descend)

- Moods can affect the level of symptoms, particularly anxiety, impatience and irritability

9. This is a situation where it would be wrong to 'drain' energy. What the patient needs is more energy so acupuncture or herbal treatment here would be 'tonifying'.

- After a long period, the condition may continue to arise even without these moods.

- The symptoms are often better from shifting position.

- Pulse: wiry

- Tongue: either unchanged or a little red on the sides

Aetiology of Large Intestine Qi stagnation

Qi can stagnate in the Large Intestine for a number of reasons:

- From Liver Qi stagnation, ie impatience, irritability, anger, frustration, emotional upset

- Emotions before, during or soon after eating, even if concealed, have a destructive effect on the digestion and Large Intestine Qi. For example, if you get disturbing news whilst eating, it can stagnate your Qi – also your Stomach Qi (chapter 11).

- Poor dietary routines such as eating while working, including
  o eating while working at a computer,
  o eating in a hurry,
  o eating as you drive, especially if you are hurrying
  o eating while not sitting – ie as you stand or walk or snatching food to eat as and when convenient, or eating too little, then rushing, then eating too little again: also snatching food to eat as and when convenient,
  o eating too little, then rushing, then eating too little again.

All these upset the vegetative processes that our digestive tracts prefer. Of course, millions of people the world over
have jobs that give too little time for the leisurely meal I advocate: that is understood! But that does not mean the advice is wrong. If, for a time you find your eating routines are

poor, then you will know why when you start getting the symptoms described.

- • If Lung Qi is weak, which it often is in elderly people, in those who have suffered prolonged disease, or after pulmonary disease. Lung Qi weakness can also arise from sadness and worry. These and other emotions are frequent causes of disease, including Qi stagnation. See chapter 9.

- Additional factors that lead to Large Intestine Qi stagnation (often including constipation) but arise from slightly different causes and have more extreme symptoms, include:
  – Eating large meals too late at night
  – Syndromes called 'Damp-Heat' and 'Heat' in the Large Intestine, usually caused by eating too much hot, spicy, rich and fat food or red meats – lamb and beef, alcohol, or in an extreme case...
  – from Fever when Heat is said to' obstruct' the Large Intestine.

What HAPPENS NEXT if Large or Small Intestine Qi Stagnation continues for too long?

If this kind of Qi is prolonged, then further conditions appear, often involving changes in the anatomy, as they become conditions recognised by Western medicine.
First, mainly connected to your Large Intestine:

- Elasticity in your large intestine weakens and you may find bowel motions become less reliable unless you eat a very careful diet

- – Diverticulitis
  – Irritable Bowel Syndrome can recur
  – Polyps may develop there or in your nose

- You always have a sniffle, or too much mucus in your nose which sometimes becomes sinusitis

  These symptoms arise because, in Chinese medicine, the Large Intestine channel reaches up to the face and nose. Other symptoms occur due to its partnership with the Lung.

- You often get more mucus after eating the wrong foods

- You start getting what appear to be allergies to dust and animal fur etc, needing anti-hystamines

- You become more prone to colds
  – So you start taking nutritional supplements

- Your lungs gather phlegm and a wheeze, leading eventually to a diagnosis of asthma

- Your skin gets dry or itchy in cold weather, diagnosed as eczema

- If Heat arising from some other syndrome in Chinese medicine transfers to the Large Intestine, you may get
  Colitis. Here the Qi stagnation over a long period made the large intestine more susceptible.

Second, mainly connected to your Small Intestine:

- Qi stagnation here more easily turns to Heat:
  – Inflammatory conditions, Crohns, Colitis
  – Bleeding
  – Ulcers, intestinal
  – This can transmit to the Heart, causing increased excitability and a tendency to manic states, insomnia,
  anxiety, mental instability and the inability to decide on the best action to take

– Tooth and gum problems because the Small
Intestine Channel crosses the cheek and jaw

*What can YOU do to help yourself if you have Large or Small
Intestines Qi Stagnation?*

A/ EMOTIONS. Work out what the originating cause is, and if
possible, solve it. However, admitting powerful emotional
causes or patterns of illness to yourself is not always easy. But
if you can, it will help, because as you may have realised, there
are plenty of people with Irritable Bowel Syndrome who started
off with just a little Intestines Qi stagnation. Had they sorted it
out early on, their IBS might never have developed.

So if it is emotional in origin, what to do about it?
First, remember that your symptoms are a form of trapped
energy: your energy! They have a huge potential for good. If
you can accept that, it makes finding a solution easier
and possibly even fun!

Ultimately, if the cause cannot be avoided, you may need
to move away from the (job) situation if that is the problem. If it
is a matter of pride, be prepared to swallow your pride and to
move on, perhaps allowing yourself to grind a few teeth.

But suppose you cannot move on? Because that is the
only job you can get? What then?

• Sooner or later you must face up to the problem or
  persons concerned: learning to be assertive and to say your
  piece can be enormously beneficial. Bullies get their
  way because nobody faces up to them.

• However, pick your moment. It is usually better to face these
  people when there are just the two of you present – unless
  you fear physical violence of course, when you will need
  friends nearby to call on if necessary.

• Also, rehearse your arguments. Read 'The One

Minute Manager'[10]. This, although written for employers
and managers, can be adapted to your advantage.

- Then practise what you plan to say many times until
  you have it off pat. And when you do say it, say it slowly,
  politely but firmly, looking the other party in the eye. Do not
  rush it, whatever you do.

- If it does not work first time, do it again. And again.
  After talking it over privately with the individual, you may
  be able to refer to it publicly if the bad behaviour continues.

- Office politics. Nobody likes them (well, those who are good
  at them seem to, obviously) and they can be destructive in
  many ways. Unfortunately, you need to keep your antennae
  up. Ideally try not to become identified with any one group.
  Although this can be a position of weakness, it keeps your
  options open. That means that your Qi is, ultimately, less
  likely to stagnate.

·

*Joining a group gives you strength only for a while. Eventually it
will stultify and the more you have become identified with that
group the harder it will be to exert your individuality: to move your
Qi. Read more about this in chapter 4.*

·

- The particular kind of problem that seems to produce Small
  Intestine Qi stagnation often comes down to a conscience:
  what is right, what is the best way of doing things.
  Consequently, passive aggressive behaviour[11] towards you
  or in your workplace may twist you up. This makes for a

10. The One Minute Manager by Ken Blanchard, Harper
11. Passive aggressive behaviour includes, to your disadvantage, behaviour by others such as
    procrastination, intentional inefficiency, sullen or negative behaviour, and similar
    destructive attitudes. It also includes superiors remarking to inferiors that 'I have been
    watching your back for ages, resisting pressure from all sides'. It can extend to 'Don't
    worry about me, you go ahead with it – I'll be fine'.

paranoid workplace: everyone fears being betrayed or outmanoeuvred.

– Problem people usually have difficulty handling their own anger and emotions. Their passive aggressive behaviour relieves them of the need to face up directly to situations.(Another name is 'negative aggression'.)

– Apart from quitting, you have several ways forward. One is to learn to endure the problem and not to let yourself become sucked in. Your department or team will not be anything like as efficient as it could be but that may be the price of keeping your job.

– Do realise that you probably are not the only person writhing under the yoke of the passive aggressive behaviour. Others also hate it. This means that where you work will not be 'normal'. It will be artificial, even somewhat insane. You will have to accept it and float above it. The problem is that you and others can all too easily start to behave the same way, which can be disastrous for the work, the business and eventually, you and your psyche.

– Start talking to the individuals concerned.

– Acknowledge that it may not at first go well! But you need to say how you feel about it and how it has upset you.

– Read chapter 8 on Liver Qi stagnation to find out other ways to deal with this.

– Learn Negotiation and Assertiveness skills

B/ FOOD. Because usually the problem is psychological in origin, the following may or may not help. Often patients attribute their problem to allergy or sensitivity to something: it may be a food or a perfume, a medication or vaccination.

It may also be a chemical in your environment, a toxin or illness your mother suffered from when you were in her womb, and much else. While I am sure any one of these is sometimes the originating cause, I have not seen it often as such.

More often in the cases I have seen, it is psychological, but reaches a point where an allergen exacerbates the condition and is assumed to be the cause of it.

What ELSE YOU CAN DO TO HELP YOURSELF

As you will have read, above, problems with Intestine Qi stagnation can cause food Stagnation or Accumulation, or turn into Heat. The following deal with these problems to some extent, but are in most cases palliative.

By the way, unless you have a fully developed disease or condition such as advanced IBS, green vegetables are your best source of fibre – better than from grains.

- If you know what the allergen is and can avoid it, do so at least until you improve.

- Taking something to cool the heat or inflammation can help in the short run, including
  – Aloe Vera juice (do not expect it to taste nice, it is a herbal medicine!) which you can take raw several times daily.
  – Cucumbers: half a cucumber, three times daily between meals.
  – Sweet lassi, without the ice in it. This assumes you have no sensitivity to dairy food. Lassi is made with yogurt and most people are less sensitive to yogurt than to milk or cream. Make up a supply and take several tablespoons of it three times daily.
  – Green tea, slightly cooled, several times daily.
  – Mint tea, several times daily.
  – Eat small quantities of Sauerkraut. This is made from cabbage, prepared and fermented to enhance the natural enzymes and yeasts. You can buy sauerkraut, ready-

made, in glass jars fromshops that specialise in middle or eastern European food. Eat it uncooked and unpasteurised if you can (becausecooking kills or destroys some of the nutrients). You can liquidise it but it will still not taste wonderful. Hold your nose and swallow half a glass, three times daily. Do not cook it before taking it, though you can warm it by adding warm water, or add a little ginger. It still will not taste great, however. (Unless you were brought up on it!)

Sauerkraut is cooling. In addition, it contains fibre, which helps your bowels. It also supplies a sour taste to your diet, which may help regulate your digestion and your health in general.

– Organic cider vinegar: a tablespoon in warm water, twice daily. No sugar. Like sauerkraut, it is cooling and supplies the sour taste, but it contains no fibre.

– Pro-biotics: some of the above naturally contain pro-biotics but in small quantities. You can buy them in a more concentrated form as yogurt or concentrated in powder or capsules. The latter mostly avoid any problems with sensitivity to dairy foods. Seek advice from a reputable health food shop about which to take and how often. If you prefer to take yogurt, you perhaps should add a little ginger to encourage your Spleen Qi which otherwise might be drowned in all the coldness that comes with yogurt.

More Self-Treatment for Intestine Qi Stagnation

Exercise helps almost all forms of Qi stagnation. Try Yoga and Tai Chi, both of which slow you down and have to be learned over time.

• Play: with children or pets – very natural and fulfilling. This works better for Small Intestine Qi stagnation because it diverts the Small Intestines' natural Fire energy outwards.

- Take up a musical instrument. Learn to play something different. Small Intestine Qi stagnation might benefit more from percussion and modern pop music instruments, (more Fire-like instruments) whereas Large Intestine Qi stagnation people might benefit more from Classical music instruments, especially the wind instruments (i.e. using the lungs) – but play what you enjoy, not what it says here! [Moves Small Intestine Qi on to Metal from Fire. If for Large Intestine, benefits the Lung, the partner organ.]

- Learn to meditate: stilling your Mind will help you with the discomfort[12]. The breath method steadies the Lungs, descends Qi and balances and controls Liver Qi, which is often a cause of Large Intestine problems. [Earth]

- Breathe deep and slow to regulate bowel actions – see appendix 7.

- Learn to go slow; to enjoy life as it happens to you. It takes practice if you are out of the habit. Putting aside your cell-phone or tablet for some hours a day would be a start. Also see the note on Rest, below.

- If your body has absorbed an allergen that is exacerbating your problem, it may take time to detoxify yourself. What that means is that it may take some time for your body to neutralise and breakdown the chemical and excrete it. It does not take forever, but may take many days. During that time, eat a simple diet, with plenty of purified water. In some cases your body may have come to depend on the substance in question and you will feel initially worse as you detoxify yourself, with headaches, tiredness, aching joints, skin dryness or spots etc. (Signs mainly of Yin deficiency.)

12. See http://www.acupuncture-points.org/meditation.html

- For some, it is possible that poisons in your teeth
  (e.g. Mercury and some other more modern fillers) can
  be major sources of contaminants in your system,
  seriously affecting your Intestines[13].
  It is a bigger commitment, but replacing the
  questionable fillings with less dangerous substances may
  improve your health in the long term. You may need to see a
  specialist dentist who can suggest the right order in which to
  extract your teeth. Some specialist dentists insist that getting
  the order right can make a huge difference to the outcome.

- Rest. Your Intestines are also part of your Earth Phase in that
  their energies assist the Stomach (chapter 11) and Spleen
  (chapter 13) to nourish and provide Qi for your body.
  Modern life is probably more rushed than it was until 40
  years ago, and 24 hours days, working shifts, constant use of
  our eyes on computer and smart-phone screens drain both
  Qi and Blood.
  We give ourselves too little time to sleep. Stop reading and
  looking; close your eyes; listen to some slow, gentle or
  relaxing music and allow yourself to take at least one short
  sleep (less than 30 minutes) during the day. It is unlikely to
  affect your sleep at night, but during it you will allow your Qi
  and Blood to recover and this will help all your energies –
  and confidence.

Treatment

- Of course, *acupuncture and Chinese medicine* can
  help conditions arising from this syndrome. The
  theory understands the factors causing illness, how our
  bodies react in illness, and how to help. Major psychological

13. The official line, at least in the UK, is that mercury in fillings is in such small quantities that
it cannot harm you, and that modern composite fillings last half as long and anyway upset
your endocrine system. Many people dispute this position. For more information, search
"mercury amalgam poisoning" on the Internet.

issues often have their counterpart in the Energy Organs. Balancing and restoring the affected Energy Organs increases your health.

- *Neurolinguistic Programming NLP* May help you learn better ways to express emotions that might otherwise stagnate and cause you pain.

- *Autogenics* May help you understand and control your symptoms.

- *Massage and sometimes manipulation* by an osteopath or chiropractor. These help the nerves in the spine that 'supply' the areas causing pain and free up blood flow to them. Likewise Reflexology.

- *Dental treatment* for Mercury – see above.

In general, I suggest that you take only one form of treatment at a time, and give it a chance, ie give your chosen therapy time to work. Otherwise, because treatments may be covering the same ground, your body's Energy may get confused. Alternatively, if you feel much better, you will not necessarily know which treatment is working and which one(s) therefore to stop!

.

If emotional issues are at root the cause of your problems, seeing an experienced psychologist or counsellor may help. After reading this chapter, read also chapters 9 (Lungs) and 10 (Heart).

.

The next chapter is on the Spleen Energy Organ. Its function lies at the centre of the four phase energy system. It provides a vital core function.

Spleen Qi Stagnation

In Chinese medicine, the Spleen is in its own way as important as the Heart, the Lungs, the Liver and the Kidneys. Its function is vital to your health. This is less the case in Western medicine, where the Spleen, although important, is not seen as so intrinsically important and can be removed in some cases.

However, if you think more of its function in Chinese medicine, its importance makes more sense. When it goes wrong, you definitely notice it. If it is not working, nearly everything else eventually goes wrong too.

Fortunately, it is very long-suffering, which is just as well because it has a big brother who frequently loses his temper and kicks it around – the Liver.

Essence of Spleen Qi Stagnation

Should you read this chapter?

- Yes, if you are a worrier, a manager or an administrator
- Yes, if you are in the caring professions, or have to care for someone
- Yes, if you get too much mucus or phlegm

- Yes, if you have to use your intellectual powers to work, and do not break up the working day with short bursts of exercise

- Yes, if you eat or drink too much for the exercise you take

- Yes, if bits of you are starting to protrude (for example your belly or varicose veins)

- Yes if you tend to get obsessive about things

In this chapter you will read about:

- The functions of the Spleen in Chinese medicine

- Its direction of energy flow

- Symptoms of Spleen Qi deficiency, often leading to or caused by stagnation of Qi elsewhere

- What happens when Stagnating Spleen Qi turns into something else

- Spleen Blood deficiency

- Damp

- What happens when Spleen Qi descends

- What happens when Spleen fails to transform

- Liver Blood deficiency coming from Spleen Blood deficiency

- Why you get Spleen Qi deficiency

- What you can do to help yourself if you have Spleen Qi deficiency

- Food and Spleen Qi

- What treatments help Spleen Qi

When an Energy Organ fails to maintain its flow of Qi, you often also get problems along the path of its channel of acupuncture.

Spleen functions

Traditionally it is said to 'transform and transport'. It takes what comes from the Stomach, turns (transforms) it into Blood[1], fluids and Qi (Energy), and moves (transports) these round the body.

In Chinese medicine it is said to send energy upwards to the Lungs and the Heart. But Spleen Qi also holds things up, in their place.

The Spleen is like an administrator who takes stock of what is needed, arranges to put it right, keeps everyone in order and everything in place.

She (Sorry! Could be a 'He' of course!) tidies up the mess and moves it away for disposal. Then she sends clean Blood and Qi up and around the system.

When Spleen Qi fails or weakens, perhaps because of Qi stagnation or from some other cause (there are a number of them), things do not move as they should, they do not get repaired and they may fall down. Or out.

For example,

- Varicose veins often start along the Spleen channel in the legs when the individual is a worrier.

- The abdomen loses its elasticity and protrudes where the patient eats too much and cannot process it properly.

- If the individual eats too much 'bad' food, and does not chew it properly, or eats in a rush, not giving his digestion time to digest, food will be poorly digested.

- The result is often phlegm. This builds up and may 'overflow' into the lungs. You notice this when someone always clears

---

1. Your Spleen Energy organ does not actually make Blood, but it provides some of what is needed by your Heart Energy organ to make Blood. See http://www.acupuncture-points.org/blood.html

his voice before speaking. Also, read again the page on 'clear' and 'turbid' Qi on page 32.

- When the Spleen energy fails to send clear Qi upwards, one of the symptoms is prolapse of internal organs; the protruding (beer) belly mentioned above.

- Another is loose stools because the Spleen energy cannot hold them up (and in).

- A third example of this can be a loose cough with lots of mucus. You notice that after certain foods (usually junk food, sweet food, cold or dairy food, but there are other possibilities, and it may also depend on your genetic inheritance or blood group), the cough worsens or there is more phlegm in the throat and/or nose.

Avoiding foods that do this will help reduce the problem, though may not always cure it. To cure it requires treatment because the symptoms may have become a permanent feature: chronic.

.

CHRONIC?
Your body cures itself best through acute illnesses such as a high fever, major inflammation or other very sore reaction – this can sometimes be dangerous but it's quick. Western medicine is very good at suppressing these symptoms, leaving us with chronic conditions. Your body cannot usually cure chronic conditions without help from outside.

.

In the developed countries of the world we often do not notice the effects of what we do to our bodies. For example, we probably know that coffee makes us more alert, so is good to take after a huge meal unless we intend to go to sleep. But that huge meal, including the pudding, puts a considerable strain on our digestion, i.e. on our Spleen and Stomach Energy Organs. If they cannot handle it, we shall get indigestion and we shall know why. But we may also get phlegm which arrives, sometimes within minutes of eating the wrong food, but more often not for some hours – even the next day – afterwards, by when we may not realise the cause of it. If we habitually get phlegm, we should carefully consider whether it comes from or is made worse by what we eat.

The Spleen energy's time[2] is between 9am and 11am. This time immediately precedes the Heart time (11am – 1pm). It is as if the first thing the Heart needs to be sure of before taking over is that the system is in good running order.

When you get someone who feels weak in the forenoon, even though he ate a good breakfast, suspect that the Spleen energy may be faulty.

If you have slept well, and eaten a good breakfast, the forenoon should be when you can do excellent work, with a clear mind and reliable energy. If not, perhaps your Spleen energy is not working properly.

A Transforming and Transporting Qi

Qi takes many forms, including Blood and fluids, and even our thoughts (see B. below.) The Spleen is said to manage all this: a big job!

Most of us (male or female) do not respect this function in our bodies. We act like patronising and thoughtless men who expect their womenfolk to do everything round the home and sometimes in the garden too.

In fact, it is amazing how much work such women do, often without complaint. When they fail in their job of running the house, shopping for provisions, cleaning and tidying, sorting and cooking, sometimes advising their men,

2. This 'time' will seem like a lot of nonsense if you haven't read about the Five Element system and the Chinese Clock (Chapter 5 and appendices 4 and 5).

loving and nourishing the children, and on top of everything else providing free sex ... their men notice pretty fast!

Then, unfortunately, their men have been known to admonish or (in the past) kick them. The Chinese seem to have noticed it too, because in Chinese medicine there is a destructive energy cycle[3] based on the Five Element system (see appendix 4). In this, if the Liver Energy Organ is misfiring, it often hits out at the Spleen Energy Organ.

As we grow older, our energy diminishes and we pay more attention to our digestion. With age and experience, we learn how to guard this vital Spleen energy function. Take care of what and how you eat and you could live much longer!

This transforming and transporting function actually covers just about all the other Spleen functions listed below.

B Houses the Intellect[4]

This means how we process information and think things through – working with its partner, the Stomach. It is not how we decide what we do with our lives, or how we reach decisions and assert ourselves; it is not our memory.

It also provides most of the energy for thinking. When you are exhausted by events or activity, (not merely tired, but exhausted), you want to rest or sleep: not to have to think. After a good sleep, you can start thinking again. The Spleen provides the wherewithal, the Qi and the Blood service your brain to recharge your synapses to enable coherent thought to begin.

'Deciding' is more of a Gallbladder and Liver function (chapter 7), and sometimes a Small Intestine function (chapter 12),

---

3. This destructive (or "K'o") cycle, based on the 5 Element system explains how a parent Energy Organ can imbalance its grandchild Energy Organ. It shows another way Chinese medicine has developed to get people healthy again.

4. Hence, over-thinking, boredom, obsessions, worry, constant anxiety etc all deplete the Spleen and lead to stagnant Qi.

depending on circumstances. 'Memory' comes mostly under the Kidney function but is also supported by the Blood.

The default way of thinking for the Spleen is to be helpful. It is a wonderful quality! People like this if asked for help often cannot say "No!" As a result, they can be taken advantage of, which leads to worry, anxiety, guilt and exhaustion.

This exhaustion makes Spleen Qi stagnate, leading often to weak digestion, loose stools and more importantly, Spleen Blood deficiency which itself often then leads to Heart Blood deficiency – see also chapter 10.

C Controls Blood, Muscles and the limbs.

This follows on from A. above.
With a healthy Spleen and excellent Blood, you will have –

- Good mental powers of thought

- Well-nourished skin

- Excellent eyesight

- Strong nails

- Good powers of recuperation

- Attractive musculature, strong limbs

- A reliable heartbeat that is well regulated

- The ability to heal fast, to recover from shock quickly

- Good colour

- Good sleep to feel great in the morning

- … plus far more than I can cover in this paragraph.

D Manages or controls the raising or ascending of Qi.

The Liver also ascends Qi, but cannot do it properly without a healthy Spleen. Mainly this means that you can think clearly and quickly, absorb information fast and cope well in adversity.

E Is said to open into the mouth, controls saliva, and manifests on the lips.

Full, healthy lips suggest a healthy Spleen. People who chew or pick at their lips often betray the beginnings of Spleen Qi stagnation.

Symptoms of Spleen Qi stagnation

In the literature of Chinese medicine, there is little mention of Spleen Qi stagnation. In my opinion, this is not because it does not exist but because its symptoms tend to be included in other forms of Qi stagnation, e.g. Liver Qi stagnation.

Also, many Spleen Qi stagnation-like syndromes are dealt with under other headings, such as Spleen Qi deficiency, Spleen Qi sinking, Blood Deficiency of various kinds, Cold Damp invading the Spleen, Spleen and Lung Qi deficiency.

The syndromes mentioned in Italics above are all different kinds of Spleen problems. Diagnosing them correctly and precisely helps your acupuncturist or herbalist know what to do.

I have tried here to isolate and bring out what I believe are specifically Spleen symptoms arising from Spleen Qi stagnation. First, symptoms common to all kinds of Qi stagnation, which are covered in Chapter 7, include:

- A distending or bloating sensation somewhere in the trunk, but with Spleen Qi stagnation, this occurs mostly first in the abdomen, but can begin in the throat where it feels like a lump that you cannot swallow.

- Some people feel as if the back of their throat is pressing upwards and forwards onto the root of their tongue, blocking the throat and making it harder to swallow.

- It can happen if you are nervous or worried or suddenly confronted with the unexpected, or embarrassed.

- The feeling may then move its location into the chest

- Low spirits, negative outlook

- Impatience or irritability – may feel panicky

- Mood swings

- Deep sighs, deep breaths even when inactive

- Yawning even when not tired and frequent attempts to 'catch the breath' even when there is no other sign of difficulty breathing, faster breathing

- In this syndrome of Spleen Qi deficiency, the muscles behind your thighs – under the Bladder channel – are OK. So ascending is not so bad. Descending puts more strain on the anterior muscles lying under the Spleen and Stomach channels. If, say after an accident or illness, your thigh muscles are weak, doing leg-extension exercises may be sensible for a little while, but move on to squats as soon as possible because squats strengthen both front and back thigh muscles, toning Stomach, Spleen and Bladder channels, so providing more stability. Squats require you to balance, always good for Liver and Kidney Qi.

- However, make sure you get help from someone who can show you how to do the squats with good 'form'. Good form means you won't hurt your back, won't fall over, and will improve faster.

- Pulse: often wiry

- Tongue may be a little red on the sides and swollen and/
  or pale in the centre and towards the front.

If those are the basic symptoms, most of which apply to all forms of Qi stagnation, what about other symptoms applicable to Spleen Qi stagnation?

Here is where Spleen Qi stagnation rapidly turns into other Spleen syndromes. These are longer-lasting than the basic Spleen Qi stagnation and without help can quickly become chronic or hard to shift.

You often find symptoms of Spleen Qi deficiency, or Spleen Blood deficiency mixed in with other symptoms. In effect, you can say that these feel like tiredness (being Spleen Qi deficiency) and the longer-term effects of tiredness as it undermines your body's ability to renew itself (Spleen Blood deficiency).

Spleen Qi Deficiency symptoms

- Tiredness is common. Arms and especially the legs
  feel constantly weak and tired. You find it becomes an
  effort to walk, to ascend or descend stairs or hills. Curiously,
  although it is hard work to climb there may be more anxiety
  about descending. This is because when descending you are
  mostly using your quadriceps muscles, on the front of your
  thigh: when climbing, you also use the muscles at the rear of
  your thigh, which the Bladder channel runs through. (The
  Spleen and Stomach channels run down through
  the quadriceps muscles so if their channels are weak so also
  may be the muscles under them.)

- Tiredness may be noticeable even in the forenoon
  (because, in Chinese medicine, from 7am to 11am approx is

when your Earth Phase Qi should be at its best. If your Earth Phase Qi is under-functioning, the Spleen may not be able to keep you performing well at those times. You like lying down for short naps.

- During Bowel Movements you can feel worse: and it may be hard to retain stools, leading to embarrassment. Your stools are usually loose, which means they lack clear firmness and are probably a bit runny, though not very smelly. (They become offensively smelly if you have eaten Heat producing foods, like curry, or if you already have Heat in your interior[5] as well.)

- Poor appetite and tendency to snack. If you eat at all, you instinctively prefer easily digestible foods, often sweet, and refined carbohydrates (eg crisps, alcohol, sweets, puddings). These give a quick lift to energy but later you feel more tired and want another snack. This tendency to snack on easy carbohydrates leads to weight gain. From the Western medical perspective, these snacks raise your blood sugar levels very fast. To protect your brain your body responds by pumping insulin into your blood to counteract this sugar excess, but this converts the sugar into fat.

- You put on weight fast: tendency to obesity. In young women this looks more like voluptuousness, but do not get carried away by your good fortune!

- You will find it hard to shed the weight later on so learn to be firm with yourself from the start. Try to take plenty of exercise and take care with your diet. It is all too easy to get into bad habits. Stop-Go dieting is a source of fortunes to

5. 'Heat in your Interior' is a pre-existing form of Heat arising from some other chronic condition. For instance, it could come from Heart Heat transmitted to your Small Intestine or, in a woman, from Damp-Heat in her womb from a pathogenic factor, perhaps a Sexually Transmitted Disease (STD).

publishers, and it will be YOUR money and YOUR body they make money from.

- Often you pick your lips or nose or chew your lips. Occurs if you are worried, or even if you are just thinking intently. You may also bite your fingernails or the skin on your fingers.

- Thinking is an effort and it is hard to think things through. You frequently feel a bit depressed or sad. In effect, Clear Qi is failing to rise up to your head to help you deliberate soundly.

- Many digestive problems, including discomfort or distension after food, loose stools, indigestion, noisy rumblings, gas (either up or downwards). In extreme conditions food may weigh like a stone in your abdomen after eating.

- Phlegm and Catarrh. This affects the mucous membranes in your nose first – usually – then builds up in your throat and starts to invade your lungs. Turbid Qi, in the form of phlegm, isn't transformed and so builds up. What this means is that soon after eating, (or if it is a large meal, even during your meal) you will notice a slight dampness in your nose. You may need to blow it, in which case a transparent or slightly white mucus will appear. This is a direct result of over-stressing your Spleen Qi. Either you have eaten too much, or you have eaten foods that your Spleen cannot deal with properly at that time. As the dampness increases, phlegm then starts to affect your Lung Qi.

- Pulse Empty

- Tongue is pale and, with Qi stagnation, may have indentations along its sides.

What HAPPENS NEXT if Spleen Qi Stagnation is not resolved?

As the condition continues it progresses to more serious states, some of which may be recognisable as discrete diagnosable conditions in Western medicine.

For example, you get piles (haemorrhoids extending down from the anus or rectum) and varicose veins, perhaps from sitting too long and not taking enough exercise. This may not seem important if your doctor has convenient remedies.

However, in theory this is more serious than you think. Why? Because it is a deterioration in your body's anatomy, which is harder to change than mere transitory, even if painful, symptoms.

Once an elastic band has been stretched too far, it won't return to its former shape. Fortunately, your body does have powers of recuperation and repair, but they are not inexhaustible.

Of course, some people have an inherited tendency to these ailments. In that case, Spleen Qi stagnation will hasten the arrival of the inherited malfunction. For them it is all the more important to take care of their Spleen Qi! Other syndromes can arise from Spleen Qi stagnation, one of the chief being Spleen Blood deficiency:

Spleen Blood deficiency

In addition to the Spleen Qi deficiency symptoms mentioned above you may get the following Blood deficiency symptoms:

- Poor sleep. With Spleen deficiency, you wake up around 2am or 3am. Often you will remain awake for several hours.
  (Why? In Chinese medicine your Mind – your Shen – is said to rest in your Blood when you sleep. If your Blood is deficient,

your Shen cannot rest comfortably in it, like a bed that is too short for you.)

- Sleep may be un-refreshing unless you continue to stay in bed and sleep between 7am and 11am, the Chinese clock times for the Spleen and Stomach, when they come back on stream and can help make up for the deficiency.

- Tendency not to obesity but to lose weight or be thin. Not enough Blood to fill you out.)

.

Weight loss is one of the signs a doctor considers in diagnosing cancer, but there are many other causes of weight loss, so please do not fret. Prolonged weight loss without adequate explanation though is always to worry.

.

- If you are a woman, your periods may cease or become very short or meagre. (Not enough Blood.)

- Your joints may ache. (Not enough Blood to feed or repair them.) 'Arthritis?' wonders your doctor.

What else HAPPENS NEXT as your Spleen Blood becomes deficient?

If Spleen Blood becomes more deficient, possibly exacerbated by Qi stagnation, you may get other signs of Spleen Blood deficiency as it progresses into more serious conditions including Internal Wind and Liver Yang rising.

These additional conditions may approach (but it would be unusual to get all of them!) conditions recognised by Western medicine:

- Headaches, often from temple to temple. Often like little hammers. ('Cluster headaches'? 'Migraine'?)

- A sense of emotional vulnerability or over-sensitivity, and a dislike of company, perhaps fearing rejection. You are easily discouraged. Some may accuse you of cowardice.

- The tendency to become obsessive about things or about something in particular. Of course, you will not see it that way! – You will regard your concern as being perfectly sane. Others may think you have gone OTT.

- Excitability and a nervous or anxious disposition. Easily frustrated or vexed; fidgety; restlessness.

- Trembling of your fingers

- Poor co-ordination

- Facial tics including of the eyelids

- Photophobia – dislike of strong light such as sunlight

- You will feel worse during your menses (because, if you have menses, you are losing blood which you are already short of)

- Palpitations, if Blood deficiency also causes Heart Blood deficiency

If you also become susceptible to what is called 'Damp'[6]*, a further range of conditions arise.*

- Swelling, probably initially often round knees (because the Spleen cannot do its basic function of transforming and transporting, so fluids build up)

- If you are a woman, you may get leucorrhoea, a discharge, profuse, albuminous, which can feel like warm water trickling down (because the weakened Spleen cannot hold things in place, nor can it prevent damp conditions building up)

- Apthmous ulcers in your mouth. This is when you get not

6. http://www.acupuncture-points.org/damp.html

merely Damp but Heat too. These swellings are
partly because of Damp. Can be Candida Albicans – 'Thrush'.

- Diarrhoea (because the Spleen Qi cannot hold things
  in place). If Heat is present, this diarrhoea will be urgent and
  with a strong smell.

- Pulse: Fine or Choppy

- Tongue: pale and thin

*What happens if Spleen Qi, instead of sending energy up, allows it
to fall?*

If Spleen Qi lets things fall down because it fails to send energy
upwards, there will already be signs of Spleen Qi deficiency.
You may not have noticed them, or you may have thought they
were normal for your age, or you may have overlooked them
because you have had them for so long that you cannot
remember when they started.

Signs of Spleen Qi failing to ascend might include (but are not
limited to):

- Varicose veins, especially along the pathway of the Spleen
  channel, which runs down the medial anterior thigh and leg.
  But varicose veins anywhere are partly because Spleen Qi is
  failing to hold things in place. Veins tend to stand out more
  on thin people. This is not necessarily because of Spleen Qi
  failure. But in heavily muscled people who weight train
  excessively, if their veins do not hide away within a few
  hours of exercising, this may indicate overuse of Spleen Qi
  through over-exertion and over-strain.Actually, over-lifting
  and other sports where there is great effort can strain what
  is called Kidney Yang. As Kidney Yang supports Spleen Qi the
  latter also suffers. Over-enlarged veins that have lost their

elasticity are one sign of this syndrome. What's the explanation for varicose ulcers? They start as varicose veins (from Spleen Qi deficiency) but the additional onset of Blood stagnation leads to the appearance of internal Heat, giving the ulcer.

- Bruises and trauma that fail to mend suggest Spleen Qi falling.

- Beer belly: or enlarged abdomen hanging down and outwards.

- Sagging posture – not able to hold a proper erect position. (And men, this can apply to your erections too though there are other, usually more important reasons for erectile failure.)

- Prolapse, anywhere, for example of the womb, stomach, anus, bladder or haemorrhoids (piles). Nowadays we recognize that long-distance air travellers can get venous thrombosis if they do not move enough. The same goes for sitting anywhere for too long.

- Abdominal distension after you eat, with the tendency to obesity

- Loose stools and frequency of urging to stool

- Frequent urination or urination on coughing or sneezing

- Very profuse menstrual flow (menorrhagia) from weakness.

- Bearing down sensation, often in the womb, mainly before periods. This sensation can sometimes be felt down into the thighs. This bearing down sensation does sometimes occur in other places, e.g. the lumbar area.

Q. Why do you get Spleen Qi descending symptoms?
A. The same reasons you get Spleen Qi deficiency symptoms.

However, a frequent additional cause is that of being required to stand still a lot or to walk very slowly for long periods of time.

Walking fast for a while, or running on the spot, or putting your feet up, or doing one of the upside down yoga postures, can each alleviate this a bit if your condition is not too bad.

Sitting, un-moving, for too long, can prevent Spleen Qi moving Qi and Blood around. Long-distance air travellers are warned about this, but anyone sitting still for too long is at risk of venous thrombosis, when the Blood moves so little that you get Blood Stasis[7], a syndrome recognised in Chinese medicine.

.

*If you have been sitting glued to this book and here you still are after more than 300 pages, **please get up and go for a walk!** In fact, abandon the book for today and **do something completely different.***

.

What other problems might arise starting with Spleen Qi deficiency? Given that Spleen Qi transforms and transports, what happens *when this function fails?*

1. If it does not transform, you start to get Blood deficiency mainly of Heart Blood [because the Heart is the Mother of the Spleen via the 5 Element system – see appendix 4 so if the Child – Spleen, fails, it over-strains the Heart. However, in the Four Phase diagram, the picture is clearer because the Spleen is at the centre and all the other Energy Organs depend on it].

The main additional symptoms of Heart Blood deficiency are palpitations, more insomnia (or sleep often disturbed by dreaming), occasional dizziness and poor memory.

If you are female, your periods will reduce in amount or frequency. As with Spleen Qi deficiency you will have

7. http://www.acupuncture-points.org/blood-stasis.html

a tendency to worry, to get anxious, and your stools will be loose.

Why the palpitations? – you ask. Because, lacking blood in quality (ie Blood) even if not in quantity, the Heart has to pump more vigorously, or desperately, to enable good blood to do its job round the body. *Like a speedboat's propeller out of the water, it whizzes too fast from time to time when there is insufficient resistance from the Blood, because of its deficiency.*

What about the dreaming? Because your Mind (your Shen, controlled by the Heart), which should rest quietly in your Blood during sleep, finds its bed – the Blood – rather uncomfortable and un-welcoming, so cannot sleep deeply and keeps dreaming and half-waking.

2. Another kind of Blood deficiency caused by Spleen Qi deficiency is *Liver Blood deficiency*.

.

Deficiency-type conditions nearly always improve from rest. In this case, i.e. Liver Blood deficiency, closing your eyes gives time for your body to replenish Liver Blood so helps headache and tired eyes.

.

With Liver Blood deficiency you do not get the palpitations but you do get most of the other Spleen Qi deficiency symptoms, plus little black spots in the eyes, called 'floaters'; your vision is not so good (e.g. at night) and your eyes tire easily.

For example, long hours in front of a computer screen or cinema or TV are very tiring and give you a mild headache that improves when you close your eyes.

With Liver Blood deficiency you may also get muscle cramps, and finger and toe nails that are brittle or crumbling, discoloured, scaling, soft, splitting or thin. Your skin will probably be dry too.

3. Alternatively, the Spleen fails to support the Lungs, [of which it is Mother via the Five Element system]. This then gives both Spleen and Lung Qi deficiency.

In addition to the other Spleen Qi deficiency symptoms, you get Lung deficiency symptoms like shortness of breath, a quiet or fragile voice, an occasional cough, sweating when you would not expect to, and the tendency to catch frequent colds. This can become a chronic condition, though it usually responds very quickly to acupuncture.

4. Spleen Qi fails to 'transform' Damp. Damp is like thick fog, tiring and heavy, its moisture weighing you down. This can be like post-viral fatigue, M.E etc, with aching[8].

Aetiology of Spleen Qi deficiency. What makes this worse or causes it to start?

- Besides stress leading to worry and anxiety or, as the Chinese call it, 'over-thinking':

- Eating an inappropriate diet for your metabolism. Usually this means cold, raw, iced, fatty food. Not properly chewing and over-eating make it worse.

- Bad eating habits bring it on, including snacking instead of eating properly sit-down meals, and rushing meals. It also includes eating when your belly is already full ofbeer or similar. See below for some suggestions for how you can help yourself.

- Exposure to damp living conditions, like a damp basement, or a damp climate where you cannot get properly warm, rested and dry between periods of damp exposure.

- Chronic disease of any kind, or being ill with a disease for a long time, tends to weaken your Spleen making you more

8. For more on this see http://www.acupuncture-points.org/chronic-fatigue-syndrome-acupuncture.html

susceptible to Spleen Qi deficiency symptoms, and to Spleen Qi stagnation.

- Lung Qi deficiency can lead to this. You have Lung Qi deficiency if you are always catching colds, your voice is often weak and you have a slight cough (often worse as you get tired or after eating), you are short of breath and you do not like cold weather.

- Lung Qi deficiency can lead to this because the Lung and Spleen Energy Organs work closely together to provide you with blood and energy.

- Weakness in one often leads to weakness in the other. There is another reason too, which is that in the Five Element system the Spleen is the Mother Energy Organ for the Lung.

- Overwork affects Kidney energy, which also weakens Spleen Qi. Overwork here mainly means over-thinking. Students studying too long or into the small hours become susceptible to this. Of course, being young, they manage better for longer than older people, but the lack of sleep and over-use of Liver Blood (used up staring at computer screens, television and other screens, and reading) drains and weakens the Spleen.

What can You do to help yourself if you have Spleen Qi deficiency?

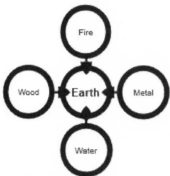

[*Observations over the centuries by the Chinese culminated in what we call the Five Element or Four Phase system. When reading the following, you do not need to understand this system fully but when and if you do study it you will understand why the following applies. Read more about it in appendix 4.*

For the Earth element, this system of thought suggests what might benefit people with Spleen and Stomach problems. For Earth, all the other Elements have to be considered – Wood, Fire, Metal and Water. The following uses some of those ideas. Most references to the Five Element/Four Phase system in this section are in square brackets in case you want to skip over them.]

A If your problem is caused by Qi stagnation...

... you must find out what emotion is causing this, because if you do not sort this out nothing else you do, even if right, will work for long:

- Frustration: inability to make progress, or to reach targets set for you. This becomes a big worry for you.

- Too many jobs to do, even if you enjoy them and want to do them. In other words too many balls to keep up in the air.

When you started, you had the energy and time to do them, and you thought you were organised! Now keeping up with them is harder and you start sleeping badly (waking up around 2am or 3am for several hours, when you may sweat a bit too.)

- Anger. Anger from worry and tension directly implicates your Liver Qi which is said to 'attack' your Spleen causing Spleen symptoms.

- A situation of negative aggression at work

- Worry or Anxiety or Grief: not so easy to 'sort out'. Do the other things explained below to maintain as much health as you can until you get over your loss. Also read the suggestions made under the Lung Energy Organ (chapter 9).

- Reminder: Qi stagnation is trapped energy: your trapped energy: though its symptoms may be unpleasant it is a huge source of potential for good when you allow it to move or to change you.

B Diet and eating habits.

[Food and nutrition are at the heart of the Earth Element.] It is very important to get your diet right. Food can make you ill, by which I mean that you should not merely avoid foods containing artificial substances (herbicides, fungicides, pesticides, colourings, flavourings, preservatives ...) but you should eat food with the right energy for your particular needs.

Getting your diet right can make a huge difference to how you feel. However, you have to adapt it to circumstances. What suits you on a cold day may be quite different to what is best for you on a warm day.

Also, if you are ill, Chinese medicine often suggests foods quite different to those you should eat when well.

.

For those of us with a tendency to Spleen Qi problems (most of us!), this means mainly eating foods that

- are not sweet to taste (but there's more to this than meets the eye), and
- you should eat most of your food warm.

What is the wrong kind of food for your metabolism?

There are many theories about finding your own food type.

They vary from those based on your blood type to Sheldon's somato-typing[9] which has many similarities to the Ayurvedic[10] systems of classification. There are food combining diets and diets that concentrate on protein and reduce carbohydrate. For weight management, there are hundreds of suggestions, from taking what are in effect diuretics (not recommended) to – short-term – eating just one food-type. There are brown-rice diets and what is currently reckoned to be the best overall diet, the Mediterranean diet.

The first thing to realise is that what suits someone else may not suit you, and ideally, you should experiment cautiously to discover what does suit you.

If you are serious about finding a diet that suits you, read Dr Mercola's Beginner's Nutrition Plan[11]. Whichever diet plan suits you –

- Chew well, and take your time to eat food.
- Do not eat in a rush. Make meals a time to relax.

9. Atlas of Men, William Sheldon, 1954
10. Ayurveda: ancient Indian health and life system.
11. http://www.mercola.com/nutritionplan/beginner.htm

- Do not eat on the job, snatching food as and when you can.

- Do not eat large meals before you go to sleep.

- Try not to eat when you are exhausted. If exhausted, have a small snack while you prepare your meal, to give you some energy. Ideally, then rest a little before eating, to recover your energy.

- If you are chilled or very cold, ideally get warm first. For example have a warm bath or shower, or sit with your back to a radiator or beside a fire. Eat only when you are warm.

- Eat in gentle, courteous company if possible.

- For Spleen type problems, Chinese tradition favours cooked food, eaten warm. The reason given is that this does not chill your stomach. Your stomach needs a level of heat to function – we would probably call this stomach acid in the West but this is not what the Chinese theory means. They meant Stomach Yang, which is a more inclusive term meaning the ability to 'cook' what you eat. Like a downpour of rain on a fire, cold or chilled food may dowse your Stomach's flame or seriously weaken your Stomach's ability to digest what you eat. That means you are advised to *avoid food or drink that is*:
  - Raw
  - Cold
  - Iced or chilled. If you must eat raw, cold, iced or chilled food because not to do so would damage relationships, try to drink or eat something warm before and then again after the cold dishes/drinks.

NB This advice is for when you have Spleen Qi deficiency. When you are well, some raw food, such as salads made of fresh vegetables, is both good for you and not a challenge for your

Spleen. However, on a cold day when you are feeling chilled, eat warm, cooked food[12].

Conversely, on a very hot day when you are hot, you may be able without mishap to eat some chilled or raw food even when you still have some Spleen deficiency.

Also avoid:

- More hot or spicy than you are used to

- Very oily or fatty food. This is not to say that fat in food is bad for you (though hydrogenated fat is definitely bad for you). You need fat, including saturated fats and omega 3 and omega 6 unsaturated fats which your body cannot manufacture for itself. Many modern diets suggest you reduce the saturated fat in your diet. Increasing evidence points to saturated fat as being necessary for health[13].
  • Sweet food or sweetened food, even if sweetened with artificial sweeteners. Sugar and sweet food definitely damages Spleen Qi and sweeteners fool it for a while but introduce other problems.

How the ancient Chinese classified food

So far I have not mentioned the actual nutritional qualities of food, the vitamins and minerals, the protein, the carbohydrate etc.

The Chinese lacked our scientific knowledge for what constitutes adequate nutrition. They got round this by suggesting you eat food from five basic food groups.

Since nearly all their food became cultivated only over time, the implicit presumption was that all food they ate would be what we now call organic and, in the case of meat, free range. It therefore lacked antibiotics, herbicides,

---

12. For more on hot and cold foods, see http://www.acupuncture-points.org/hot-foods.html
13. Am J Clin Nutr. 2010 Mar;91(3):535-46. doi: 10.3945/ajcn.2009.27725. Epub 2010 Jan 13

pesticides, fungicides and artificial fertilisers. The five groups were based on the Five Element or Five Phase system that classified food by its appearance, smell and, particularly, taste[14].

Element or Phase	Flavour	Taste examples
Wood	Sour	Vinegar, lemon
Fire	Bitter	(Bitter) coffee, almonds, watercress
Earth	Sweet	Carrots, rice, chicken, breast milk
Metal	Pungent	Ginger, garlic, cinnamon
Water	Salty	Fish, pork, seaweed

More on this question of Food

You will notice in the table above that sugar does not appear under Sweet, nor salt under Salty. Instead, I have given examples of the foods that are regarded as being of the nature of the taste, even if they do not always taste as such.

For example, the ancient Chinese perhaps lacked anything in quantity that was sweet as we think of it (though of course bees existed, but probably were not husbanded for their honey as they are now, nor was honey used often except as a treat) except in the natural form of food.

Chew a few raw grains of rice for a little while and you will soon notice the sweet taste as it emerges from the interaction between the rice's carbohydrate and the enzymes in your saliva.

More important to them was that the foods in question seemed specifically to encourage the Energy Organs of the Element in question (for example, the Kidney and Bladder in the Water Element) to function properly when taken in balance with the other tastes.

It would be ridiculous to suggest that eating one grain,

14. http://www.acupuncture-points.org/nutrition.html

seed or drop each of coffee, sugar, pepper, salt and vinegar would constitute a healthy diet. Instead, for health, you needed to eat regularly foods selected from each group.

Selecting foods this way meant that, because they were all what we now would call organic, the foods chosen would then supply all the vitamins, minerals, proteins, carbohydrates and fats necessary for health and contained enough fibre to pass peaceably through your intestines.

It may have been rough and ready, but it was still a highly effective way of choosing foods, and easy to remember. However, please do not assume that if you have weak lungs you should just cram yourself with ginger, cumin, cinnamon and garlic. For health you need balance. Too much or too little of any flavour leads to imbalance.

For instance, you would probably eat more pungent foods if your Lungs were invaded by an external pathogenic factor and assuming you wanted to disperse the energy trapping your Lung Qi. From this perspective, it makes sense to eat garlic when catching a cold, or perhaps in advance to ward it off – though even that is a little risky because too much might make you sweat at the wrong time so making you more susceptible to the cold virus before you had developed fever.

This question of the tastes does raise an interesting question, however. Antibiotics do not work against viruses but modern science has found that some nutrients, taken at the right time, may be partially effective. For example, Zinc lozenges may shorten a cold[15]. This might suggest that Zinc should come at least partly under the Pungent taste. However, as the report referenced showed, too much zinc produced side effects like nausea and an unpleasant taste [adversely therefore

15. Science M, Johnstone J, Roth DE et al. Zinc for the treatment of the common cold: a systematic review and meta-analysis of randomized controlled trials. Canadian Medical Association Journal, May 7 2012

affecting the Lung's Mother, the Earth Energy Organ – the Spleen and Stomach].

I cannot however, see Zinc on its own being suggested by Chinese medicine for colds. Firstly, though it is a mineral necessary for life, it is a concentrated extract of food so in itself not a normal food.

Secondly, if foods containing it are eaten (seeds and nuts usually contain lots of it, for example) it comes ready-packed with a range of other ingredients that make it palatable and digestible.

Thirdly, if used as concentrated zinc it would be combined in a formula with herbs – which are themselves concentrated foods – to balance and promote its action.

A bigger question is how concentrated extracts of foods or herbs, based on their Taste and action in Chinese medicine, might be used to treat modern diseases.

So far, lessons using pure extracts of herbs have not been learned by practitioners of Western Medicine. For example, an extract (artemisinin) of Herba Artemisiae Annuae has been used to treat malaria. Mosquitoes adapt to it so it is losing or will lose its effect.

Had the original formula been used, in which the herb was used in its entirely and often in a formula with other herbs rather than as an extract, this resistance might not have occurred. After all, the herb has been used successfully this way for hundreds of years.

Artemisia's properties include, in Chinese herbal medicine, the ability to clear fevers from deficiency, to clear what is called Summer-heat with low fever or unremitting fever and to check malarial disorders[16], *without resistance occurring*.

16. Chinese Herbal Medicine Materia Medica 1986, Eastland Press Chapter 2.

C Stability and Rest

[Stability, rest and family support are very Earth-like qualities in the Five Element system.]

Avoid very Yang influences (see Chapter 4) and give yourself time to benefit from Yin resources. We all started in a womb, where everything was provided. We just lay there, slept and grew. Food was pumped directly into us via the umbilical cord: no need to choose or chew it. It was safe, warm and comfortable – a very safe Yin environment. Try to emulate this for yourself at home.

- Go home or somewhere safe, warm, quiet and comfortable where, if possible, your needs can be met.

- This usually means lying down and being fed what your body needs.

- Simple foods are, traditionally, rice gruel and chicken soup – tasty, easily digestible and nourishing.

- If you wish, listen to quiet, restful music that is not too intellectual. You do not want to have to think about it because thinking hard uses up Spleen Qi!

- Sounds of the sea and waves on a beach, or of rain falling on a forest, are very restful to many people. There are many cell-phone apps that can provide this sort of sound.

- Lie somewhere that has mellow, quiet colours and is not too bright. Strong light and bright colours use up Liver Blood. As Liver Blood comes from the actions of the Spleen when it transforms food, bright colours that strain Liver Blood eventually drain the Spleen.

- Avoid people who are needy. If you are in the helping professions, your life is made up of helping others. If you are ill, you yourself need help so do not feel guilty about avoiding those who normally depend on you.

- Even if you are not in the helping professions, try to cut yourself off from being in demand all the time. Switch off your cell-phone. Move the landline telephone to another room and tell someone else to answer it and not to disturb you every time.

- Keep warm. Put a warm wheat bag, or hot water bottle, on your stomach.

- Do not receive visitors until you feel stronger.

- Sleep.

- As you get better, to begin with take only gentle exercise. Do not rush back to the gym or into competitive sports.

- As soon as you can tolerate them, eat a small amount of food from each category, avoiding sugar or sweetened food.

- Include pro-biotics that populate your digestive tract with beneficial micro-organisms to help your digestion and immunity. (However, do not take them as chilled yogurt, but if you have no other source, take it with something warm e.g. in warm soup.)
  Why did not the ancient Chinese include yogurt in their diet? Probably: not enough milk, and the microorganisms occurred naturally in many foods along with dirt both of which probably increased their immunity. Nowadays, city-dwellers buy from supermarkets which preserve food, even fruit, by specially treating it to irradiate microorganisms, good or bad, and dirt.

- Try to avoid medicinal treatment, especially treatment that kills the good microorganisms in your body, such as happens with antibiotics.

- Learn techniques to relax your muscles. There are

many books and internet sites that tell you how to relax muscles [muscles are said, in Chinese medicine, to be 'ruled' by the Spleen]. Progressive muscle relaxation, for example, makes you use your Spleen-centred thinking facility to gently tense then relax all the muscles in your head, body and extremities.

D Exercise

Exercise usually means vigorous movement, preferably of the whole body, walking fast, or running or as in physical sports. However, if you have deficient Spleen Qi, much lighter exercise is appropriate, until you have rested and recovered enough.

How often and for how long should you exercise? Ideally, you should exercise daily and for a minimum of 20 minutes during which you move fast enough to get slightly out of breath. But you could do different levels of intensity on different days, light one day, heavier or more intense the next. Start with very light exercise: gradually increase its intensity.

One form of exercise that particularly benefits [the Earth Element and] the Spleen is gardening – see below.

E Activities

[The Earth element often benefits from Fire qualities – Fire is the mother of Earth in the Five Element system – and from moving its energy towards Metal.]

Although recovering and maintaining your energy is paramount, you will normally benefit from warm, cheerful, loving people with good humour and a positive attitude. [i.e. Fire people at their best.]

- Warmth in almost any form is beneficial, including from the Sun,

- Hot stones [Hot Stone treatment is great for most Earth people],

- Moxibustion[17] on appropriate acupuncture points (see Treatments below),

- Hands-on loving massage,

- Tuneful music

- Warm colours, eg warm-coloured flowers round your home

- Gardening [an Earth pastime if ever there was one] is a wonderful occupation for you. Even a few potted plants on a sunny window ledge will help your spirit.

- Handicrafts and repairing things. Get out your pliers and woodworking tools, needle and thread, and make and mend things round your home.

- Keep a pet, preferably one that you can touch, stroke and which enjoys this and returns the favour. Learn to look after it properly and to respect its needs.

F The future – but start now!

[For Earth, Metal is the future, or where you can direct stagnating energies.]

- Start thinking about what you can leave out of your life, jettison, throw away, discard or give away – even sell.

- Clean up and tidy your home and work-place.

- Learn to meditate – see http://www.acupuncturepoints.org/ meditation.html

- Learn to breathe properly. Your Lungs and Spleen work closely together. Helping one helps the other. See appendix 7.

17. http://www.acupuncture-points.org/moxibustion.html

- Go hill-walking or travelling to see a bigger picture.

What treatments help Spleen Qi Stagnation?

- Acupuncture and Chinese medicine know how to treat this condition.

- Gentle massage, done by someone with knowledge of the acupuncture channels. Hot stones, moxibustion and other warming treatments will feel great.

- If you are in a situation of frequent emotional strain, seek help from someone sympathetic but dispassionate, for example a friend or experienced Counsellor or therapist. However, deep 'talking' type therapy may be counterproductive when your Spleen energy is very low because it makes you do even more thinking – which is the last thing you need!

- If you have a constitutional tendency to a weak Spleen, Chinese medicine should help. Get advice on your diet. In extreme cases where you are clearly always deficient in an important vitamin, for example, you may need to take that vitamin for a while. However, take advice on the best way to take it so that you absorb what you eat and therefore do not waste it.

- If you can, go on holiday to somewhere that they really understand how food, if each meal is adjusted to your needs, can quickly promote healing. Just remember that what you are given to eat may not be what you are used to. If taking extra vitamins this way, try to find a source that makes them from organic foods, i.e. not manufactured from chemicals, and which supplies them in balance with other food extracts.

- Emotional Freedom Technique can help with the tendency to

worry, but in my experience is less effective with the physical side of the syndromes mentioned here.

·

The next chapter is on Bladder Qi stagnation. Fortunately, it affects few people, but when it happens, it is painful. Read chapters 14 and 15 together, since both relate to the Water phase.

CHAPTER 14

Bladder Qi Stagnation

Bladder Qi stagnation takes one main form, and if you get it, you may need help. It can be very painful.

Essence of Bladder Qi Stagnation

The most common person having Bladder Qi stagnation has a nervous system that has been made very sensitive to stimuli, not necessarily all the time, but in certain conditions, being for example after:

- Accidents
- A disturbed liver function
- Exhaustion
- Neuralgic pains
- Overwork
- Social drugs like tobacco
- Strong emotions like fright or rage, jealousy, from bad news
- Surgical operations
- Vaccination

This condition often generates a feeling of fear, great anxiety and nervous tension. Read more about it in chapter 15, on Kidney Qi. In this chapter you will find out about:

- The Bladder Energy Organ's time
- The direction it sends Qi
- The emotions that affect the Bladder
- The commonest symptoms arising from Qi stagnation – Damp-Heat
- What YOU can do about it
- What treatments help

Bladder function and time

The Bladder time is between 3pm and 5pm every day. Its function in Traditional Chinese Medicine is broader than in Western medicine. This time (and also between 3am and 5am) is sometimes when Bladder Qi symptoms are worse.

It acts as a store for the fluids of the body, and then after transforming those not needed, stores urine before it is excreted. That storage function is reflected in the length of the Bladder channel. It is the longest channel, with 67 points lying along it from your eye over the top of your head down your back to your foot. It has important relationships with all the other Energy organs in the body.

For example, on your back it has special points that work directly on each of your Energy Organs. From a Western physiological point of view, the Bladder channel runs down alongside the spine and spinal cord, from which nerves branch out to all parts of your body, including your lungs, heart, kidneys, gastro-intestinal tract, your womb, your arms, legs and your skin. If your spine, spinal cord and nerves are in good condition, your health is likely to be better.

Bladder moves Qi downwards

When it stops moving Qi downwards, you get the inability to urinate, with retention of urine, with uncomfortable swellings, possibly pain: swelling in your joints, for instance. You may get swelling on the medial (i.e. the nose) side of your eyes, or a sense of fullness in your head, possibly headaches and other signs of energy not moving down from your head.

Other signs might be cloudy vision, mucus in your eyes, tooth pain, vertigo, and a sensation of eye pressure. Some of these are signs of Turbid Qi not descending. See chapter 1, page 32.

Emotional strain and Bladder Qi stagnation

Bladder Qi Stagnation is not much recognised in Chinese medicine, but there are a range of emotions which affect your Bladder Qi in a particular way. These emotions are connected with the Water Phase. They include long-term:

- Fear
- Sense of persecution
- Jealousy
- Suspicion
- Subjection to negative aggression (see also chapter 12)

When these emotions, or ones similar to them, affect the Bladder Energy Organ, the energy usually eventually turns into what is called Damp-Heat in the Bladder. This

Damp here arises partly from the Spleen Energy organ, because these emotions also make you 'over-think': worry!

Over-thinking weakens the transforming function of the Spleen, leading to the build-up of Damp that deploys to the Bladder. The Heat either arises naturally within the Bladder when Damp exists there or perhaps comes from transformation of mental energy (eg fear) into physical Heat.

.

It may seem a strange idea that 'mental' energy can transform into 'Heat' in the body, but it's been noticed by Chinese medicine for millennia. It's not that hard to understand because if someone gets very emotional or angry, they often get hot. Where that heat ends up is very important in Chinese cause disease.

Symptoms of Damp-Heat in the Bladder

Nearly all the symptoms are felt in the bladder itself or on urination:

- Burning Pain when urinating

- Urgent need to urinate frequently

- Blood in the urine (from Heat which burns through to release blood)

- Urination may stop in mid-flow and be hard to restart (a symptom of the Bladder energy not being able properly to descend, and of Damp obstructing the natural flow of urine)

- Urine is discoloured: often a strong yellow colour or turbid (from Heat). It may eventually produce small stones.

- Fever and /or a sense of heat

- Thirstiness but little desire to drink (from Damp in the system blocking the sense of thirst)

- Eye pain, inflammation, discharge or discomfort:

this symptom I have noticed but it is not in the classic
picture of this syndrome. (The Bladder channel begins
just medial to the eye and I have mentioned some of
the symptoms under 'Qi not descending' properly, above.)

.

This is an example of turbid fluids not being sent down – see
Chapter 1.

.

Also,   Damp-Heat   in   one   organ   can   cause   it
elsewhere. Discharges from the eye are sometimes also caused
by Stomach Heat, see chapter 11.
Are there any other reasons for these symptoms?
Excessive exposure to damp cold conditions can produce this
reaction in Yang-type people i.e. those with good circulation.
Even people with poor circulation can get it if their body reacts
to the Cold by producing Heat symptoms.

What HAPPENS NEXT if Bladder Damp-Heat is unresolved?

In susceptible patients, notably the elderly, prolonged Damp-
Heat in the Bladder eventually begins to drain their Yin
resources, such as those of Kidney Yin. This can signal the
appearance of symptoms recognised by Western medicine.

• Kidney Yin deficiency makes them restless, prone to
  hot sweats in the night, with back ache and sore joints,
  loss of memory and concentration, loss of teeth and
  hearing and a range of other symptoms often associated
  with ageing.
  o These Kidney Yin deficiency symptoms of
  poor concentration, anxiety, restlessness and memory loss
  may indicate dementia. This restlessness is a form of
  Wind, caused by deficiency. The Wind caused here is from

deficiency, like children running amok in a classroom when the teacher leaves.

- Kidney Yin deficiency can lead to an apparent excess of Yang, with high blood pressure and headaches and a sensation of *Heat*. (Heat from deficiency.)

What can YOU do to help yourself?

If the problem comes from emotional strain, you must address that first because otherwise the symptoms will return, whatever else you do.

Unfortunately, as you age, your ability to change your circumstances gradually diminishes. You cannot easily go out and get another job, or move from where you live to avoid the situation that makes you fearful.

With less strength you become more susceptible to suspicion and jealousy, and may feel forsaken or persecuted, the very emotions that generated the energy that produced this syndrome.

If, unfortunately, you cannot change your situation and the damaging emotions it produces, then you will be sorely tempted to see your doctor. If you have typical symptoms of Damp-Heat in the Bladder he will think you have cystitis from an infection.

Take it from me that when he takes a swab of your urine your doctor will discover microbes in your bladder! Just about everyone has microbes in their bladder, but in healthy people they are easily held in check by the immune system. He will then feel fully justified in prescribing antibiotics[1] and he will be most persuasive. You will find it hard to refuse.

1. Although perhaps now he will not, given that many bacteria have become resistant to antibiotics. Since most doctors, trained in orthodox Western medicine, learn only to use modern medicines to treat disease, he may not know how to help you. If experienced, perhaps he will look to some of the older remedies used before antibiotics were developed. They include acupuncture!

A complication is that when you have had this syndrome for some time, whatever the reasons for it, you will feel drained by it, your immune system will be weakened and you will be harbouring even more microbes. Almost all antibiotics have a primary cooling effect, which is why you will be glad of them. Their secondary effect (for more on Primary and Secondary effects of drugs see chapter 8), however, weakens your Kidney energy, especially your Kidney Yin energy and your Spleen energy[2].

So you get kidney or renal problems in addition to those you started with, with the doubtful additional pleasures of damp in the form of candida from having used the antibiotics.

What can YOU do about this, assuming you want to avoid antibiotics?

- Drinking water is an obvious solution, except that the amount you need to drink may be considerable and neither what you feel you can swallow (remember you may be thirsty but you probably do not want to drink too much) nor what your kidneys can easily manage.

- That said, you must try to drink more fluid. It does not have to be cold water. It can be warm, as in tea, which tends to have a gently cooling effect as well, even when drunk hot.

- If you have a prolonged fever, then you should seek therapeutic help, even if from your doctor who will undoubtedly have ways to help you in the short term.

- Some foods, and juices like cranberry will increase your need to urinate. However, the following foods traditionally help to clear damp-heat conditions:

- – Fruit: umeboshi plum (a Japanese salted

2. For more on the energetic effect of modern medicines from the Chinese medical perspective see http://www.acupuncture.com/herbs/pharma.htm

plum preparation), bearberry, bilberry,
blackberry, blackcurrant, blueberry, cranberry, raspberry,
all unsweetened, of course, (because if sweetened,
the Spleen energy to clear Damp may be compromised), and
preferably taken warm.o Beans: kidney beans, correctly
cooked, of course.- Vegetables: celery, asparagus, Chinese
cabbage, (I would add sauerkraut).- Herbs, spices: tamarind,
gentian (can be taken in Swedish Bitters, but, I would better
say, without the alcohol additives), goldenseal,
meadowsweet, nettle. Wikipedia lists other bitter foods such
as "cocoa, South American mate, marmalade, bitter gourd,
beer (due to hops), bitters, olives, citrus peel, many plants in
the Brassica family, dandelion greens, wild chicory".

.

Most of the herbs and foods listed here deal just with the Damp-Heat. They do not deal with the Qi stagnation causing it. Whilst there are Chinese herbal formulae for Qi stagnation, they palliate, not cure. So, you still have to sort out the underlying problem.

.

- You may notice that some of these foods have a bitter taste.
  In Chinese medicine, the bitter taste helps to descend
  energy, clear heat and dry damp.
  o Probiotics taken several times a day. Please
  notice something about probiotics, however. Many
  probiotics come in yogurt, which Chinese Medicine regards
  as being very cooling. Although you have a damp-heat
  condition, if you otherwise tend to be chilly, too much
  cooling food will not help. So do not take too much yogurt.
  Instead, buy the probiotics in tablet or capsule form and
  swallow them with warm water.

- Avoid highly spiced food, hot foods, chilli, pepper, etc. They encourage heat in your body and may irritate your bladder even more.

- Avoid damp and phlegm-producing foods. So reduce dairy food, and stop eating sweet or sweetened food[3].

- Exercise? Well, you probably will not feel able to take much exercise given your urgent need to urinate frequently. But there are some stretching movements that tone the Bladder channel and may help.
  – One of the most famous yoga asanas is Paschimotthanasana where you sit on the floor, legs straight out in front of you and, trying to keep your back straight and head upright for as long as possible, lean forwards at the hips, eventually touching your toes with your fingertips and flattening your chest against your knees and thighs. If you have never done yoga before, I suggest you get someone to help you before you start! And certainly, get advice if you have a history of bad backs: good advice can show you how to begin safely. This asana stretches the Bladder channel.
  – Other asanas that calm and rest the nervous system benefit you in the long run, though your discomfort may mean you cannot do them until after you recover.
  -*Appendix 10* describes a simple series of moves specifically designed to keep your spine flexible and in good condition. Once learned, the moves take less than 2 minutes to do and can be done several times a day or when you feel tired and need to be alert. People say that they help to keep you looking young!

3. For much more about phlegm see http://www.acupuncture-points.org/phlegm-after-eating.html or read my book 'Yuck! Phlegm!

What treatments may help?

- *Acupuncture and Chinese medicine* understand this syndrome and practitioners have treated it for millennia.

- Bowen technique can also help.

- *Herbs from Western herbalists* do not use the same theoretical background as Chinese medicine practitioners, but what they do may have the same effect, even if they come at it from a different perspective.

- *Homoeopathic remedies* prescribed by an experienced homoeopath often deliver fast results. However, the homoeopathic process often looks to treat other parts of your symptom picture to prevent recurrence.

- An old solution is *hot fomentations* on the abdomen and lower back to ease the pain: nowadays we might suggest a warm bath or abdominal compress.

.

Bear in mind that deep fears producing this condition cannot easily be treated successfully long-term unless you find a way to change the situation generating them.

.

Now please chapter 15, which describes the closest the ancient Chinese doctors came to describing what we might now call the effect of inherited genetic features and burnout. Some of what they concluded may surprise you.

Effects of Kidney Qi Problems

Kidney Qi is important! Not just for its own symptoms, but because if your Kidney Qi is not reliable, it leads to other forms of Qi Stagnation.

Essence of Kidney Qi picture

Should you read this chapter? You probably should!

It affects everyone. The modern pace of life, with its demands for instant responses, gives your Kidney Qi no time to recover. Less developed societies, moving at a more sedate and physical pace, do not seem to develop Kidney Qi problems so much or so early.

Underlying this Kidney picture is the emotion of fear. This fear includes anxiety about results, about what people think of you, about the future, about your family, your finances, your position and job: anything really. It is made worse by the need to be always ready, always perfect, always fit, always alert.

Long periods of being 'stretched' like this deplete your Kidney Qi, which makes you susceptible to other forms of Qi stagnation. In this chapter you will read why your Kidney Qi is so important:

- The bedrock anchor and resource of your health
- The Kidney time according to the Chinese Clock
- Relationship between Kidney and Heart
- The Kidney Qi direction of flow
- 'Pre' and 'Post Heaven'
- Kidney 'Jing-Essence, a most important topic!
- Men and their Jing
- Women and their Jing
- Roots of Kidney Qi 'stagnation'
- Excess Kidney Qi
- Sexual Life both in Ancient China and now in the West
- Sex and Fire Energy
- Overuse of your Jing
  -In Women
  -In men
  -Masturbation
- What happens to frustrated Sexual Energy
- The symptoms of frustrated Sexual Energy
- Who suffers from frustrated Sexual Energy
- Causes of Kidney Qi deficiency
- What you can do about Qi stagnation arising from Kidney Qi deficiency
- A rare kind of Kidney Qi excess
- What treatments help Kidney Qi deficiency

As you can see, there is more here than in most chapters. After reading this you will understand why the Chinese attitude to, the Kidney Energy Organ underlies so much good sense in Chinese medicine and explains so many questions.

Kidney Qi acts as an anchor and resource. When it runs down:-

- you age!
- Mental energy deteriorates and we get nervous more quickly making us more prone to anxiety and/or conditions such as
  -Cramp
  -Frequent urination
  -Headaches and/or tinnitus (noises in ear)
  -High Blood Pressure
  -IBS (Irritable Bowel Syndrome)
  -Insomnia
  Irritability and angry outbursts
  -Muscle tension
  -Nausea
  -OCD (Obsessive Compulsive Disorder)
  -Palpitations
  -Perspiration when no obvious reason for it
  -Phobias
  -Teeth grinding
  -Tiredness and exhaustion
  -Trembling
  – your memory weakens,
  – you recover from illness or trauma more slowly and, in due course
  – your hair thins,
  – your bones thin,
  – your hearing fails and
  – your teeth fall out or need more treatment.

- When your teeth fall out you cannot eat properly and you age even faster. Who wants that?

- Breathing: you cannot 'catch' or hold your breath easily. Your Kidney energy should *'grasp'* Qi as the Lungs *'descend'* it.

- Panic? Always feeling nervous, as if a panic is not far off? It could be because your Kidney Qi is not *stabilising* you.

- In Chinese medicine your Kidney energy is the **bedrock** of your health ... What you do to sustain it will help your life be healthier and longer. In fact, the default concept here is that of strength. When you discover that you cannot maintain this inner image of yourself, you panic, you go to pieces, you lose your strength and will-power. Unfortunately, it is possible to drain this bedrock quite fast and to use up the reserves it husbands for you.

- So it is a resource worth preserving. With strong Kidney Qi you remain vibrant and adaptable, eager to learn and play, positive in outlook and usually strongly sexed. Good Kidney Qi helps your creativity and resourcefulness.

- Purifies Blood. Another action of Kidney Qi (called Kidney Yang) purifies Blood and sends the purest part upwards and outwards as moisture to nourish your lungs, eyes, thinking and skin. So dry skin, (for which weak Kidney Qi is only one possible cause out of many), may be due in part to Kidney Yang deficiency. But predominantly, Kidney Qi holds things down and helps to steady your 'ship'.

Let's look at some of those ideas more closely.
Stabiliser
Kidney Qi acts as a stabiliser, an anchor for your Qi. What that means is that when Kidney Qi is deficient, energy ascends, often as mental or physical instability, heat or pressure. As you grow older and your Kidney Qi diminishes that instability increases.

You find your balance becomes less reliable, you tend to fall or tip sideways when you get up, your heart pounds more when excited or anxious. It can also appear as a slight tremor or trembling in your fingers, though there are other reasons for this too.

Instability appears in lapses of memory, temper and hearing, and as thought processes slow. You find that you take longer to recover after acute illness or trauma. Your bones break more easily, your joints grow stiff, and the major stabilising muscles in your trunk, front and back, grow weaker, giving you a protruding abdomen and a sore back. You get anxious more easily. In short, you grow old.

Energy not held down, rises up That rising heat is felt for example by menopausal women during hot flushes and by others as a sensation of pressure or warmth in the head or ears. This starts off by happening later in the day but may eventually be present all the time.

Hypertension A doctor may diagnose high blood pressure when you report continuing headaches, caused by Kidney Qi not holding Qi down, allowing Yang energy to

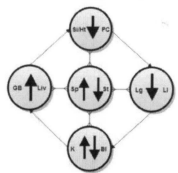

ascend when it should not.

Kidney Qi has both a holding down and a raising up function. You may remember the diagram from Chapter One on the natural flow of Qi – see also on the right here. Not only does Kidney Qi hold things down, it regulates the 'descending' of fluids, as when we urinate.

If you are healthy it does it in a controlled fashion, meaning you urinate when you are ready. However, if depleted you find yourself peeing involuntarily, for example from debility as you age or sometimes when you cough or sneeze.

And that is not all! Other forms of Kidney Qi and its effect on Qi stagnation we shall cover later.

Kidney Time[1]

The Kidney energy takes over between 5pm and 7pm . This, and from 5am to 7am, may be times when Kidney Qi problems manifest strongly. However in this case, Kidney Qi problems also often occur during Bladder Qi 'clock' times, between 3pm and 5pm and 3am to 5am.

I believe one of Chinese Medicine's greatest contributions to understanding health is in its thinking about the Kidneys. In Western medicine we think of the kidneys as merely a filtration plant, keeping the right level of substances in the blood, sending what is not needed to the bladder for excretion.

Over the last 120 years, Western Medicine has realised the important relationship between the kidneys and the heart. When blood pressure builds up, the normal procedure is to stimulate the kidneys to excrete more fluid. (In addition, of course, doctors may prescribe a range of other medications including beta-blockers to calm the mind.)

.

The ancient Chinese did not have the means to measure blood pressure any more than we did, but they certainly recognised how weak Kidney Qi allowed the Heart energy to overact dangerously on health.

.

1. See Appendix 5 on the Chinese Clock for more about this.

Kidney and Heart The connection between your Kidney and Heart has been important in Chinese medicine for at least the 2500 years they have been thinking about it.

The Kidney both Ascends and Descends Qi

The Kidney is the only Energy Organ that has both a descending and an ascending function. It can push things up when other organs are letting them fall, and hold things down when other organs would otherwise let them ascend.

What that means is that the stronger or more stable your Kidney energy, the more stable and resilient you are in the face of problems, whether they tend to make make you hyper or hypo.

Kidney Qi *descending* function It sends down, or holds down, what might otherwise rise too fast. It helps you catch your breath, hold your breath, and breathe deeply. It acts as an anchor for the Heart, steadying and controlling your thinking, particularly outbursts and restlessness.

It helps to hold you down in deep, good sleep, though good sleep also needs adequate Blood and a calm Mind. Foundation The Kidneys are also the foundation of your physical ability to renew and conceive, and mentally of your ability to concentrate and remember. They are said to house your will-power. This is your ability, having decided on an action, to carry it through, to persist, to endure setbacks, to keep going.

Kidney Qi *ascending* function Another part of their function is that together with the Spleen energy, they help send upwards what is pure and clean, to nourish the thinking. This sending of 'pure' upwards is an important action described in chapter 1.

You will notice that their time of day is the early evening (5pm – 7pm, when day turns to night -at least at the equator), and that the opposite time, 12 hours later, is when morning approaches. That opposite time we explained earlier: that of the Large Intestine, the function of which is to eliminate unwanted matter from the bowels, an important purifying, detoxifying process. The Large Intestine Qi, in Chinese medicine, amongst many other important actions, clears Heat from the skin and sends Qi downwards.

In the morning, then, the Large Intestine clears your head and cools you down from the vestigial torpors and warm humidities of sleep. At the opposite time of day, the Kidney sends clear Qi up to maintain your concentration and memory. It also supports your Liver Blood in providing clear vision in the dark.

There are acupuncture points on the Large Intestine channel that help clear the head, in terms of both blocked sinuses and of unhappy thinking. It brightens you, makes you aware and more level-headed.

The Kidney function, or one of them, is to help eliminate unwanted matter from the Blood. In terms of attitude to life, it steadies you as you approach night, providing the emotional resources you need to cope with unknown adversity. If you like, it deploys all the genetic adaptations that you have inherited and strengthens your Blood to spread them round the body. If it is not working properly, some of your inherited or acquired traits may let you down.

What does that mean? Under stress, you may resort to self-destructive tendencies: what should be clear, pure Qi ascending to the brain turns out to be grimy and contaminated, messing with your mind and inclining you to bad habits. You see this in people who have taken mind-altering drugs for too long. Their thinking gets confused, they lack purpose and direction in life, and their bodies weaken.

Sadly, this can also happen to people on prescribed medication, after a while.

Kidney Qi *Stagnation* is not much discussed in the literature of Chinese medicine. Indeed it is usually ignored or considered under different headings. Indeed, most practitioners would argue that Kidney Qi, being a resource, does not stagnate. However, there are serious implications for Qi stagnation elsewhere when Kidney Qi either gets weak or is unbalanced and blocked.

Kidney Qi, Yin and Liver

Every Energy Organ has a Mother! (This Chinese idea comes from the Five Element system – appendix 4.) If that 'Mother' Energy Organ is stable and strong, the 'Child' Energy Organ will be more secure; less inclined to show Qi stagnation symptoms, for instance.

The Liver is the 'Child' of the Kidney. A strong Kidney Qi, including Kidney Yin and Yang, means that you will be less inclined to Liver Qi stagnation and other Liver syndromes like Liver Blood deficiency[2] or Liver Yin deficiency[3].

Blueprints for your Life Kidney Qi is like the energetic structure on which everything else depends. It houses the spark of life. It is like the electric grid supplying power for the system. It is there from the start and for the system to commence there has to be an initial spark for it to kick into action at conception, even if the foetus then needs the mother's energy to maintain it.

Pre-Heaven Life depends on the presence of that initial spark which comes with the interaction between sperm and ovum. This union and the nine months of pregnancy are described in Chinese medicine as the 'Pre-Heaven' stage .

After-Heaven As life starts outside the womb, the so-called 'After-Heaven' phase, other factors come into play to provide power for the circuit. These include Qi from food and from air. Many other kinds of Qi are important then of course, not least love from the child's parents. As life carries on, what we do either strengthens or weakens our Kidney Qi.

2. http://www.acupuncture-points.org/liver-blood-deficiency.html
3. http://www.acupuncture-points.org/liver-yin-deficiency.html

Kidney Jing

Kidney Jing-essence is like the reserves of Kidney Qi. It is almost as if at birth you arrive endowed with a bottle of this precious stuff, and use it up through life. This Jing maintains life during major, exhausting, diseases or events, especially long chronic diseases and high fevers, when your Stomach and Lungs cannot provide enough Blood and Qi.

At these times, you draw on your reserves of Kidney Jing. High fevers can occur during acute disease that penetrates into the Qi level of the body, affecting Lungs and the Stomach. The Lungs and Stomach normally provide the defence energies your body needs. When the Lungs and Stomach Energy Organs do not function properly, perhaps because the disease prevents you eating and breathing enough, your body uses Jing to keep things going.

·

How disease penetrates into your body is the subject of a huge amount of thought in Chinese medicine. For instance, there are what are called the 6 Stages[4] and the 4 Levels[5].

·

The Defensive-Qi level is the first level most disease encounters as it enters, something like the way your immune system first combats disease. The Qi level is the second, ie the next deepest level, where your body tries to stop disease.

·

How Much Jing do you have? At birth, your body receives 'just so much' Jing. In health you do replace this, a very little at a time, but the Chinese say that you need the equivalent of 8 pints of blood to make one drop of Jing (they were not talking literally here!). How much Jing you have at birth depends on:

4. http://www.acupuncture-points.org/six-stages.html
5. http://www.acupuncture-points.org/four-levels.html

- The health history of your biological parents, grandparents and earlier forbears

- The health and age of your biological parents before and at the time of your conception

- Your mother's health while you were in her womb including

- – What she ate and drank – both quality and quantity
  – What diseases she had and how they affected her
  – What medication she received
  – What social drugs she took (alcohol, tobacco etc.)
  – What trauma she suffered

- How easy was your birth process

Jing drains rapidly in seriously high fevers or in chronic long-lasting conditions and, for example, in major trauma: I would include battlefield stress and similar. Prolonged high nervous or emotional tension can drain it too.

Men and their Jing Men also expend Jing during orgasm, i.e. emission of sperm. When men are young they have huge sperm supplies and remake it fast. As they get older, or if they have too many emissions, they use up their Kidney Jing. This in turn can weaken their Kidney Qi's ability to maintain power and stability in their system.

Women and their Jing In addition to high fevers and those other conditions mentioned above, women use it up faster than they can remake it:

- when they have too many babies close together without allowing for recovery between them, or

- if they lose blood heavily and consistently at or between periods, and perhaps …

- … if they return to full activity too soon after giving birth.

- Breast-feeding too many babies at a time might do it too.

Of course, how well a woman copes with this depends on the quantity of Jing she arrived with at birth and her overall health and how she manages her life.

·

Johann Sebastian Bach had seven children by his first wife (three survived to adulthood) and thirteen by his second (six survived to adulthood). That he was such a hard-working and productive composer and musician (a genius too), and that he had so many children, probably with lots of sex in between, says much for the supply of Jing he was born with.

It also suggests that hard-work, as long as you do not overwork for too long, does not harm your Jing much, if at all.

But it may have been hard on his first wife. She died suddenly: we do not know why. His second wife gave birth to their last, thirteenth, child when she was 41, which must give hope to many modern couples, although one presumes that those who did survive childhood then were perhaps hardier, or at least luckier than the others.

·

When Kidney Qi is seriously weakened, the system's energy cannot flow because there simply is not enough underlying power to support it. So Qi slows down.

The roots of (Kidney) Qi 'Stagnation'

As you will have discovered from reading this book, when Qi slows or weakens, it leads to stagnation.

·

Think of a fast flowing river that produces clear fresh drinkable water. Now put its water into a reservoir and slow down or stop water entering and leaving. After a period of time, the water will become brackish, stale, contaminated. If it fills with weed, when you open its sluice-gates it won't flow quickly and will lack force, and it certainly won't be clean. That is like what happens when Kidney Qi 'stagnates'. (There are some similarities between this and Blood Stagnation.)

This stagnation can occur anywhere:

- In the Bladder it can lead to poor control over the bladder, or inability to urinate, with consequent pain and with a tendency to Damp-Heat (Chapter 14).

- In the Liver, it leads to a sensation of stretching or distension, emotional pressure etc. (Ch. 8).

- In the Spleen, it can lead to build-up of phlegm (Ch.13) ... and so on:
  – With Kidney Qi deficiency, there is fear and anxiety, leading to tension, a main symptom of Qi stagnation.
  – Weaker Kidney Qi means that Qi cannot move the Blood leading, more often than not, to coldness and poor circulation.
  – Kidney Jing supports the brain function and memory so, with less Jing, mental acuity deteriorates. Unable to concentrate and think things through, anxiety increases.
  – Kidney energy supports hearing, and with Kidney Qi deficiency, hearing reduces and tinnitus increases.
  – Kidney qi provides support for the lumbar area. Weak Kidney qi means backache.
  – As we have said, lowered Kidney Jing means less sexual energy, and for men, less desire for sex and less ability to produce and ejaculate sperm.

Men! I am sorry to say that as you grow older, your body produces less sperm, and your ability to ejaculate as frequently as when you were young also reduces. But – perhaps you knew this. Since Chinese medicine was almost entirely practised and thought about by men for thousands of years, there has been plenty of time for Chinese male doctors to think about this.

That means that a considerable amount of time and energy, (waning, of course) went into trying to compensate for reducing Jing; everything to do with maintaining youth, beauty and vigour, including sexual vigour. This area of thought is still a great moneymaker for Chinese medicine. Unfortunately, this has meant the death of many animals, whose vital parts were and are still prized for their supposed efficacy in promoting sexual prowess.

It remains very doubtful if any such claims were ever in any way valid. What was valid was that if people could be persuaded that they fulfilled the claims made for them, animal parts could be sold at great profit: extremely effective marketing to individuals who, as women have long since recognised, lose just about all their critical faculties when sex is involved.

With Kidney qi waning, its child , the Liver, also starves. *As we know, Liver Qi stagnates all too easily. But Kidney Jing is more supportive of Liver Yin and Liver Blood than of Liver Yang[6], so what happens more often than not is that lacking Yin energy, there is a relative surplus of Yang, which means irritability, high blood pressure and headaches: indigestion too. (Chapter 8.)*

Kidney Yang supports Spleen Yang. *If Spleen Yang is weak, your digestion weakens, you get diarrhoea, weak limbs, tendency to worry and much more. (See chapter 13.)*

·

Sorry! The two paragraphs above in italics are a bit technical. Just remember the seesaw. If one side is too light, the other will seem too heavy. If Yin is weak, available Yang will seem strong, so you get Yang-like symptoms.

·

A weakness in Kidney Qi leads to many kinds of Qi stagnation.

6. http://www.acupuncture-points.org/liver-yin-deficiency.html, http://www.acupuncture-points.org/liver-blood-deficiency.html, http://www.acupuncture-points.org/liver-yang.html

Is there such a thing?

There are several schools of thought about this.

1/ Kidney Qi excess is neither an excess of Kidney Yin nor of Kidney Yang but a general surfeit of both together. This tends to happen most during or just before the teenage years when, in healthy children/teenagers, being in balance and abundant health both boys and girls have superb complexion and energy. In boys especially this can show up as very pink cheeks. However, this can be confused with an excess of Yang over Yin too, so please do not assume that every pink-cheeked child has Kidney Qi excess.

With Kidney Qi excess, the whole of the cheek is a strong healthy pink whereas when there is an excess of Yang over Yin the pink colour extends just over the malar bones. Such Kidney Qi excess children are usually strong-minded but by no means difficult. They just know what they want and can get it! Sexual energy after puberty is usually strong.

They have good energy and endurance. When they get ill, they rapidly produce strong reactions and high fevers. Unless poorly disciplined when brought up they are by no means hyperactive. They are healthy!

2/ An excess of Kidney Qi. This form of 'stagnation' does not really exist and could have been placed elsewhere in this book because it also affects Liver Qi and Heart Qi. I have put it here because it emanates from Kidney Qi even if the consequences go elsewhere.

In Chinese medicine, sexual energy is the physical manifestation of Jing. (Purists will scold me for this as they take a slightly different view but I do not want to over-complicate matters.) Firstly, the Chinese thought a healthy sexual life very important for health. They did not think much about what might happen if sexual energy was underused, or frustrated. They most certainly did think about what happens when you over-use it. Indeed, if you read just about every Chinese classical book on longevity and health, what they're really talking about is maintaining good sex for as long as possible!

When you have read the next bit, you will understand why all these books were written by men!
There are two important distinctions here, that between men and women in overusing their sexual energy, and what happens when they do not get enough sexual activity:

- Overuse of Jing

- Underuse of Jing

Both situations can lead to Kidney Qi stagnation, plus other types of Qi Stagnation.

Sexual life in Ancient China ('Ancient' China may be inaccurate: at least up to a century ago would perhaps be better in this context.) The Chinese thought a fulfilled sexual life was necessary for health, and in fact it went further: they thought abstinence was bad for you.

At certain periods of history in China, however, such as those which followed the Confucian way of thinking, society disapproved of public displays of affection (this is still inpart the case in modern China amongst older people) because these were thought to threaten the sanctity of family life.

During these periods, disease was not infrequently due to sexual frustration.

Sex and Fire energy

Sexual desire depends on adequate levels of what is called Fire (actually 'Minister Fire'). You need Fire for a healthy life. Lack of sexual drive shows you probably have a lack of Fire. For men, after having sex i.e. after ejaculation, their desire is reduced but recovers as their Fire builds up again.

This Fire, the Fire that provides sexual energy, is different from Fire caused by Wind and Heat, which can produce conditions like mania.

What happens when sexual desire increases? This Fire is said to blaze, increasing Yang energy. Actually this increase of Yang also increases Blood (a Yin energy) which flows and engorges the sexual organs. At the same time, the Fire warms you. With more Yang and more Yin, you feel more powerful, more integrated, more excited and energized. It is a great feeling.

Indeed, this powerful flow of energy can overwhelm your more cultivated instincts and lead to uncontrollable demands on your sexual partner. Nowadays, circumstances surrounding what is subsequently seen as rape can be hard to disentangle, if at least for a time, one party thought both wanted sex.

The power source for this Fire is at source your Jing.

Maximum tension between Yang and Yin is reached just before orgasm. Orgasm discharges the Yang energy, and this discharge promotes the free flow of Qi, flooding away any Qi stagnation. That is why good sex relaxes you!

Overuse of Jing – Women

The ancient classical books on Chinese medicine (for example the Su Wen) discuss the onset of puberty. For girls, they say that at 14 (nowadays we might make this earlier), the 'Ren Mai opens, the Chong Mai[7] flourishes, menses begin and the woman can conceive'. This means that when a girl's reserves of Yin and Blood mature, she can conceive.

The energy that produces this is controlled by Kidney Qi

7. Ren Mai and Chong Mai are the names of two of the 'Eight Extra-Ordinary Vessels' which control, stabilise and unite all the acupuncture channels.

and comes from Kidney Jing. It manifests in girls as her eggs, her ova. As we now know, every healthy baby girl is born with a huge supply of ova, dormant.

These wait for the maturing of Ren Mai and Chong Mai before they start to be released. After that, she will release one monthly for up to 35 years, making a total of more than 400, out of an original supply of over 6 million that by birth had reduced to a million.

By the time she reaches puberty, the number of ova in waiting has probably reduced to 300,000. These gradually degenerate unless used, and by her menopause none are left. Her ova are a direct display of her Jing. Even with 300,000 left at puberty, she has plenty! She only needs 400. No matter how much sexual activity she enjoys, she will not lose Jing as a result of losing extra ova: they are doled out, one a month, come what may. So she cannot over-use her Jing this way.

She can lose it in other ways, however. First, she can lose Jing – a little – by severe loss of blood. This is because a small amount of Jing is needed to create Blood. To replace heavy loss of Blood requires that her body draws on its reserves of Jing. (Also, it takes a considerable quantity of Blood to manufacture more Jing, so losing much Blood depletes her ability to renew Jing reserves.)

What the Chinese call Blood is more than the red stuff we call blood: it includes the character or personality, and the ability to concentrate and remember, endurance and other strengths too. Blood is relied on by many Energy Organs[8].

Jing is needed at the last stage of making Blood when the red stuff, nourished with oxygen by the lungs, passes through the Heart and becomes Blood. This final transition needs Jing. So a major loss of blood leads to a loss of Blood. Making more

8. Read more about Blood at http://www.acupuncturepoints.org/blood.html

Blood requires more Jing: extended loss of menstrual blood (menorrhagia) for example can be very Jing-draining.

Secondly, exhaustion. Long periods of any activity, notably including illness and fever that takes more out of her than rest and nutrition can replace, will lead to a drain on Jing.

Prolonged labour of child-birth would be one way of draining Jing. Heavy physical work or over-straining is similar: too much prolonged pain that exhausts her can do it too.

But not too much sex! (Unless it leads to the draining of Jing mentioned above.) However, women who have too many babies too close together, i.e. without allowing themselves to recover properly between births, or who are malnourished during pregnancy, can lose Jing as their bodies scrape around for the means to produce the child. Nature fixes it that the baby's health takes precedence over the mother's health so she uses up her Jing to balance the books.

Pregnancy can also be a tremendous restorative for women. Indeed, sometimes a woman whose health has been poor until pregnancy, becomes healthier after it. Here one supposes that the additional energy of the child helps the mother recover.

But to take advantage of this huge present potentially donated by mother nature, the mother should take care to rest properly towards the end of her pregnancy and, in particular, after it, when others should preferably look after her as if she were an invalid or convalescent – for at least a month![9]

This is not to be confused with when a woman only feels great during pregnancy. This, as a rule, happens to women who are normally Yin and Blood deficient. During pregnancy the baby in the womb provides the Yin necessary to compensate for her normal deficiency.

Men and Women

As we all know, sex releases tension. As sexual

9. This practice is still greatly respected in many parts of Asia.

excitement builds, Yang energy increases, only just held in check by Yin energy as the pleasure and anticipation of orgasm grows.

This tension between Yang and Yin, expressed throughout the body, can lead to euphoria and a sense of power. The need for this experience can become addictive.

Men

Every time he ejaculates, a man uses Jing. His testes can produce vast amounts of semen, especially when young, but it takes Jing to make semen. Too frequent ejaculation is draining.

As he ages, the less Jing he has and the longer it takes to make more. In men, the 'art of love' is to maintain this state of excitement for as long as possible because when ejaculation occurs, tension is released. A number of ancient classics describe the benefits, mental, physical and emotional, of prolonging this tension, and how to do it.

They describe the benefits of stopping short of ejaculation. Nowadays it is becoming common knowledge, though somewhat easier to describe than to practise: but if one can practise it, it often leads to a sense of strength, and better self-control.

Young men make semen faster than their elders so can repeat orgasms with more abandon, which is perhaps just as well as young men have plenty of tensions, many of them sexual.

Women

For women, the sexual tensions can be a whole-body sensation far beyond that localised to the genitals. That whole-body commotion often continues in a lesser form after orgasm, and because she has lost no semen, no Jing, in the right circumstances she can repeat the experience again and again until replete or exhausted.

For women, as Fire stirs, it affects the Mind. But the way

it does this is through her Heart and Pericardium. The Heart has a direct connection to a woman's uterus (via a special channel called the Uterus Vessel Bao Mai).

During orgasm, contractions of the uterus discharge all her gathered Yang, releasing the Fire. Although ejaculation for men can seem a powerful experience, a woman's uterus has the power to push out a baby and is a hugely powerful muscle. So a woman's experience of orgasm can, when it embraces her whole body including her uterus, be a far greater experience.

Orgasm releases other tensions too. Worry, sleeplessness, anxiety, anger and many other emotional sources of tension are all relieved, even if only temporarily. This state of abandon eclipses other tensions, at least for a while.

Masturbation

So on that score, masturbation is a great way of releasing tension, both pleasurable and effective. For men, however, Chinese medicine counsels against too frequent loss of semen, because of its connection with Jing: frequent masturbation is not advised.

Of course, making love with another is beneficial in so many other ways that it does not really compare with masturbation, but masturbation still has benefits unless it leads to a solitary life and the inability to form satisfactory relationships.

With another human being, sexual love-making involves plenty of physical activity as well as the tenderness and benefits of exchanging love. That physical activity also helps to release both sexual and other tensions, and makes mutual love-making better than masturbation. As you will have read earlier in this book, physical activity is a great way of releasing Qi Stagnation.

Abandoning oneself to someone else's ministrations can

also be hugely exciting and satisfying, and engenders trust and a deeper relationship.

So sex is good. I have mentioned, briefly, the dangers of addiction and exhaustion (potentially more dangerous for men than for women). Sex can be bad too, when it leads to transfer of disease. Please practise safe sex, with consideration for others.

What about frustrated or unfulfilled Sexual energy? Whereas excess sex is definitely a potential cause of disease – see above – apparently the Ancient Chinese entertained no such worries about not getting enough! Or so it might seem.

As we have seen, as sexual desire builds up, it increases Fire in the body. This Fire is wonderful stuff! It is exciting, warming, energising, empowering and addictive. When, after a build-up, it is released, it is enormously satisfying. But what happens when this Fire lacks a proper channel for release?

As mentioned, if there is sexual desire, there is Fire. A healthy body produces Fire. Humans do not much mention it in relation to themselves but female mammals of all sorts are referred to as being in 'heat' when, during their reproductive cycle they are ready to become pregnant. Often their sexual organs will swell and consciously or unconsciously they will display themselves more as they seek to make themselves more attractive. In other words, they seek a mate and may become more aggressive or ostentatious.

One sign of this, in both sexes, is increased secretions and odour: musk. Many humans are self-conscious of their body odour at these times, and seek to hide it with artificial fragrances.

If their bodies' natural attempts to get attention are frustrated or, being by agreement 'attached' as a human to another there are circumstances that do not relieve the tension build-up, women often get enlarged and painful breasts, cramps and spasms in their abdomens, irritability, increased sensitivity in the genitals and so on. What are these if not the same symptoms of Fire in the lower pelvis? (Actually they are also signs of Qi stagnation caused by the build-up of Heat.)

And when it comes, you cannot easily get rid of it, though hard physical work or exposure to cold can dampen or use it up temporarily. This Fire easily affects the Heart, which means it easily affects the Shen, the Mind. Healthy young men think frequently of sex, we know! – Fire affecting their Minds. This Fire energy is distracting, and easily inflamed.

Asceticism is practised in various religious or monastic settings. The ancient Chinese were rather suspicious, even disapproving, of Buddhist nuns who practised abstinence. In Christian traditions, the description 'temptations of the flesh' shows the difficulty that monastic traditions had with Fire.

Of course, if either Jing energy is low or there is a lack of Fire, sexual desire will be low and there will be no problem.

Well, actually, there will be a problem for many, because low Fire leads to lack of confidence and assertiveness, self-dissatisfaction, anxiety over health, fears of impotence, fear of failure, grief over wasted opportunities, worries about desirability and a whole lot more that you will easily appreciate.

So when ordinary mortals with strong sexual energy cannot fulfil their sexual needs in the way that they want to, it causes problems.

What sorts of problems? What does Fire do when not channelled in a healthy, fulfilling way? Fire unable to move is a form of Qi stagnation, in this case relating to Kidney Qi. Obviously, there will be sexual frustration and unfulfilled desire. Fire then accumulates with the tendency to become pathological. This pathological accumulation of Fire becomes Heat. Heat inflames, dries, forces energies to rise, blocks the free flow of Qi up and down, and leads to Qi Stagnation in the pelvis area.

The next stage is that Heat begins to rise up the body, sometimes creating an upward draft of Wind. This upward flow of energy is said to 'harass' the Shen, to disturb the Mind, perturbing its tranquillity. What kinds of symptoms might this lead to?

- Distraction, lack of concentration, agitation

- Tension in the pelvis

- Sometimes pain or cramps in abdomen or lower back.

- The tension usually ascends but in very tired or over-stressed women it can also be felt in the thighs.

- Later this tension can flow to wherever the patient commonly experiences stress and pain, for example the shoulders, or neck, sides of the head or forehead, those being the areas covered by the Gall Bladder channel, the most commonly affected channel

- A sensation of heat, both in the pelvis and upwards (Heat rises): this Heat in women can lead to
  – spotting menses, and/or
  – coloured and/or thicker discharges and/or
  – dysmenorrhoea (painful menses) and
  – menorrhagia (heavy menses)

- In women, the Heat transfers to the breasts which may swell uncomfortably making them very sensitive.

- Women sometimes exhibit increased cleavage just before their menses, partly as an (unconscious) form of display and partly, it is arguable, to dissipate Heat.

- Fire in men may not be experienced as heat but as a desire to expose the genitals and/or to reduce underwear or clothing: in effect you could say this is the body's energetic way to cool the area, to dissipate Yang-Heat Qi. (Modern society strongly disapproves of this exposure by men, attributing it to either mental instability or perversion. I think Chinese medicine might say it was an unfortunate expression of excess Heat energy.)

- Sensation of heat in the upper body

- Mentally, the mind is agitated – perhaps more obvious in men but potentially both sexes – mania, exposing the body, restlessness, inability to concentrate, disturbed behaviour

- Mania (from Fire engendering Wind), leading to manic, destructive (including self-destructive) or uncontrollable behaviour

- Sensations of heat and cold, almost like the onset of a fever

- Emotional: perhaps more often in women – loneliness, yearning and pining, depression.

- Dislike of tight clothing around body or neck

- Some kinds of acne may be exacerbated by this Heat

What classes of people might often suffer from this?

In the West, what classes of people might we expect to see affected by this, assuming the individuals had Fire and sexual desire?

- Widows, widowers and those previously in satisfying sexual relationships which, ended through separation or death, have not been replaced, or where sexual energy – Fire – exceeds the availability of willing and desirable partners

- People with very poor interpersonal skills who cannot develop reciprocal relationships

- In the past, and perhaps now, in those parts of society

not expected to have sexual relationships including
– Disabled but not ill people including the wounded
– Single sex schools
– Nunneries, monasteries, cults
– Servant 'classes'. Many societies do not like the
word 'servant' now, but developed countries are full
of immigrants who are prepared to work at the lower
levels of society and who, for a time at least, may lack
sexual partners
– Prisoners
– Elderly (admittedly an ambiguous description)
– Patients in care homes or hospitals
– Sports people in training (though by no means in
all traditions)
– Members of the armed forces when at war

If this Fire is not allowed to discharge through sexual release, it leads to increased Qi stagnation with all the symptoms already discussed in this book.

What are the causes of and what HAPPENS NEXT if Kidney Qi deficiency continues?

Listed above are some of the causes of Kidney Qi deficiency, so I have put them in again here only briefly. What follows includes some conditions that are recognised by Western medicine.
    Causes

• Inherited or what we might now call genetic weakness

• Weakness and impotence from too much sex. Though this normally applies more to men than to women, there are situations where it applies to women.

• Severe or chronic disease

- Age
- Overwork. Although the example given above of Bach, who produced prodigious amounts of music at a time when it all had to be written and copied by hand, suggests that hard work does not hurt, overwork is a different matter. This is often described as burnout[10].

.

The great Italian composer Rossini composed 37 operas in 19 years, 35 of them in about 14 years to the age of 32. "When a man has composed 37 operas he begins to feel a little tired" Hiller quotes him as saying. After that he composed almost nothing, though he lived until 76. Admittedly he had some domestic issues, but finance was not one of them. I think he just burned out. 'Burn-out' is definitely on the spectrum with Kidney Qi and Jing exhaustion.

.

- What may be normal for one person may be extreme overwork for another
  – Overwork is probably OK in short bursts if followed by adequate rest and recovery, especially in the young. Overwork by older people, without adequate rest, drains their Kidney Qi fast.
  – Kidney Yin deficiency occurs more often in those whose work is intense and intellectual.
  – People can train themselves to work harder. As their minds and bodies adjust, they can do more, just as an athlete takes time and training to achieve peak fitness, strength and ability. But even athletes need rest and food.
  – Heavy physical work, like heavy lifting, drains Kidney Yang though again, as you build up the work, you can do more and within reason it stimulates Kidney Yang. Heavily draining

10. For example as referred to by Herbert J Freudenberger 'Staff Burnout' Journal of Social Issues 30 (1974) 159-65

Kidney Yang will eventually draw down reserves of
Jing. Weight-lifting, for example, is known to
boost testosterone levels when done with proper form
and adequate rest and nutrition. This does not mean
that testosterone is exactly the same as Kidney
Yang, however, but there are similarities.
– The pleasure of bringing up babies and children is one
thing but it is counteracted by sleepless nights
and emotional exhaustion from trying to maintain
order when parents have busy demanding jobs;
children exposed to media see and want more and more;
and the break-up of the nuclear family means that
traditional support structures are missing. Parents here
grow old fast, evidencing Kidney Qi and Jing drainage.

Too much mental work or excitement can drain Kidney Yin too, especially if done without proper rest and recuperation and under stress. Many situations of extreme conflict qualify for this condition.

Many of these symptoms are signs of WIND, generated from deficiency of Kidney Yin. The Wind appears as restlessness, anxiety, tremor, shaking and dizziness.

• Prolonged over-excitement leads to nervous exhaustion This
  is like the hyper-arousal often noticed in people with post-
  traumatic stress disorder but noticeable also in some
  people after drug misuse, especially when trying to withdraw
  from the drug.
  – Anxiety, on-edge
  – Cannot relax
  – Concentration is difficult
  – Dizziness
  – Headaches
  – Insomnia, nightmares, disturbing dreams
  – Irritability

    – Phobias
    – Sense of isolation
    – Shaking
    – Sweating at night (plus sweating at other times too)

- As the Kidney deficiency leads to other forms of
  Qi stagnation, e.g. Liver Qi stagnation, there may be a
  stuffy, 'cannot breathe' or distending sensation in the chest,
  and indigestion with stomach upsets. These are mostly
  from Yin deficiency and in particular from Kidney
  Yin deficiency.
  o You see this for short periods in young children
  when, before a visit say to Disneyland, they cannot sleep. If
  that state is prolonged indefinitely, you will understand
  how draining it can be.

- Emotional strain
  – Any strong emotion, even 'joy[11]', if prolonged for too long,
  may damage Kidney Qi. For example, my children used to
  enjoy watching horror movies around midnight, and one
  could hear the in-drawn breaths, the tension released and
  the laughter. But it did not help them sleep and it did not
  make for equable temperaments the next day, so we
  allowed it only very occasionally.

- Prolonged anger, fear, grief, worry, jealousy, envy, desire for
  revenge etc can all damage Kidney Qi. (Of course, prolonged
  anger also affects the Liver, Grief the Lungs, Worry the
  Spleen and Stomach and so on: see under the relevant
  chapters.)
  • Memory loss; dementia; Alzheimer's disease
  • As you read under the Essence at the start of this
  chapter, the pace of modern life stretches us. This constant
  drain eventually depletes our Kidney Qi.

11. Joy, here, though it may be pleasurable, can be a problem. The more it borders on mania,
    the more of a Qi draining problem it becomes.

Modern medicine keeps us alive for longer when we might have died before. It behoves us to keep fit and, if we want to be healthy when we are older, to regulate how we live life when we are younger. Our constitution predisposes how we react to and survive stress.

What can YOU do to HELP YOURSELF if you have Qi stagnation arising from Kidney Qi or Jing problems?

[Observations over the centuries by the Chinese culminated in what we call the Five Element or Four Phase system. When reading the following you do not need to understand this system fully but when and if you do study it you will understand why the following applies. Read more about it in appendix 4 and chapter 5. For the Water element, this system of thought suggests what might benefit people with Kidney and Bladder Energy organ problems. For Water, the main Elements to consider here are Metal, Earth and Wood. The following uses some of those ideas. Most references to the Five Element or Four Phase system in this section are in square brackets in case you want to skip over them.]

For problems arising from Kidney Jing or Qi deficiency

This is when your sexual energy is low, you often feel tired or discouraged, you may have backache, difficulty hearing, poor powers of recovery, thinning hair and so on. You may also be irritable and unable to relax. All this makes you worried if not

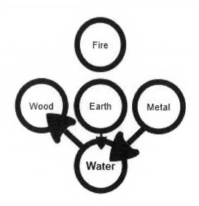

fearful, tense, prone to accidents and insomnia. So, what to do?

- Rest often

- Desist from over-activity! Relax more!

- Men should reduce the amount of sex they have. In fact, they should stop ejaculating altogether for a while.

- Sleep more or more often. If you cannot sleep through the night, take short naps through the day or early evening. If you cannot sleep during the day, seek treatment, see below.

- Take gentle exercise only. Learn Yoga but avoid the standing-on-one-leg poses until you feel stronger. Many Yoga poses stretch and tone your muscles, building endurance and inner strength. Pilates likewise.

- Avoid standing still, or walking very slowly. Do not carry a heavy weight, such as a child, on your shoulders or in your arms.

- Avoid heavy lifting, even that of full shopping bags.

- Get plenty of warm but not excessive sunlight.

- Keep warm. Wear more. Avoid getting chilled. If you do get chilled, take a warm bath to get you warm, then go to bed to sleep for a while. In hot climates, prolonged sweating – because of the heat – can also drain you.

- Do not over-eat, especially when you are very tired. If you are very hungry, eat a small snack first (perhaps some nuts, or a little soup) as you prepare your meal. Then eat the meal slowly.

- Eat a good diet, including many nuts and seeds, Nature's richest supply of zinc and other sperm and blood nutrients.

- Take time over your meals and do not work at mealtimes.

- Reduce prescribed medication and exposure to

poisons, herbicides, fungicides, pesticides and other environmental chemicals if you can. Any form of chemical or medication has to be metabolised by your liver, and as your body detoxifies itself it uses up your Qi and Blood. You need that Blood to make more Jing.

- Learn to meditate and to calm your mind.

- Learn techniques to keep your spine flexible. (Your spine and spinal cord and brain are all strongly connected with your Kidney Qi.) Yoga, Tai Qi and the gentle exercise for toning your spine described in appendix 10 may help.

- Consider learning autogenics, and use the benefits of noise to soothe and nourish your Kidney Qi. [Kidneys rule your ears and hearing.] What is the right noise? Slow gentle music is good, probably classical. Try the noise of the sea, or rain on leaves, preferably with bin-aural hidden beats which help you rapidly enter a deep almost trance-like state where your mind slows down and enters the self-healing process more powerfully.

- Try to remove toxins from your system. Read the remarks in chapter 12 about dental fillings.

- Try to resolve arguments or old issues with antagonists.

- Socialise, not so as to attract sexual partners, but for friendship and conviviality. If you are introverted (q.v. Carl Jung's definition of the word), go somewhere away from company or in the company of only very close friends. [This uses the Fire Element to control the deficient Water Element.] Socialising exchanges your Qi with that of others. Obviously, this moves your Qi and helps to prevent it from stagnating.

- Visualisation. Take lessons in this. [The most powerful energy you can use is that of the Mind, supported by Qi from the Lungs. The Mind is housed by the Heart

which is in the Fire Element, and Visualisation is mainly a
Fire Element process.]

- Reduce the amount of social drugs you take,
  including alcohol.

- You may be interested to read some of the books written by
  the ancient Chinese sages. A good place to start is
  'The Secret of Everlasting Life' by Richard Bertschinger,
  pub. Singing Dragon 2011. This book is Daoist.

- Learn to breathe properly. [Good Lung Qi supports
  Metal, the Mother of Water, the Kidney Element.]

- Consider moving from where you are, if the
  opportunities for your Qi to move are not served by where
  you are. Qi stagnation of any kind, though it can feel
  unpleasant, is a form of trapped energy, with huge potential
  for good!

General Ways to improve your skills and resources

Your [Water element] Kidney qi signifies your resources, skills
and will power. What can you do to help yourself?

- Yoga and Tai Qi are ancient ways to strengthen your system.
  Pilates is a modern adaptation, but Tai Qi still has major
  benefits because it involves a range of movements to stretch
  your capabilities, gently exploring your limits.

- The Bladder channel runs down the back of your
  body besides your spine. The Kidney channel runs up the
  front of your body, and partly up the front of your spine.
  The spinal health exercise in appendix 10 is very
  appropriate to the health of your spine and nervous system.
  However, if you have back pain or spinal problems, approach
  it carefully. Doing it is not a competition – just you!

- Meditation and rest. Meditation, in particular, centres and stabilises you. See http://www.acupuncturepoints.org/meditation.html With the needs of your Kidney and Bladder Energy organs in mind, meditation is best done sitting upright.

- Where possible, take time and/or learn how to repair your clothes and possessions rather than always throwing them away or buying replacements. This act of putting things right is stabilising and diverts your mind from worrying.

- If you garden, the process that most matches your needs is that of mending and oiling garden tools, repairing chain-saws, lawnmowers, garden fences and brickwork – but avoid heavy lifting. Weeding and applying compost are also good. These activities nurture and support the process you need to help recover your Kidney Qi.

- In your home, get into the habit or tidying storage spaces, putting things in order, repairing broken possessions. [This recognises the importance of your Metal phase for your health and mental well-being.]

- Learn new skills. Wintertime is the most appropriate time of year to do this.[Utilising the Metal element, the Metal element being the Mother of the Water phase] Seek advice about the most essential matters in your life for future success. Ask an experienced mentor to guide you. Mentoring is different from Counselling. You may find helpful the works of people who formerly did what you do.

Considering Your Future, ways to help yourself

[Arising from the Mother-Child law in the Five Element system, Wood is the Child to Water.] Because Kidney Qi stagnation does not exist of itself, but only through its effects on other Energy

Organs, releasing Kidney Qi stagnation to the next phase is a nonsense.

However, the Liver Energy organ bases its health on the Kidney Energy. From the seeds that have rested in the ground over winter comes the effulgence of Spring. Consequently, the clearer you are about the next phase of your life, by when your Kidney Qi will have recovered, the more you can do to prepare for it while you rest. Use this waiting time to consider your options.

Many people with weakened energy, including those with myalgic encephalitis, post-viral syndrome or sequellae from debilitating illness, can use their convalescence to consider deeply what they really want out of life. One part of this is to contemplate how, in future, to avoid dissipating their energy again; what physical or mental symptoms to be careful of to prevent the recurrence of their debilitating circumstances.

Arising from Kidney Qi excess

By this is meant overall 'excess' of Kidney Qi – not the excess of Kidney Yang over Kidney Yin. This problem is rare in developed countries and may only occur in young people.

- Learn how to socialise, not just to attract sexual partners, (though that is what you will feel like doing when you reach sexual maturity), but to increase you attractiveness for and experience of a wide range of possible partners.

- Take plenty of exercise to help dissipate tension and heat: competitive sports are better than lone sports, but any sport is better than none. Dancing is great!

- If you have not reached sexual maturity, throw as

much energy as you can into learning and education, sports and travel.

- Try to get as much sleep as you can. If you are growing, you need it, even with excess Kidney Qi.

- If you have reached sexual maturity, try to discipline yourself to spend a reasonable proportion of your time using your energy to improve your circumstances, whether through working or education. With excess Kidney Qi, the world is at your feet, perhaps more than you realise.

- Try to avoid hazardous or violent activities that you may feel inclined to practise. If you must pursue them, make sure that help is at hand should you injure yourself. Bear in mind that violent sports cause injury, which not infrequently leads to long-term dependence on your family and the (possibly expensive) health services, not to mention jeopardy for all your hopes in life.

- Do not take drugs, as you may be tempted to, when you realise that you recover from them faster than do others. Just make it a rule in your life not to get started. Such a rule is easier to keep than trying to stop once you have started.

- Do not assume that your constitution is proof against anything, including inclement weather. You, more than many, may be able to avoid disease but when it does strike, you may get it more acutely, with a very high fever for example. If the invading pathogen is powerful, your body may put up a considerable fight, which if prolonged, may drain you. Do not be goaded by peer pressure into taking stupid risks.

What treatments work for Qi stagnation arising from Kidney Qi deficiency?

The answer to this question has been the subject of intense thought by practitioners of Chinese medicine for 3000 years. I cannot answer it comprehensively here because whole books have been written about it, so I merely give some suggestions. Do realise that this kind of deficiency takes time to put right, and the older you are, or the more deficiency you start with, the longer it may take.

- Chinese herbal medicine
- Counselling to help you resolve any emotional, anxiety or fear issues
- Acupuncture and moxibustion[12]
- Spine: See an osteopath or chiropractor to get your spine in good shape. Also see appendix 10.
- Healing – an exchange of Qi. Read The Medium, The Mystic and the Physicist by Lawrence LeShan.
- Nutritional advice from someone trained in Chinese medicine. There are many foods that are said to help Kidney Qi but I have noticed that giving a list of them tends to make people eat nothing but the ones on the list which is also unhelpful. In general, therefore, take advice.
- Learn Tai Qi, Qi Gong and meditation, preferably from someone knowledgeable and experienced. 'Touching hands' is a Tai Qi training method which is both relaxing and connecting: you exchange Qi with someone else.
- Lifestyle advice
- Advice on a graduated exercise regime

12. http://www.acupuncture-points.org/moxibustion.html

- Take advice on how to avoid circumstances that lead to further drains on your Kidney Qi.

- What I believe does not work, except in the short-term, is taking prescribed medication that suppresses[13] your symptoms, but does not cure the underlying condition. I would only suggest such medicine if you were very old or infirm, when orthodox prescribed medication may dull pain and tiredness, and when you may not mind the secondary effects of the drugs.

Kidney Qi Excess

I have no advice to give for treatment for Kidney Qi excess except to suggest you seek help with any relationship or work issues arising from exuberance that you cannot otherwise resolve. Parents of children with natural Kidney Qi excess should take care to ensure their offspring do not injure themselves and that they do get the best education possible.

Summary

Kidney does not have any separate syndrome in Chinese medicine for Qi stagnation, but several of its syndromes easily lead to it. These include –

- Kidney deficiency

- Kidney Jing deficiency and

- Kidney excess.

You have also read about how to help yourself and what treatments may help.

The next chapter is on a hugely important Energy Organ, much

13. http://www.acupuncture-points.org/suppression.html

abused these days from lack of restraint in describing others –
particularly online. Its Qi can stagnate when our relationships
don't work as we would wish.

CHAPTER 16

Pericardium Qi Stagnation

There is no very obvious organ in your body for the Pericardium: it is a place. But Chinese medicine puts considerable emphasis on its importance for establishing healthy relationships and for stabilising your metabolism.

Essence of Pericardium Qi Stagnation

Should you read this chapter? Yes, if you have suffered a sudden change in an important relationship, or feel very insecure in your dealings with other people.

In this chapter you will read about

- Location of the Pericardium
- Function and History of the Pericardium
- Time of the Pericardium
- An exercise to support it
- Pericardium Qi stagnation
- What YOU can do to help yourself
- What treatments help

Location of Pericardium
The pericardium is the space round the heart organ so is not actually a physical organ that you can point to.

Function of the Pericardium
To understand this you have to see what the ancient Chinese made of it. Initially they thought that you could only treat the Heart itself via the Pericardium. One of the great books of acupuncture[1], written probably 2500 years ago, states that the Heart has no acupuncture points other than those along the Pericardium channel. However, just as modern science questions everything, so did the Chinese and Chinese medicine has developed and changed greatly over the centuries. The Heart channel is now considered to exist, with its own important points.

History of Pericardium Function
The Pericardium's function has not changed much, which is to protect the Heart from adversity, from emotional exposure to stress, and from physical disease. It was thought to be like the band of courtiers in a medieval court, including what we had now call the Diplomatic Service. They protected the monarch and dealt with affairs of state on his or her behalf.

For us, it has an important function in that it enables us to relate to people. Communicating with, and giving support to and receiving it back from our peers and community bring us back to Earth. It is other people who keep our feet on the ground! As babies, when ill and old we rely on it. Innovation is hugely boosted by good communications[2].

It is not so easy to see how an area of the body could do this, but if we think of the Pericardium as including the diaphragm and the membranes which separate the heart from the lungs and the diaphragm, which keep the area sliding smoothly one bit over another, we may get an idea of what is meant. This relationship with the diaphragm makes the

1. Huangdi Neijing
2. The Data-Driven Society, Scientific American, Oct 2013 p64

Pericardium have properties within both the upper part of the trunk, the chest, and that below it, being the epigastrium and the hypogastria, the space below the umbilicus.

Why? Because the movement of the diaphragm expands and contracts the lungs above, and massages and moves the small and large intestines below. As it opens the space above it compresses the space below, and vice versa. The diaphragm has an important relationship with the lungs. When we speak or sing, we learn to breathe in and then expel the breath over the vocal chords at various speeds: fast and we speak loudly, slow and we speak softly. Part of this comes from how we contract and expand the muscles of the chest of course, but the base of the chest is the diaphragm, which needs to work in tandem with the chest muscles.

Abdominal breathing, which we learn to help keep ourselves calm and to steady our voice, uses very little chest muscular action: it all comes from control of the diaphragm. When we stick out our abdomen without breathing in, we are partly using our diaphragm muscle to make the movement.

As you would expect from a book on Qi stagnation, how we control and move Qi is vitally important. The Lungs govern Qi, so if we can learn to breathe properly we increase our ability to control and move Qi, to prevent Qi stagnation anywhere, and we reduce our susceptibility to health problems from stress. See appendix 7 for more on this important subject of breathing.

The diaphragm muscle is in many ways controlled by the Pericardium. Because the diaphragm has such an important role in breathing, anything that helps our Pericardium Energy organ also helps our Lungs.

Pericardium time

The Pericardium 'manages' Qi between 7pm and 9pm, exactly 12 hours after the times of the Stomach, with which it has an important relationship[3]. This time, and that of the Stomach, are sometimes when Pericardium Qi stagnation symptoms manifest.

A Diaphragm Exercise that supports the Pericardium

There is an important yoga exercise, called Nauli that strengthens the breathing, strongly moves and massages all the abdominal organs, and helps to keep digestion healthy. *NB See the last paragraph below in these italics to check WHO should NOT do this!*

On an empty stomach and after evacuating both bowels and bladder, it involves emptying the lungs of all air, as far as possible, then, in a stooping position with hands on thighs, pulling in the abdomen. In fact you do not initially pull in the abdomen, you contract the diaphragm. That pulls in and up the contents of the abdomen into the lower chest space vacated by the (emptied) lungs. This creates an empty space in which you can contract and move the central anterior muscles of the abdomen. This pulls and rolls the underlying small and large intestines, the bladder and womb, providing an important cleansing function for them.

This exercise is NOT recommended without practice under instruction, nor if you are pregnant or trying to become pregnant and during your menses. However, after your menses it is great to cleanse the uterus and lower pelvis space.

A gentler form of this, available to all, is abdominal breathing, as in appendix 7. Some of the abdominal moves learned in belly-dancing are also great!

When the Pericardium is in good health, it helps keep your breathing steady and deep. It maintains physical condition in your abdomen, and of course, with these, your Heart Qi is more likely to perform well. When the Pericardium fails to function properly you feel unhappy with

3. For instance, the Pericardium and the diaphragm lie immediately above the Stomach physically, so movement in one affects the other. Also several acupuncture points on the Pericardium channel have an important effect on the Stomach's descending function.

yourself, depressed or dejected, probably stuffed up, sometimes nauseous, and often constipated.

Does Pericardium Qi Stagnation exist?

As you have read, we do have Heart Qi stagnation as a syndrome in Chinese medicine, but not Pericardium Qi stagnation. Partly I think this is because it is hard to separate out its functions from those of the Heart and of the Liver. Also it is because there are a number of Pericardium syndromes arising from emotional strain that are more specifically described under different names.

Little bit of technical stuff. In writing this book I realised it would be impossible to ignore the effect on the flow of Qi caused by emotional strain on the Pericardium without including a chapter on the subject. So in effect, I am contending that some of the Pericardium syndromes amount to different forms of Pericardium Qi stagnation. The following is my attempt to define some of the symptoms of what I shall call Pericardium Qi Stagnation. In doing this I shall probably make some purists a bit cross. But as they already know all this stuff and anyhow this book is not for them, they will have to forgive me. I.e. Too bad. First, though, you need to know what the Pericardium does in Chinese medicine.

Functions of the Pericardium Energy Organ

In the centre of the chest, around the Heart, of which it is called the 'Heart Protector', the Pericardium envelops the Heart. Because the Heart governs the Mind (the Shen), the Pericardium is important for the healthy working of the Mind.

In particular, that means not just the Mind and its emotions but the Blood necessary to feed the Mind.

This matter of 'Blood' is important in Chinese medicine. Qi and Blood are the two basic forms of energy in the body. They depend on each other. Blood feeds and steadies, Qi leads and moves.

A famous horseman who had just won a world-class horse-jumping competition was asked by a journalist:

"How important is the horse?" (he meant, in winning the competition). The horseman just looked at him and said: "Well, the horse is very important!"[4]

Qi leads, Blood carries and supports. An important maxim in Chinese medicine is *'Qi is the leader of the Blood, Blood the mother of Qi.*[5]

Treated like an organ, the Pericardium is important in its function of producing and moving blood through the Heart and then moving on this Blood that now has life in it. This 'moving' side helps the Lungs and the Heart. The Heart houses the Mind. When we panic, our heart-beat increases. If our pulse increases for no reason, we shall probably get anxious. In Chinese Medicine the Mind is not what we think of as the mind in Western science, when we think of the brain and how well it computes. That idea is only part of what is meant in Chinese medicine. The Mind is more like our personality or consciousness: it is probably not possible to find an exact equivalent in Western science. (Appendix 3.)

The Pericardium helps maintain the equilibrium of our emotions. The Pericardium is said to be mainly involved in development of relationships with others. For this to be successful we need a satisfactory sense of our self-worth, (or at least so proposes modern Western psychology). In Chinese medicine, this self-worth equates to healthy Blood and a mutually supportive balance between the different Energy Organs.

This balanced sense of self-worth, embodying a balance

---

4. If someone can tell me which horseman this was, I shall be grateful. Possibly Harvey Smith?

5. The red stuff becomes Blood (capital B) only once it emerges from the Heart. Read more about Blood at http://www.acupuncturepoints.org/blood.html

between the different Energy Organs and within the Heart, is presented to the outside world, acquaintances, competitors, colleagues, friends and lovers by the Pericardium. If our relationships go wrong, the Pericardium takes the strain. If our emotions, especially those involved in relationships, let us down or are unbalanced, the Pericardium energy is intimately involved. This means that points along the Pericardium channel are often used by acupuncturists to help us recover our emotional equilibrium[6] in the face of some new kind of relationship.

In Chinese medicine there exist connections between the Heart, the Pericardium and the Uterus. When a woman is very upset, she may experience menstrual irregularities, or even the loss of her menses.

Pericardium Qi Stagnation

Pericardium Qi stagnation symptoms are usually classified under other Energy Organ Qi stagnations, but following from the above functions of the Pericardium, we can list the following. Some of these symptoms are of Pericardium Blood deficiency because that usually occurs as part of the picture:

• Sense of isolation, usually from thwarted, lost or failed relationships. You can easily feel the emotional energy building up, as with the analogy of the motorway 'standing wave'. It is as if the motorway simply isn't wide enough.

---

6. I have often used points on this channel to treat people suffering from relationship problems. It has also been useful where someone has fallen madly in love to their possible detriment; where a woman cannot adjust to the news that she is pregnant (another kind of new relationship); where her body appears to be complaining about the pregnancy whatever she may feel about it; where after the baby's birth she has depression: from the Chinese medical perspective she has then to adjust to a new person in her life, outside her womb.

- Depression and inner sadness usually arising from unfulfilling relationships

- Weeping, tearful or moody

- Menstrual changes or amenorrhoea arising from relationship problems

- In the chest, a blocked or oppressed feeling or pain

- In the throat, sensation of a lump that can neither be swallowed nor hawked up to be spat out

- Sighing, or the taking of large breaths when you are not exercising, or yawning when you are not tired, or much more yawning than usual when you are tired, or breathing faster than normal

- Shortness of breath as the Pericardium fails to support the movement of Qi

- Appetite is reduced and you may even feel some nausea, though eating may help it

- Cold hands, pallor and dizziness as the Pericardium fails to support the movement of Blood

- Frequent waking from sleep, or inability to sleep deeply for long, with disturbing dreams, from Pericardium Blood deficiency

    Frequent Waking? And once you wake, the clear Qi does not ascend (see Clear and Turbid' Qi in the Introduction) so you don't find it easy to think straight

- Anxiety and tendency to be easily frightened from Pericardium Blood deficiency

- Palpitations – the feeling that the heart is beating faster and more urgently in the chest

- Sweating because Pericardium fails to support or control Lungs via the Four Phase cycle.

What HAPPENS NEXT if Pericardium Qi Stagnation continues?

These symptoms can turn into a more alarming syndrome when the emotional strain leads to Fire with additional or alternative symptoms, some recognised in Western medicine, such as:

- Palpitations: heartbeat may be fast and even stop and start at irregular intervals
- Ulcers in the mouth or on the tongue
- 'On-edge' all the time: restlessness
- Feeling of heat in the chest
- Red Complexion (can become eczema)
- Fast breathing (acute anxiety attacks)
- Thirst and sometimes a bitter taste
- Very Heavy Periods (menorrhagia)
- Some foods and drinks can predispose us to this syndrome. These include heating foods such as very spicy food, too much red meat, very fatty, greasy or deep-fried food, and alcohol.

What can YOU do to help yourself in either of these situations?

Although you have palpitations, these symptoms do not suggest heart problems though if ignored, in some cases much further down the line you may get Blood Stasis[7],

---

7. http://www.acupuncture-points.org/blood-stasis.html

which can be serious. If you are still at the 'just started' stage then:

- When a relationship breaks up, or you lose a partner or loved one – and the same applies to the death of a loved and loving pet – it does take time to recover. Do not prevent yourself from grieving. It is a natural way to help you overcome your loss. Read chapter 9.

- Finding a replacement (partner or pet) is not always easy but is a time-honoured way of overcoming the problem.
  – It is better not to rush into new relationships with potential partners. Too many have married in haste, to repent at their leisure.
  – However, dating agencies, including online agencies, have created many very fulfilling relationships.

- Family or friends can sometimes help to suggest suitable partners. With family and friends behind you, the new relationship may have more chance to last.

- Learn to express the emotions you feel. However, for some people, those with an excess of Fire – for example, slightly manic people – showing emotions even more vigorously can be counter-productive because Fire in excess disturbs the Heart even more.
  – For this kind of person, learning to talk quietly about the situation may be better though it is not easy for them to do this. They need to take vigorous exercise to use up the fuel behind the Fire.

- As with other forms of Qi stagnation, exercise can be really helpful in moving Qi and the Blood and releasing emotional tensions. I recommend walking over hills.

- Avoid very fatty or greasy food, and reduce alcohol.

- Sleep can be enormously restorative. This is one of the very

few occasions when, if you cannot see an
acupuncturist or practitioner of Chinese herbal medicine, I
might recommend that you ask your doctor for medication
to help you sleep for a couple of nights. But not more than a
couple of nights!

- Any technique that helps calm your mind may be
good. Meditation, once learned, can be very conducive
in temporarily 'turning off' the ceaseless round of
disturbing thoughts.
– Emotional Freedom Technique can be wonderful here. (See
Appendix 6)

- There are excellent tapes or CDs with white noise or
the noise of the sea superimposed on an almost
inaudible double beat. The difference between the speed of
the beat in left and right ears produces a much lower beat
that your brain appears to recognise. This new beat can be
at a rate that mirrors the electric wavelengths your brain
uses when asleep. By listening to the sounds through
stereophonic headphones your brain is induced to slow
down, if not sleep. If you learn to meditate while using these
CDs you may find you can quickly sink into the mental state
described at times when the Cds aren't available, simply by
doing the meditative breathing.
– Listen to music that mirrors how you feel. Sad music will
not always be appropriate. Try lighter stuff too.

- Learn to breathe using both your chest muscles for
your upper lungs and your diaphragm for your lower lungs.
– Doing the 'bellows' breath (ask a yoga teacher) forces your
Lungs and Pericardium to perform better, moving Qi and
Blood around.
– Likewise, alternate nostril breathing, as taught in
many yoga classes, is very calming. Whether this
exercises alternate sides of your brain I do not know, but

the effect is very steadying. From a Qi stagnation perspective you are moving Qi (breath) through different sides of your nose, affecting the Lungs, Governor, Large Intestine and other channels, all important in managing your Qi movement.

- Do stretching toning exercises to bend and twist your spine in all directions. This helps the nerves supplying all parts of your body, including your brain, to work better. See Appendix 10.
  – Keeping your spine flexible like this helps you to be alert, to think better and consequently to get tired and sleep better. That helps you take better decisions and to come to terms with your situation faster.

- Seek sunlight on your skin, (not excessive or burning)

- Warm companionship. Try to continue socialising and entertaining, one of the best ways to move your Qi.

- Go to the movies or the theatre, even the opera. Operas are full of situations involving loss, separation, renewal, love and life, with music to match.

- Literature is full of great stories that may help you come to terms with your situation. Ask a librarian! And the Internet is full of suggestions.

- In the long-term (not much use short-term) learn some NLP, neuro-linguistic programming, which helps you learn how to deal with people

- Go on a course in negotiation skills

- Long-term, learn autogenics

- Learn Tai Chi, especially 'Touching Hands'.

- Read Chapter 10 on the Heart Energy Organ.

What forms of treatment help?

- Acupuncture is often excellent
- Chinese herbs help greatly
- Treatment to help your spine flex better (appendix 10)
- Learn Emotional Freedom Technique (appendix 7)
- Massage on your back, abdomen and feet
- Counselling
- For very short periods, your doctor may be willing to give you a hypnotic medication that helps you sleep (though I do not really approve of this but have seen it work well.)

Having read this chapter, now please read chapter 10 on the Heart because Pericardium and Heart work closely together.

·

The next chapter is on the politics of pharma and how it may be affecting you.

CHAPTER 17

Pharma-Politics

Qi stagnation is excellent business for pharmaceutical companies. Why?

In its early stages, stress – appearing as Qi Stagnation – produces discomfort. Unless cleared by resolution of the stressors, or for example by exercise, it builds up. Many people are not good at tholing[1] it. Just remember what the typical symptoms are, and then consider a few of the ways it moves on to further symptoms.

A typical symptom is of pressure, pressing, tightness, tension or distension. This distension is not always easy to recognise as such but many people experience it as the need to stretch, to move, to shift around, as a constriction, as the need to take a deep breath. It comes with other symptoms, like frowning, grinding teeth, fast breathing, sweat, tensing hands, swearing, and so on, as I have tried to explain. It is very common.

If Qi continues to stagnate, it moves to shoulder, neck or head tension, with headache; to abdominal cramps and wind; to digestive disturbances including heartburn;

---

1. To thole something is to endure it. Thole is an old Scots verb with Norse, German and Roman roots. I like it because it almost means putting your thoughts into a hole, where of course they thrust around but under control as you adjust to the situation.

trouble sleeping; need for alcohol or tobacco or other social drugs to relax; to frustration vented as anger, even rage.

There can be a craving for junk food; for sweets, crisps and alcohol and tobacco, now also other social drugs. Premenstrual women often experience this along with symptoms more specifically related to the onset of their menses.

Depending on which Energy Organs are affected, we can make predictions as to where the energy will go next and the symptoms it is likely to produce as the problem internalizes into pathology.

Any number of pharmaceutical and other drugs suppress these symptoms, making excellent money for the manufacturers. They include:

- Alcohol
- Analgesics – painkillers
- Antacids
- Anti-inflammatory medications
- Appetite suppressants
- Beta blockers
- Laxatives
- Muscle relaxants
- Sleeping pills
- Social drugs
- Stop smoking patches and treatments
- Tobacco
- Tranquillisers

This symptom suppression has short-term benefits for

both user, pharmacist, shop and manufacturer but, if the drug is taken for too long, long-term shortcomings for the user. Very few of these drugs produce addiction nowadays. Older drugs did, like Librium. But that does not mean that people do not start and then continue to take them as a matter of course. For instance, we know how damaging paracetemol can be if taken in quantity.

What is not so obvious is any long-term effect of using medication regularly, (though we are told there is no such long-term effect, until we know better after they've been used long-term).

That does not mean it does not exist, just that damage to users has not been noticed. Usually if a drug is having a long-term 'beneficial' effect you find that you gradually need more of it to achieve the same results as before.

This means your body has learned to adapt to it so you need more to get results. That is often how people become alcoholics or addicted to tobacco. But it also happens with paracetemol and antacids etc., where need and addiction can look much the same.

Learning to adapt to those drugs does not mean all is well. Your body still has to metabolise the medication: your liver has to break it down, your kidneys have to filter the results and excrete them. This is work for your body, which makes it less able to do other things. Some medications do not mix, possibly confusing if not poisoning you.

Worse, because a symptom is suppressed, the disease process may eventually go deeper. Your body is not able to preserve the symptom on the exterior or at less important levels for ever. If suppressed, the symptoms progress deeper, requiring more powerful medication to deal with new symptoms.

- A smoker's sore throat becomes a smoker's cough

- A smoker's cough moves on to failing lungs
- Neck tension becomes an ongoing headache
- Heartburn suppressed may lead to insomnia or stomach valve problems
- Insomnia suppressed may lead to depression
- Abdominal distension becomes irritable bowel syndrome

All these 'deeper' problems require deeper acting medication: good for doctors and good for pharmaceutical manufacturers.

Of course, we should not forget the damage we do to ourselves either. All those junk foods, those crisps, sweets, refined and processed foods, soft drinks, sugars and artificial sweeteners, all so tasty and addictive, can have over time a devastating effect on our general health and, amongst other metabolic processes, our ability to maintain healthy insulin production. The outcome is often obesity.

In Chinese medicine, these junk foods disrupt the Spleen and Stomach energies, then the Lungs, Kidneys and Liver. Gradually many of us become insulin dependent diabetics.

Diabetics have many further problems. Potentially:

- Amputation of limbs
- Arterial problems
- Circulation problems
- Eye problems and blindness
- Heart attack
- High blood pressure
- Kidney damage and failure
- Obesity
- Stroke

Treating these conditions makes splendid news for pharmaceutical[2] companies! But it is bad news for a government which has to pay for it through its National Health Service. And the government and its people do have to pay for it, either in terms of providing prescribed medications for the ill, or supporting people too ill to work, or in terms of people's lowered capacity to work or defend themselves.

With consequential lowered income people pay a lower rate of income tax and may need more social benefits. They are like the aged in this regard, and in terms of yin and yang, (chapter 4) there is no difference.

Pharmaceutical companies have huge marketing and powerful lobbying departments. They do expensive research and naturally need to show positive results and to hide 'un-conducive research outcomes'.

Disease Creep

Because the health model we use in the West supports the idea that the only true medicine is that which gives drugs, often to suppress symptoms, or cuts out unhealthy organs or irradiates diseased tissues, we do not deal with the underlying signs of disease, nor often notice disease 'creep'.

The Western health model often fails to see connections between symptoms that are more obvious to practitioners of Chinese medicine. It is not that we can eradicate Qi stagnation. Stress and Qi stagnation impel us to change, to improve and work better.

But always suppressing its symptoms will weaken us and ultimately make us more ill, and more dependent on medication and the support of the health, social services and possibly State income benefit.

When what we might have learned to do instead would be 'thole' it when it is mild, to eat, sleep and exercise better

2. Though we should marvel at and be grateful for what Western medicine can do when working to its strengths.

so that we could thole it when it is worse, and to seek non-suppressive treatment when we cannot thole it. What we certainly should not do is sacrifice ourselves to medicine's tender but insidious grip. That makes shareholders rich and the rest of us poor.

How to deal with this?

- Education to help people understand Qi stagnation and learn how to deal with it better

- Showing people the consequences of their actions

- A system of rewards that makes both economic and social sense, promotes the desire to create and adapt, to improve one's lot, and encourages those able to shift for themselves to do better

- Setting out a sensible regime for people to follow

- Recognising how difficult it is for those already well down the road of suppression or disability or stuck in a poverty trap to recover their position and

- Establishing systems to deal with their predicament

All much easier said than done!

Returning to the ideas about Yin and Yang in chapter 4, and putting the subject of this chapter under scrutiny, we could say that

- the pharmaceutical manufacturers as a group are Yang in their ability to 'work' the system;

- the government and the people are Yin, slow to change but adaptable to persuasion;

- individuals with ideas will always be more Yang than large pharmaceutical manufacturers. New ideas, or old

ideas adapted to the times, can circumvent the
established ways and the Establishment;

- ultimately, however, the government has to become
more Yang and legislate to change circumstances so the
people
(Yin) are better educated. Better educated people know how
to better their lot;

- that requires change. Change is a Yang word
because although Yin does change, it changes slowly.
Change often means movement. The ability to move is easier
for younger generations than for older ones. Young
people need to be aware that they can often improve their
lot by learning new skills, by moving to where there is work
or by inventing new ways to make money;

- older people have experience and wisdom. Many can adapt
their lives to do new, possibly challenging activities, and
provide benefit for their community either by care-work or
entrepreneurially. How fortunate we are that, for all its
problems, the Internet is increasingly adapted by and for
innovative older minds to make money for people whose
bones are too old to do hard physical work or to move their
addresses. To keep their Qi moving, if able to, older
generations should continue to work or do activities that
move their Qi economically. They will feel richer in many
ways.

·

*Returning to the analogy of the standing wave on the motorway
in the Introduction, by education and adaptability we widen the
road, make it more resilient, and provide more ways for the traffic
to leave it so the traffic jam never starts.*

·

- that money creates wealth. As long as that wealth is

kept within a state or exchanged for equal value with
producers in other states, the government and its people will
benefit from the jobs it creates or the tax it enables
the government to levy.

The price to pay for this?

Increased change and the willingness to accept this. And
vigilance to ensure that Qi, in the form of Money, Goods, People
and Ideas, can flow freely, thereby creating wealth more easily
for all. That state will then be stronger and better able to
withstand international and political vicissitudes[3].

---

3. But what will actually happen? Yang individuals will come up with new ways to make
   money from Qi stagnation. If these are medicines or drugs, then ultimately they'll make
   money and the rest of us will be the poorer, both monetarily and in our health. However,
   if they can invent ways to help us without using medicines or drugs, then something new
   will have been created, probably adding greatly to their and our wealth.

CHAPTER 18

Conclusions

This book has been about Qi stagnation and its consequences for our health. When it stagnates, it produces symptoms that resemble what Chinese medicine calls Wind and Heat, disturbing the normal actions of the body's Energy Organs.

Unresolved, those forces cause long-term disease. The Chinese model provides an understanding of both early and later stages of stress, unlike the Western medical model that looks mainly at the later stages.

Whilst the ways of resolving Qi stagnation proposed in this book work for many, for those in slavery or captivity, or unable to help themselves or to be helped, one can have only compassion and express the expectation that, such are the ways of Yin and Yang, no condition is unchanging for ever.

For health, our Qi needs to circulate: not too fast, not too slow. It needs to circulate smoothly both within us and with our environment. Circulating Qi with our environment is vital for life:

- We need to eat food, one form of Qi,

- We have to breathe air, another form of Qi and

- To make a living we need to have jobs or businesses that are needed by our community and which pay us money or exchange our efforts for the means to live (another form of Qi) and

- To live happily we need companions who return our affection and with whom we can have mutually caring, respectful relationships (still further kinds of Qi).

- Many would argue that we need a respectful and grateful relationship with the world that made us, and with our God if we have that belief (the ultimate Qi flow-return[1])

We can learn ways to keep our minds in a relaxed alert state. We can keep our bodies healthy with strong immune systems with the right diet, living conditions and exercise. This keeps the Qi moving in our bodies and encourages it to resist disease without over-dependence on medication.

We can keep our spirits in good condition by allowing ourselves to show off, to create, to improve living conditions for all. This allows our Qi to manifest itself outwardly.

We can promote our position in our environment and country by the right attitude and service. This promotes the movement of Qi between ourselves and our employers, employees, friends and acquaintances.

Those who refuse to work or participate in their communities ultimately prevent their Qi from circulating. This leads to dependency, too much of which leads to Qi stagnation because Qi here flows only in one direction – it is not returned.

A country has to be strong to be able to maintain that flow of Qi in one direction indefinitely. It is like leaving a water tap

---

1. I remember talking to an ex-prisoner of war who had spent nearly 4 years in the Japanese prison camps in WW2. He maintained that those who preserved their sanity best were those who had an ongoing relationship with their god.

running all the time. The water runs to waste. In a country with big reservoirs, this does not much matter. In dry countries it does matter.

For trade, a country must both give and receive. For health, Qi must flow, not too much and not too little. If the balance tips too much in one direction, it will lead – eventually – to Qi stagnation, because it is not being returned.

We see international Qi stagnation in many forms. Politician grapple with it all the time, always seeking advantage or trying to keep it circulating.

Chinese medicine developed a Qi model centred on the individual and his health, but it used a sort of political model – the Energy Organs, with an Emperor, a Prime Minister, a Chief of the Armed Forces and so on – a hint about the larger picture of the way Qi should flow.

The Chinese understanding about the way that energy should flow did not just cover the way Qi flows when an Energy Organ is healthy, but also the flow round the Five Element/Four Phase system. Stagnation in one Element could be helped not just within itself but by encouraging movement round the cycle.

Just as there are acupuncture points that can encourage Qi to flow from one phase to the next, so there are actions we can take.

In health, we take them naturally, as when people temporarily enjoying their Fire phase (e.g. Red Nose day parties) give money (Metal phase) to charity (Earth phase). Appreciating the phase relationships may enable us, when ill, to move our Qi onward, facilitating recovery.

Their model makes us each responsible, to a large extent, for ensuring that our individual Qi can flow. It makes us individually responsible, in the first instance, for our health.

As we mature, it makes us responsible for learning how to help the Qi of our family and community flow. We have responsibility for our community and ultimately for our state or country.

As chapter 4 attempted to explain, our country is made up of individuals who, working together or through their appointed representatives, should aim to reduce the environmental stressors that make some parts of society more constitutionally vulnerable.

But it starts with us.

Finally ... Now you've read this book, *please review it!* It aims to be not just informative, but *useful.*

If you think others would benefit from it, please post your opinion somewhere prospective readers might see it, such as on Amazon. Here are links to the North American site (https://www.amazon.com) and the UK site (https://www.amazon.co.uk).

- Click on the link (either amazon.com or amazon.co.uk – or of course, your own country's equivalent)

- Type "Qi Stagnation – Signs of Stress" into the search box at the top of the Amazon page

- When a picture of the book appears, click on where it says 'review' or 'reviews', then

- Click on "Write a customer review" and say what you think about it:

- You can give it 5 stars out of 5 – if you think it merits them, of course!

I hope you will be positive and constructive, but if you have major criticisms or reservations, I would like to know! Then I can improve it for the next person.

Let me know via http://www.acupuncture-points.org/book-review-contact-page.html .

PART I

APPENDIX 1 - WHAT IS QI?

To be frank, nobody knows, so you may wish to skip this appendix!

I did electrical engineering at university, though it was not a high point in my career. It has left me with an enquiring mind which I sometimes use.

The history of the development of the concept of Qi, at least in the West, goes something like this. Let us suppose that early humans developed something like a reverence for life when they understood death. What was the difference between a living body and a dead one? One obvious difference is that a living body can decide to move of its own will, and move itself.

From our perspective, we can now see that this is not a particularly good criterion on its own, because volcanoes erupt, a storm at sea can destroy boats, lightning can burn your house down and so on. They are all kinds of perceived movement.

If you cannot see where the will to move comes from, then it is magic or the act of invisible gods, spirits or devils. The basic idea also breaks down because when you are unconscious or asleep and not dead, you still move (your chest rises and falls as you breathe, you pulse can be felt, etc) but there is no sign of active volition in these activities.

What entered the body to give it life? Most early societies, at least in the West, seemed to have agreed that this came down to the breath. This began at birth and left you at death, the word 'inspiration' having both material and spiritual aspects.

Where did the breath and the energy it gave bodies come from? The Chinese called it Qi (pronounced "Tchee!"). One of the most venerated and earliest books of Chinese medicine, still in daily use as a resource, is the Huangdi Neijing[1] or the Yellow Emperor's Classic of Medicine. In this it says that Qi is made from what comes from the Heavens and from the Earth, food and water, and that it permeates throughout the whole body.

The process by which Qi is 'manufactured' in the body is clearly set out in Chinese medicine and there is a summary of it on our website at http://www.acupuncturepoints.org/qi.html

As it moves throughout the body, it leads Blood. The pathways of Qi run along acupuncture channels that traverse the whole body. The actual lines, which you can see on acupuncture diagrams, are the centres of their influence. Like a stream or river in a valley, the actual area drained by the river extends up to the watershed shared with the next river – or channel.

The original Qi (in Chinese the Yuan Qi) is said to be found between the kidneys, deep in your abdomen in front of your spine. This originates from your parents though how well it functions and how much of it there is depends on what happens in your life – upbringing, education, diet, disease, trauma etc.

Interestingly, Western science now tends to agree with this in principle, that the power of your own mitochondria, the fuel

1. Of this there are a number of translations. For example Unschuld, Paul U. (2003). Huang Di nei jing su wen: Nature, Knowledge, Imagery in an Ancient Chinese Medical Text. Berkeley and Los Angeles: University of California Press and Veith, Ilza; translator (1972). The Yellow Emperor's Classic of Internal Medicine). Revised paperback edition. Berkeley, Los Angeles: University of California Press.

power in each of your cells, derives from your parents, specifically the mitochondria of your mother.

As Qi disperses it becomes more rarified, as it concentrates it becomes more material. Ideas and thoughts are examples of more rarified Qi, while physical bodies, flesh and bones, are example of more concentrated Qi.

In nature, Qi is said to be always moving or changing or trying to move or change, and as it transforms from one state to another things come into existence or cease to exist. It is fundamental to the Universe and life.

Indeed, it may be said, more accurately, that Qi exists because of the interplay between Yang and Yin, as they transform into one another, oppose each other, depend on each other and consume each other.

Whether, and if so to what extent this equates to quantum physics, in which in this universe at any one moment a particle may or may not exist, flashing in to and out of existence, is anyone's guess. Taking all such events into account at one moment with their cumulative effect means existence as we know it and enables us to experience Qi.

PART II

APPENDIX 2 - WHAT IS CHINESE MEDICINE?

Traditional Chinese medicine (TCM) is a body of knowledge and experience about health and disease developed in China over at least 3000 years. That makes it sound as if it has been a cohesive body of understanding, which it has most definitely not been!

Note. Whether acupuncture originated in China is a moot point. Other countries, such as Sri Lanka, have strong claims to it. And it may have been used in Europe even earlier, if the markings on a 5000 year old body discovered high in the Alps where pressure or needles might have been placed are what they look like.

In any community, the first two ways of helping someone who is sick are hands-on – touch – and food. Food is kitchen medicine. Cooks gradually learned which foods did what, including herbs. Probably they were also informed by shamanic medicine. What became acupuncture, Chinese herbalism, the use of moxa and other techniques almost certainly did not start up in any orderly fashion.

Probably it was gradually assembled together once underlying theories were developed.

Over time, lacking modern scientific method, Chinese scholars developed theories based on a philosophical or universal world view, but tested by experiment and experience on real people in real situations.

Various books written between 2000 and 3000 years ago are the basis of TCM's structure but the last 2000 years have seen many experienced practitioners and thinkers refine and add to them.

Chinese medicine is a very flexible system for understanding health and treating disease. Its criteria for diagnosis of disease are often very different from those of modern medicine. In a way it is like someone who knows how to drive a car but does not know what makes the car go. Modern science is learning what makes the car go, but lacks the finesse of at least 3000 years experience in driving it.

TCM is an ancient (ancient – but continues to be worked on even nowadays) shorthand for how the body works. Modern science is the longhand version. TCM can seem like superstition and magic, only because modern science has not explained it. One day, modern science will probably be able to explain it all and perhaps improve on it.

TCM practitioners were quick to understand the advantages that Western medicine offered and to incorporate Western medicine treatments and drugs into Chinese medicine.

Western medicine has found it very hard to accept Chinese medicine, let alone to incorporate it. Many practitioners of Chinese medicine would say that the double-blind, placebo-controlled tests that Western science insists upon are not often appropriate for the way Chinese medicine works.

Why? Because Chinese medicine is individualised.

Each individual has to have treatment precisely designed for him.

There is no 'one-size-fits-all'. If a treatment does not work then the original diagnosis needs to be re-appraised. In addition, there may be a number of ways of achieving the end result. Different practitioners of Chinese medicine might have different techniques; they might stress the importance of treating the same condition in different ways or in a different order.

Indeed, a major weakness in orthodox or Western medicine and the drugs it uses is that, as pharmaceutical research shows, a particular drug may be helpful in a small number of cases but harmful when applied to everyone with a given disease, leading to many dangerous side-effects.

This happens because each of those suffering from a given disease is an individual, and cannot be treated like all the others. If all are treated with the same drug, the drug will tend to suppress their symptoms rather than cure them. When suppression occurs, the disease process is either hidden for a while or re-emerges in another form.

Dangerously, when the symptom disappears it may be hailed as a success, overlooking its later re-emergence in some other, perhaps more sinister form.

With DNA 'finger-printing', Western pharmacy may get its next lease of life, eventually enabling drug companies to manufacture drugs that really are designed for each individual.

Until that moment arrives, Western pharmacy and medicine may find it hard to comprehend and accept the sophistication of Chinese medicine. For instance, amongst Western scientists there remains great resistance to the concept of the acupuncture channels and the movement of Qi, yet applying these concepts has repeatedly helped millions of people.

PART III

APPENDIX 3 - SOUL AND EMOTIONS

The Soul in Western religions like Christianity, Islam and Judaism is singular. Each of us has only one. The problem is that Soul is the nearest word in English for Shen in Chinese. However, Shen has nothing to do with the Christian, Islam or Judaic concept.

Shen also implies no ongoing relationship with an Almighty God. The idea of an Almighty God is not present in Chinese medical thinking. It is neither confirmed nor denied and the same goes for the Western concept of the Soul.

In some ways the word 'self' is better. But that raises other questions. In Chinese medicine, Shen is the overall concept for Self or Mind.

Now prepare yourself because this next bit is a little complicated, and that is because they have had 3000 years to develop it and to compare it, for example, with the Buddhist concept of Nothingness.

The Shen is made up of five aspects. Each of these relates to one of the Five Elements or Phases. Consequently, it allows the purpose and function of each of the Energy Organs, working together, to integrate as the Shen, the Mind.

Before describing each of the five aspects of the Shen, you need to get to grips with a fundamental idea behind Chinese medicine and philosophy.

I have introduced this in chapter 4, on Yin and Yang. The interplay between Yin and Yang gives us Qi. Qi manifests in all the forms and ways of expression possible in our universe:

- A lump of stone is Qi.

- The wavelength of light is a form of Qi.

- The blood in your veins is a form of Qi.

- Likewise gravity, the Higgs Boson, porridge, fishing and all black holes whether in stockings or at the centre of the galaxy, not to mention your thoughts about all these weighty matters.

- So is the pain I feel in my ankle after skiing

- And, how you feel about all this, how your mother feels about it and the emotions expressed by anyone who disagrees with you – all are forms of Qi.

Those emotions include

- Anger

- Joy

- Worry

- Grief

- Fear

It is not just the personality, spirit or self but the body too, because unlike in Western medicine, philosophy and religion, the body is not seen as a container or prison for the soul but merely as a concentration of Qi. The physicality of the body compares with the more rarefied concentration of Qi comprising the self or the Shen or the Mind and their emotions. Whether Shen or physical body, they're just two aspects of Qi existing as you.

Consequently, just as neither Yin nor Yang can exist independently, so Shen and Body are interdependent, coexisting, co-supporting.

Analogies given by the ancient Chinese include:

- A knife's sharp edge disappears when the knife ceases to exist

- The flame from burning a piece of wood ceases when the wood is burnt

- Another analogy is that a Dance exists until the Dancers stop.

In fact, the main philosopher behind this, Zhang Zai (1020- 1077) said that Qi included Yin and Yang. *(Yes, yes, I know I said the interplay of Yin and Yang produces Qi...)* Zhang Zai also said that when Qi consolidates it has a shape, so is visible. Conversely, when it does not consolidate, it has no shape so is invisible. But, in answer to the Buddhists, who said that everything was Emptiness, he queried whether when Qi dissolved it became nothingness.

Putting it another way, he said that Qi consolidating and dissolving into the Void was like ice forming and melting in water[1].

Why is all this important?

Because it clearly distinguishes the Chinese idea of the Shen, which comes together as its five aspects integrate, from the Western idea of the Soul. That means that when the

---

1. The source for these comments by Zhang Zai is The Development of Neo-Confucian Thought by Carson Chang, Greenwood Press 1977, quoted by Maciocia G in 'The Psyche in Chinese Medicine, Churchill Livingstone 2009.

Mind, the Shen, is strongly affected for example by emotions, it can affect the Energy Organs, the Zangfu. *Conversely, imbalances in the latter will affect the Mind.*

The result is that if you can recognise the predominant emotion(s) in a patient, you may be able to diagnose which Energy Organs are imbalanced and be able to treat or ameliorate the problem through them.

On the other hand, if you know which Energy Organs are imbalanced, you have a good idea how that person's thinking and emotions may be affected. Even if you cannot ascertain the predominant emotion, you should, from a knowledge of Chinese medicine be able to discover which Zangfu Energy Organs are affected.

From then on you treat it as if the emotion with that Energy Organ needs treatment. Also, you have a means to help, because Chinese medicine aims to balance the Five Phases or Elements, and to bring more equilibrium between Yin and Yang.

By the way... this is a vast simplification of what they said, and nor do I claim to have adequately rendered the Western religious or philosophical view!

PART IV

APPENDIX 4 - FIVE ELEMENTS OR FOUR PHASES?

	Water	Wood	Fire	Earth	Metal
Process	Recovering	Progressing	Peaking	Nourishing	Refining
Season	Winter	Spring	Summer	Later Summer	Autumn
Life Experience	Germinating	Growing	Maturing	Settling and Supporting	Making Space
Negative emotion	Fear	Anger	Mania, Hysteria	Worry, Obsession	Grief
Positive emotion	Determination	Courage	Love	Support-Accepting	Researching-Letting Go
Zang-fu energy organ	Kidneys, Bladder	Liver, Gallbladder	Heart, Small Intestine	Spleen, Stomach	Lungs, Large Intestine
Colour	Black, blue	Green	Red	Yellow	White

Probably as old as the theory of Yin and Yang, the Five Element and Four Phase Systems[1] were attempts by the ancient Chinese

1. The word 'Element' is used in the West but the actual word in Chinese can also be

to explain the workings of the universe and to relate them to life. Each of the five 'elements' or 'phases' represents a segment of experience. Depending on the context, it is described as either an Element or a Phase.

Each element relates to the others in a number of ways. There are several ways of portraying the relationships between them graphically. In the most common one, all link together like a daisy chain round an empty centre.

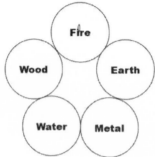

The Five Elements linked in this way are called the Five Element system or diagram – see left.

In another diagram, the Earth element is placed at the centre with the other four daisy-chaining round it. In many situations, that model, the Four Phase system, is better – see below right.

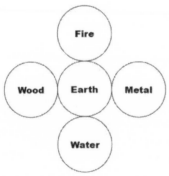

translated as 'Process', or even 'Behaviour'. I have used the word 'Phase' because, at least in terms of Qi Stagnation, the Four Phases based round the Earth Element seems to work particularly well in many ways.

Several 'laws' hold the Five Elements together.

*1. Mother – Child: each element has a maternal
relationship with the element following it.*

This is often used therapeutically and diagnostically. For
example, a baby may be sick because its mother is sick or vice
versa. If you know which is the cause and which is the effect,
you will treat the condition much faster and more
successfully by putting right the underlying cause first.

For example a case of plantar fasciitis (great pain in the heel
on any pressure such as standing) where the patient had
already tried many other methods of treatment and
was told it would take another year or so to go, was cured after

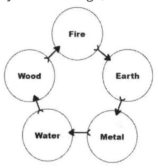

two acupuncture treatments.

The heel, in Chinese medicine, usually comes under the
Bladder and Kidney channels, which pass through it –
the Water phase. However, taking the case showed that
the problem was in the Metal phase, with a very weak
Lung pulse. Treatment to strengthen the Metal pulses
produced an immediate improvement not just in the pain
but in the general energy and outlook.

The heel channels, Bladder and Kidney of the Water phase,
needed no treatment. Here, treating the Mother (Metal) cured
the Child (Water). Choosing which to treat can make a huge

difference. Equally, sometimes it is appropriate to disperse excess energy from the 'child' in order to calm the 'mother'.

2. Controlling/destructive 'Ke' , 'K'o' or 'Ko' cycle.

In the Five Element system each element has a controlling or regulating effect on its 'grandchild' in the cycle.

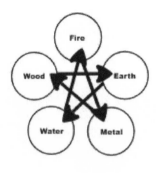

But it can also have a destructive effect on it. For example, stagnating Liver Qi (Wood) frequently adversely affects Spleen/Stomach energy (Earth). Similarly, a strong Metal (Lung and Large Intestine) can prevent Wood (Liver and Gallbladder) from over-acting but it can also prevent it from acting at all.

Some schools of acupuncture teach, or used to teach, only the Five Element system[2]. Other schools ignored it completely and their graduates were amazed when they saw its good results.

On the whole, the Five Element or Phase system seems to have lost prestige in China and gained it elsewhere. This may be because its Shamanic ideas do not accord with how the Chinese want to present their medicine.

3. The Four Phase diagram

This, in the form of a cross (see below), is probably just as

2. Each element has many other attributes not listed above, including smell, flavour, food and so on. For books on this, see Five Element Constitutional Acupuncture by Hicks, Hicks and Mole, Churchill Livingstone; Five Elements, Six Conditions: A Taoist Approach to Emotional Healing, Psychology, and Internal Alchemy by Gilles Marin, North Atlantic Books,U.S.; Traditional Acupuncture: The Law of the Five Elements by Dianne M. Connelly, Traditional Acupuncture Institute,U.S.

ancient as the Five Element
diagram. It is also known as the Organ Cosmological Sequence.

In this book I have used it in preference to the Five Element diagram, because I have found it makes more sense when explaining to patients how their Energy organs interact – e.g as between Lung and Liver, and as between Heart and Kidney.

The implications of this diagram are explained in more detail in chapter 5. However, note that each phase has a direct relationship with the Earth at the centre, both to draw from it, depend on it and to give Qi back to it.

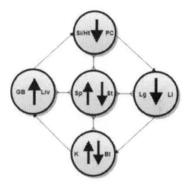

Conversely of course, Earth can have both a beneficial and an 'over-mothering' effect on the other phases.

This 'Four-Phase' diagram allows one to see how the Energy Organs that ascend Qi are together in the lower left quadrant, being the Kidney, Liver/Gallbladder and Spleen.

Conversely the Energy Organs which descend Qi are mainly in the upper right quadrant, being the Heart, Small Intestine, Pericardium (not shown on the diagram for reasons of space), the Lungs and Large Intestine, and Stomach and Bladder.

Please note that this diagram is simplified because, for example, the Kidney Energy Organ has two functions in terms of how it sends Qi! It also holds Qi down. Another example: the Liver acts not just to send Qi upwards but to keep it flowing freely. Also, like other diagrams in this book, it does not mention what is called the

Three Heater or San Jiao Energy organ. To do so would have made the book too long!

PART V

APPENDIX 5 - CHINESE CLOCK

When Qi flows smoothly, it passes along the channels in the directions shown in the table below. When it rebels, it may go in the opposite direction along the channel or, at least, not flow so convincingly. Qi Stagnation in one channel can lead to Qi in another channel not flowng smoothly in the correct direction.

Channel Flow Direction	Energy Organ	Time	Time	Energy Organ	Channel Flow Direction
Down	Three Heater	9pm-11pm	11pm-1am	Gall-Bladder	Down
Up	Pericardium	7pm-9pm	1am-3am	Liver	Up
Up	Kidney	5pm-7pm	3am-5am	Lungs	Up
Down	Bladder	3pm-5pm	5am-7am	Large Intestine	Down
Down	Small Intestine	1pm-3pm	7am-9am	Stomach	Down
Up	Heart	11am-1pm	9am-11am	Spleen	Up

The direction of flow along all Yin channels is upwards, and that along Yang channels is downwards. For example, the Heart channel's first point is in the chest area and its last point is on the small finger: Qi travels along the channel from the chest to the finger: upwards, if you imagine standing with your hands above your head.

The Small intestine channel starts on the small finger and travels downwards, in the opposite direction to that of the Heart channel. So the movement of Qi along the channels is always balanced between Yin and Yang.

Of course, the table also gives the traditional times when the Energy Organs have their 'moment' in the driving seat. Sometimes these seem very apposite but modern lifestyles, the 24 hours shift pattern, speedy travel across time zones and the availability of light all the time often make their use redundant, although sometimes it is possible by judicious use of acupuncture to reset the system.

Understanding the Chinese clock can be very helpful in deciding which channels and what points to treat.

The Direction an Energy Organ SENDS Qi

This Qi flow direction along the channels has little to do with the direction in which each Energy Organ sends Qi – up or down – in the body (see the diagram below), when in health.

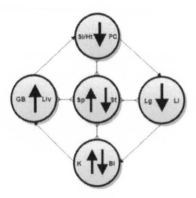

When an Energy Organ's Qi stagnates, its Qi may flow in the wrong direction (for example the Spleen may allow Qi to descend rather than ascend, see chapter 13) and there may be problems with the flow along its channel too.

This energy re-direction or 'rebellion' is more obvious and frequent than energy not passing smoothly along a channel, or even going along a channel in the wrong direction.

In this book I discuss, apart from within this appendix 5, only the mis-direction (down or up instead of up or down)[1] in which Qi is sent by an Energy Organ when that Energy Organ's Qi stagnates.

Times of the Chinese Clock

Our modern 'Western' way of life now is very different from the lives of people two thousand years ago – and even the lives of people up until recently when we got electric power and could work any hour of the day or night.

This facility to alter our once 'natural' life cycles, and to alter our pathology with chemicals and drugs, means that the Chinese clock may not work so clearly for everyone. Still, it seems to work often enough to be quite useful.

---

1. In trying to clarify this I hope I have not followed in the footsteps of the British Royal Navy's famous notice which, in stipulating how to store torpedoes, marked the boxes in which torpedoes were to be transported – "Top marked Bottom to avoid Confusion."

PART VI

APPENDIX 6 - EMOTIONAL FREEDOM TECHNIQUE

Chinese medicine's acupuncture channel theory has generated a whole range of therapies since 1970. These include Reiki, Applied Kinesiology and now Emotional Freedom Technique (EFT). EFT is not quite as easy as it seems because it may involve some soul-searching, but many people still find it very powerful. And you can do it yourself!

However, to start with, you may make more progress by asking someone else to help and show you how to use it. This appendix is not intended to explain fully how to use EFT, but to draw your attention to it, explain its basis and summarise how it works.

EFT Basis

Qi stagnation is the cause of untold misery and pain. For health, Qi should move. When it ceases to move, we get physical or mental pain. Trapped emotions are often the cause of Qi stagnation.

In our bodies there is a mapped-out network of the way

Qi should circulate for health, called the acupuncture channel system. This is different from, but gives life to other systems such as the blood circulation system, the lymph system and the nervous system. Psychologists have long recognised that if you can recognise and release trapped emotions you will feel better. Often this requires extensive therapy.

EFT uses that idea, but also uses the acupuncture channel to get the Qi moving. (In this book you will also have read of other ways to help yourself.)

There are two parts to successful EFT. Sometimes both are needed, and sometimes just the second part.

1. Identify the trapped emotion.

This is why you may not be the best person to identify the emotion. Why? Because you are the person who originally experienced it, found it so painful that you hid it away in a locker and threw away the key. Talking to someone else may help you bring it back to consciousness more easily. Once you have identified it you can learn to express the emotion positively rather than negatively, so opening yourself to change. Express this change positively as a phrase. That opens you to Qi circulation again.

The next stage stimulates the Qi circulation network in your body, releasing local blocks.

2. Tap the channels concerned.

Experience has shown that for most purposes a regime of tapping certain specific points is enough. The points generally chosen use channel entry or exit points or points near them. Many of them are on the head.

What to do? Repeat the phrase you have formulated under 1. above whilst tapping each of the points a number of times in sequence. Do this a number of times. Very often, this alone releases the block or blocks and the pain is reduced or you feel more positive and confident. Sometimes you may need to repeat the phrase and do occasional tapping.

Often you can tie the idea and the tapping into a single tap on just one point that brings to mind the whole process sufficiently to prevent the emotion from repeating.

It should be said that formulating a suitable phrase and tapping points on your body to 'anchor' the thought are used in other psychological therapeutic systems, including NLP. EFT just incorporates acupuncture channel theory as well.

PART VII

APPENDIX 7 - BREATHING

The Lungs are said to rule skin and hair as well as to 'govern' your Qi.

This whole book is about Qi Stagnation and how to get it to circulate again. In air, we have a ready source of Qi all round us. Because the first independent action we take at birth is to breathe, and because we have to keep breathing until we die, most of us think we know how to do it.

Knowing how to do it does not mean that we are any good at it. I can read a book about putting up shelves but that does not mean that I am any good at it. I may know the principles of cooking but that does not mean you would want to eatwhat I cook.

Someone who uses his body fully, through sport for example, may learn unconsciously how to do it well. You can see the lustre in their skin and hair and you just know that they are healthy and almost certainly breathe well. Many athletes would do even better if they learned how to breathe properly.

As you age, your Qi diminishes for a variety of reasons. But until you die, you must breathe. Why not learn to breathe properly and improve your life with better health?

It is easy to do! It does take a little practice but you will feel better very quickly from doing it and your skin will improve without the need for cosmetics or moisturizers. Just remember. Although breathing properly for a few minutes every day will help, you should try to do it all the time. If you sit at a desk or computer for your work, you almost certainly do not breathe properly, using both the lower and upper parts of your lungs. And if sitting much, you probably have poor posture.

Poor posture is a sign of low Qi. Breathe better, your Qi will improve and so will your posture. Likewise, good posture will keep your lungs open and allow you to breathe deeply.

An Upper Lung exercise to do in bed before rising You can exercise your lungs at any time, even abed. For example, before you get up in the morning, lie on your back (knees raised with feet flat on the bed if you like) with one or both hands on your upper chest, just below your collarbone.

By breathing deeply make your hands rise and fall. When you start, you may have an urge to yawn. Yawning opens the upper part of your lungs, so yawning is good. After every in-breath, allow your chest to relax and let the air out with a long slow sigh as you count '1'. On the next long out-breath, count '2'. With each subsequent out-breath count the numbers until you reach '10. Then repeat up to 10 again. That is enough. Now you can get up.

Lower abdominal breathing

This form of breathing is better for calming down and steadying yourself. Many forms of meditation use it to bring the mind 'down' and regulate the emotions. Unless you are using it to meditate, it is probably better to do it before you go to sleep.

A Lower Lung exercise to do before going to sleep This is best done in bed immediately before you go to sleep, having put the light out. Lying on your back, knees raised with feet flat on the bed if that is more comfortable, place one or both hands on your abdomen below your umbilicus.

Breathe slowly and steadily, so that you make your hands rise and fall from the in and out breaths. Do not worry about your upper lungs at this point. Concentrate on your belly!

Do the same counting on each out-breath as you did in the morning with the upper lung out-breaths, counting '1', '2', '3', etc on each out-breath up to '10' then starting again at '1'. Do it twice.

Then go to sleep. After doing it, resist the temptation to read or watch TV. If you go to sleep while doing it, that is fine, although try to stay awake to complete all twenty breaths (two counts up to '10'.)

PART VIII

APPENDIX 8 - HISTORY OF STRESS

Western medicine has never really decided what stress is. Various big ideas have been important but doctors tend to think the early stages, where stress builds, are less important, or at any rate, more the concern of psychologists. On the other hand, the progressed conditions, where they can diagnose disease, take more of their attention.

Over the last century, some modern psychologists have, curiously, reverted to using personality typing as a means to predict health (for examples see below under Marston and Friedman) using models not that unlike ancient astrological types of personality-typing[1].

18th Century: Neurasthenia, 'weakness of the nerves', was much discussed in the 18th Century. The idea that hard work and 'stress', as we might call it, led to diseases meant that for some, having gout was a badge of honour!

1870: Charles Mercier wrote 'Sanity and Insanity'. He thought that insanity was the product of just two factors: heredity and

---

1. This role of personality in shaping the individual's response to stress was also proposed for example by D Thomson, 'Sickness Absence in the Civil Service' Proceedings of the Royal Society of Medicine 65 (1972) 572-7

stress. Following Mercier, there were many articles about how stress made us ill, and how, if you were robust, you would need a much greater level of stress to send you mad. This thinking informed the diagnosis of 'shell shock' in the first World War.

1881: George Beard wrote about Neurasthenia and Americanisation, affirming that the chief and primary causes of the development of and very rapid increase of stress in modern civilisation were:

o Stress

o The press

o The telegraph

o Science and

o The mental activity of women (!)

1925: Wm Sadler, New York Times: thought the rising incidence of heart disease was the result of tension, the incessant drive of American Life and the excitable tendency of the American temperament. In a way, he suggested that Americans had not had time to adapt to modern life.

1928: William Moulton Marstons wrote 'Emotions of Normal People' which classified people into DISC personality types (D = Dominant, I = Inducement, S = Submission, C = Compliance). From this, predictions could be made about mental health in real-life situations, useful when interviewing job applicants. Marston's ideas led on to the classification of people into Types A, B, C, D each tending to display certain kinds of emotional responses, and the consequences for their health.

1933: V Langdon-Brown wrote 'The Stress of Modern Civilisation', discussing the loss of security, and of liberty of thought.

1936: Hans Selye wrote 'General Adaptation to Stress': Stress was mediated by the adeno-pituitary axis (later amended to the adrenal cortex). This led to wide discussion of the stress syndrome in 1950s.

Selye said there were three phases: alarm,

adaptation, exhaustion. This became the basis for much discussion. He based his theory on work where he had exposed animals to fasting, heat, cold, exhaustion etc (very crude tests) and originally he described it as General Adaptation Syndrome, but later 'Stress Syndrome'.

Selye described a range of diseases induced in animals by stress including:
- Hypertension
- Cardiovascular arrest
- Rheumatoid Arthritis
- Renal problems
- Peptic ulcer
- Diabetes

These were all diseases whose causes were not understood at the time, so were under intense scrutiny. Selye's work received many objections:
- His studies were done only on animals
- They involved extreme physical stress contrasting with stress being mostly low-grade psychological stress in humans
- Measurements were very crude, such as weighing the organs after killing the animals

His theory continues to be influential, for example in modernlectures on endocrinology.

Richard S Lazarus has written various books on this general subject, based around Selye's model. He proposed that what happened was not the main or first mediator but how you appraised the danger in the situation or your condition, then what coping methods you used. This then triggers your hormonal pathways[2].

1938: Lord Horder in 'Health and a Day' talked about the strain of modern civilisation and suggested that a prominent cause was the 'reckless, stupid, provocative, ill-mannered selfish noise' of the day.

2. Stress, Appraisal and Coping Richard S Lazarus and Susan Folkman, Springer 1984.

1949: James L Halliday 'Psychosocial medicine'. He had had to assess absenteeism records. He viewed sickness absenteeism as a barometer of society. He suggested social disequilibrium was a first stage leading to breakdown through e.g. peptic ulcer. He said a sick society couldn't cope.

1950s: Meyer Friedman did more research on the effects of emotions and behaviour on the heart, specifically concerning the Type A personality.

1966: EH Hare argued that the 'really weighty causal factors of neurosis, if they are not to be found in present stress, must be looked for in the constitution'. (Mental Health in New Towns 1966)

1967: Thomas H Holmes and Richard H Rahe introduced a 'social readjustment rating scale' that rated life events in terms of the likelihood of a major illness occurring within a year after a life event. (E.g. death of spouse, divorce, job loss etc). These explained conditions likely to cause disease and predicted the trigger for certain diseases. The scale was based on work partly done in the Air Force during the war. This scale is still in use though different countries and cultures have made minor changes to suit their own culture. Eg going to prison in Japan is a major dishonour and rates more highly than in the usual scale.

1970: Alvin Toffler wrote 'Future Shock' suggesting that the modern problems of birth, schooling, bullying, marriage, the job market, the economy etc. and even of the world, Gaia, and the cosmos, all contribute to how we live in a stressful world. He said that we are subject to future shock from the tempo of western life, its transience, rapid technological and social innovation, and a surfeit of choice for the consumer.

This manifests as a rise in organic and psychological disorders (heart, obesity, diabetes, anxiety ...) epitomised by an article in NYT by Claudia Willis in 1983:

• More aggression

- More sex crime
- Unstable power relations
- More sickness

1977: George L Engel proposed what is called the bio-psychosocial model positing that biological, psychological (which entails thoughts, emotions, and behaviours), and social factors, all play a significant role in human functioning in the context of disease or illness.

This is by no means the end of it. Many prominent psychologists have proposed personality theories, ranging from Freud (Ego Psychology) to Yuichi Shoda and Walter Mischel (Cognitive-affective personality system). All to a greater or lesser extent discuss the effect of stress on mental equilibrium.

Another strand has been not the question of constitutional vulnerability but the influence of the environment , the effect of deprivation and the costs that governments might incur if strategy involved reorganizing city environments, social welfare and working conditions. Environmental stressors include overcrowding, noise, educational inequalities, pollution and poverty[3].

Some of these strands inform the work of educational theorists like Pierre Bourdieu and Jerome Bruner[4]. They discuss the relative effects on children's attainments and, by implication, on the health of society and therefore its tendency both to cause and absorb stress; of poverty, parental involvement in their children's education; the role of the school; the role of teachers; and of government.

To this one may add a growing awareness of the role bad food plays in education[5]. Poorly fed children

3. A model of Person-Environment Fit' by John RP French, Willard Rogers and Sidney Cobb, Society, Stress and Disease iv, Working Life 39-44
Psychosocial Stress, Population, Environment and Quality of Life Lennart Levi and Lars Andersson, Spectrum, 1975. Hans Selye described these as pathogenic situations.
4. Bourdieu, P. (1986) The Forms of capital, Abingdon: Routledge Falmer and Bruner, J. (1985) Child Language, Teaching and Therapy, Oxford: Oxford University Press.

cannot concentrate so cause disarray in the classroom, learn less, probably cope less well with stress and so become disruptive in society and, if unable to find work, dependent on social benefits. All that increases the stressors on everyone else.

5. Many references. See for example: http://reap.stanford.edu/docs/nutrition_and_education/

PART IX

APPENDIX 9 - SCIENTIFIC EVIDENCE

To be frank, there is lots of evidence that Traditional Chinese Medicine works, but Western medicine accepts it ungracefully because no agreed scientific basis yet exists for it. To convince scientists and statisticians, research must follow accepted rules and meet particular criteria, a process that, for a holistic medicine, is not always easy.

Such research is not much funded (the sale of acupuncture needles makes few people rich) and pharmaceutical companies, with their huge research and development budgets, are not interested.

Still, research is done and gradually a number of Western-defined illnesses are found to benefit from acupuncture and TCM. Here are several examples related to stress or to conditions that may reasonably be associated with stress:

1. An animal study showed that rats pre-treated with acupuncture had no spike in stress-associated hormones after being exposed to chronic stress. http://explore.georgetown.edu/news/?ID=69470&PageTemplateID=295

2. "Acupuncture for chronic pain: individual patient data meta-analysis." By Vickers AJ, Cronin AM, Maschino, AC, Lewith G, MacPherson H, Foster NE, Sherman KJ, Witt CM, Linde K; Acupuncture Trialists' Collaboration.

3. Acupuncture Inhibits Sympathetic Activation During Mental Stress in Advanced Heart Failure Patients, Jnl of Cardiac Failure, 2002 Vol 8 No 6

4. Acupuncture for Headache. Advances in Clinical Neuroscience and Rehabilitation (Online Journal) 2013 Jan/Feb 12(6), 31 Jan 2013

5. Chinese herbal formula compares well with anti-hypertensive drugs. Am J Chin Med 2013;41(1):33-42

6. Yoga and Tai Qi reduce prenatal depression. Comp Ther Clin Pract 2013 Feb;19(1):6-10

7. Comparison of Electro-acupuncture and Fluoxetine in treatment of depression. J Altern Complement Med Sept 2013, 19(9):733-739

8. Treating generalised anxiety disorder using complementary and alternative medicine. Altern Ther Health Med 2013 Sep-Oct: 19(5): 45-50

9. Effects of acupuncture on high blood pressure of patients using anti-hypertensive drugs. Acupunct Electrother Res. 2013;38 (1-2):1-15

PART X

APPENDIX 10 - SIMPLE STRETCHING EXERCISES

Designed after working for 30 years with people who want the benefits of greater flexibility, improved circulation, health and immunity, more energy, a clearer head and less stress, these simple exercises draw on yoga, Tai Chi and old-fashioned gym exercises – and do not take as long!

They do not replace aerobic exercise, although done correctly they are harder than they seem at first and do work your heart and circulation. They do benefit your internal organs by means of the stretching and bending, but they do not help your body build muscle – though they do 'tone' many muscle groups. They can be done as stretches before or after more vigorous exercise.

The exercises given here do not exercise your legs, for which there are other stretching exercises not given: however, remember that walking fast for 15 minutes daily to the point where you get slightly out of breath is great exercise for almost everyone, and is probably all the aerobic exercise most people need for good continuing health. (However, people with sedentary occupations should aim every hour to walk around a bit to avoid the possibility of getting deep vein thrombosis.)

So, ideally, do the stretching-bending exercises given here, and walk vigorously daily for 15 minutes. That is all the exercise most people need to stay in good health, as long as they sleep, breathe and eat well. Wear clothes that do not restrict movement.

Ideally do these exercises barefoot or in socks, standing with feet planted firmly slightly more than shoulder width apart.

Keep feet firmly on the ground throughout: once in place they remain in the same position through all the exercises. If you have any physical health problems, and are in any doubt as to the benefits of exercise for yourself, consult your health professional before embarking on this 'regime'.

Always do the exercises in this order.

The times to hold positions, and the number of repetitions given for movements are those to aim for eventually when you have been doing the exercises for a few days. However, if you have never done them before, when you first start hold the positions for only a second or two, lengthening them each time as the days pass.

With all these exercises try to remain 'loose' in your muscles and joints, just reaching out as described. Do not try to keep anything rigidly dead straight except where indicated. If your arms are straight it is because you are stretching outwards not because you are trying to keep them straight.

1/ Bring arms up to shoulder height, loosely bent at elbow. Reach forward with right hand, heel of hand first. Stretch forward from shoulder and slowly take hand round to the right, behind you, always stretching out from the shoulder and twisting your body round though keeping legs straight and firmly planted. Do not strain! Just stretch comfortably. Turn your head so that your eyes follow your hand. When you can turn no further, stretch out a little more and hold the position for 5 seconds.

Slowly turn to the front again, keeping the stretch. Now, keeping the right arm loosely bent and still at shoulder height, concentrate on the left arm and hand, still at shoulder height. Stretch it forwards, leading with the heel of the hand, and outwards round to the left and behind, following it with your eyes as you turn your head and body from the waist.

Stretch round, always reaching out with the heel of the hand as far as you can go comfortably. Stretch a little further and hold it for 5 seconds.

Turn to the front again and repeat the move round to the right with the right hand. Repeat to the left again. Then once again each way. After all these moves face to the front again.

Each time you turn you will find you can reach further round as your spine releases bit by bit.

2/ Still standing as above, feet firmly planted, legs straight, facing to the front, place hands on hips, thumbs to the rear, and turn to the right so that your shoulders are facing right.

Now bend forwards from the hips, keeping back ramrod straight, with head up at all times, so that you stretch your neck as your chin pushes forward. Bend forwards only to the point where, to go further, you would have to bend your back, and stop there. Feel the pull in your legs and low back. Do not curl your back! Hold the position for 10 seconds then return to upright position (hands still on hips) but still facing right now lean back from the waist. Let your head fall back and hold the position for 10 seconds. Return to the upright position.

Now from the waist turn to the left, feet still firmly planted on the floor. Your shoulders should now be facing square on to the left. Hands still on hips, lean forward from the waist, back straight, chin up. Bend forward as far as possible without bending your middle or upper back or straining, and hold for 10 seconds.

Then return to upright position, still facing square on to the left, and lean backwards from the hips, letting your head fall backwards. Hold for 10 secs. Return to the upright position.

Still upright, turn shoulders to the centre position, facing forwards, hands remaining on hips, feet still firmly on the floor, legs still straight. Now lean forwards from the hips, keeping your back ramrod straight again, chin up and hold position for 10 seconds: again, only bend until to go further you would have to bend your back.

Then return to the upright position and bend backwards letting your head fall backwards. Do not strain! Do not push it too far – this is not a competition! Go only as far as is comfortable. Hold for 10 seconds.

If you do the exercises regularly in this order you will find that in time you can bend further backwards. You may notice some slight shaking or tremor in your spine in the backward leaning positions: this is normal – but can be alarming if you are not expecting it. However, do not strain! Return to the upright position. Just two more things to do!

3/ Feet still firmly planted as before, facing forwards, stretch both arms vertically upwards, again pushing the heels of your hands first, so that as you commence the following movements your palms are loosely facing the ceiling. Keep your hands nearly touching one another, arms fairly straight, reaching with the heels of your hands. (The trick is to reach with the heels of your hands, not rigidly to straighten your arms.)

Stretching upwards and slightly backwards, your aim now is to describe a huge circle with the heels of your hands as you bend to your right then down to the floor, sweeping across the floor to your left and up to your left then back to the original position with heels of hands towards the ceiling.

At all times stretch out as far as possible in whatever stage of the movement you have reached. To do this exercise properly, you have to bend from the waist and bend your back too. Do it slowly. Breathe easily. Repeat the big circle three times, then do it three times in the reverse direction, eventually ending with your hands between your feet near the floor.

4/ From the position at the end of exercise 3/ place your right hand on, or as close as without straining you can get it to, your right foot.

Here, you are stretching down towards your right foot with the heel of your right hand but now, keeping that position, stretch your left hand in the opposite direction, up towards the ceiling and turn your head so that you can look at your left hand.

In this position now try to straighten both arms so that through your shoulders they form a straight line, while you look vertically upwards. Stay here for 10 seconds, then move your right hand towards, or to touch, your left foot, still maintaining your left arm stretching upwards, head facing the ceiling. 10 seconds there.

Now bring your left hand down to join your right hand by your left foot and, with your left hand towards or touching your left foot now stretch your right arm and hand upwards towards the ceiling, turning your head to the right so as to look vertically upwards, a straight line from hand to hand through your shoulders as before but now facing the opposite way.

After 10 seconds take your left hand and stretch it towards, or to touch, your right foot, keeping your head facing the ceiling with your right arm stretching upwards for the final 10 seconds.

5/ Now take your right arm down to join your left arm by your right foot then let your arms hang vertically downwards from your shoulders to the floor. From here, just relax in this position, hanging forwards from the waist. Hold this position for 10 seconds breathing easily.

Then, very slowly, breathing deeply, bring your head up first, leading your back and body upwards to the vertical position and as you do so let your hands slide up your legs on either side, then your body and finally end in a huge final stretch, on a deep in-breath looking upwards to your hands high overhead. Then let your hands down as you breathe out.

As you move from your hanging downwards position to the huge final stretch upwards review all the main things you want to do today or tomorrow – depending on when you do the exercise.

Let your hands fall by your side. Bring your feet together, stand normally and shake out first your right then your left foot several times.

That is it! It all takes much longer to read and understand than to see and copy someone else doing it!

PART XI

APPENDIX 11 - MORE INFORMATION

Further Reading

- Five Element Constitutional Acupuncture, Hicks and Hicks, 2004, Churchill Livingstone
- The Foundations of Chinese Medicine, 2005, Maciocia G, Churchill Livingstone
- The Psyche in Chinese Medicine 2009 Maciocia G, Churchill Livingstone
- The Secret of Everlasting Life, Bertschinger R, 2011, Singing Dragon
- The Age of Stress, 2013, Mark Jackson, OUP
- How to Be a Jewish Mother, 1964, Dan Greenburg, Wolfe Publishing
- The Medium, The Mystic and the Physicist, 1974 Lawrence LeShan
- Control Stress, 2009, Paul McKenna, Bantam Press
- Stress Proof your Business and your Life, 2010 Steve Pipe and Elisabeth Wilson, Infinite Ideas
- Stress Management for Dummies, 1999, Allen Elkin, Wiley

Practitioners in United Kingdom

- British Acupuncture Council http://www.acupuncture.org.uk/
- Register of Chinese Herbal Medicine http://www.rchm.co.uk/
- Website with more information about Chinese medicine http://www.acupuncture-points.org This is my attempt to
  explain in English, sometimes in a simplified form, many of the concepts in Chinese medicine.

Other websites

- Autogenic training: http://www.atdynamics.co.uk
- Alexander: http://www.alexandertechnique.com/teacher
- Bowen: http://www.thebowentechnique.com/
- Counselling and Psychotherapy: http://www.rscpp.co.uk/
- Emotional Freedom Technique: http://www.eftacademy.co.uk/
- Hypnotherapy: http://www.hypnotherapists.org.uk/
- Management: http://www.managers.org.uk/
- Negotiation: http://www.negotiate.org/
- NLP: http://www.nlpacademy.co.uk/

Dedication

Dedicated to the author's wife, Maureen, for her love, support and forbearance.

Author

Jonathan Clogstoun-Willmott grew up on a farm (angry bulls and recalcitrant ploughs), went to school (hated it), did electrical engineering at university (never again), then became a Chartered Accountant (nearly his biggest mistake so far). Working as an accountant for 10 years made him ill. While doing accountancy he studied then practised various 'natural' medicines. This has made it possible for him to worry about people for over 35 years. He occasionally lets business colleagues lure him back into their world to enable him to maintain suitable levels of stress, via worry, grief, fear, anger and hysteria.

Jonathan maintains http://www.acupuncture-points.org
The *Chinese Medicine in English* series is published by http://frameofmindpublishing.com

1. **Qi Stagnation – Signs of Stress** (this book, first published 2013)
2. **Yin Deficiency** (first published 2014)
3. **Yang Deficiency** (first published 2016)
4. **Yuck! Phlegm!** (first published 2017)

All books are available to read on Kindle or Kindle apps and in some cases on other devices. .Softback editions may be ordered from Amazon or, in some cases, from Book Retailers.

Made in the USA
Coppell, TX
21 February 2020

16023896R00280